The

BROWN DERBY

Authentically Known Since 1926

COOKBOOK

**OVER 500 RECIPES FROM THE STAFF OF
THE FAMOUS BROWN DERBY RESTAURANTS**

Wilshire

Beverly Hills

Los Feliz

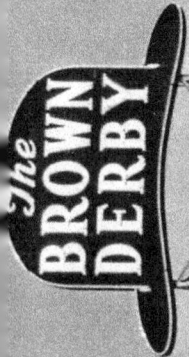

The Brown Derby Cookbook

THE BROWN DERBY COOKBOOK

Copyright © 2009 - 2014 by
M. Elizabeth Byrd

Printed in the United States of America
First Printing1949

Library of Congress Cataloging-in-Publishing Data
  Byrd, M. Elizabeth.
    Brown Derby Cookbook, The—4th ed.
        p. cm.
    Includes index.
    ISBN 978-0-9844267-2-0— HB
    ISBN 978-0-9844267-1-3— Collector's HB
    ISBN 978-0-9844267-0-6— HB
    1. Cookery. I. Title.

Publisher: The Original Hollywood Brown Derby, Ltd
Visit our website at: www.originalhollywoodbrownderby.com

Book & Cover Layout: M. Elizabeth Byrd
Book Illustrations by Douglas Bunn

PRINTED IN THE UNITED STATES OF AMERICA

1 3 5 7 9 10 8 6 4

4th Edition - November 2014

Back cover photo: *The Original Cobb Salad* (page 32)

CONTENTS

FOREWORD
to
Sixtieth Anniversary Edition of the First Edition

The Brown Derby Cookbook was first published sixty-five (65) years ago. Many, many hours of testing and evaluating went into the finished product. The recipes, simply put, are amazing. Take a little time to read, if not the entire, a portion of the cookbook. You will find that those who participated in its development were very passionate about the end results. Find your favorites in *The Brown Derby Cookbook* and try the recipes. Look for favorites of these celebrities as well: Jimmy Durante and Betty Grable (pg. 36), John Barrymore (pg. 39) and George Arliss (pg. 72) as well as Herbert K. Somborn, the founder of The Brown Derby Restaurants (pg. 134). Enjoy!

Food production during the time of the original publication was a lot simpler than today. Many foods were locally grown, produced on small farms and delivered or picked fresh. Some of the ingredients listed for different recipes may not be readily available but with a little pre-planning, many butchers and produce managers may be very helpful in assisting with your search.

The original text remains but words, phrases, symbols, etc. in brackets [ ] have been added for clarity. In today's health-conscious environment, some ingredients may be substituted or omitted. However, keep in mind that the flavor and end result may vary with any change to the recipe.

We hope that you will find *The Brown Derby Cookbook* most enjoyable. Pass it on to future generations for their enjoyment as well.

M. Elizabeth Byrd
President
The Original Hollywood Brown Derby, Ltd.

FOREWORD
to
Fiftieth Anniversary Edition of The Brown Derby

The Brown Derby, after fifty years, is a legend in its own time. Truly, an historical landmark, inseparably linked to the saga of Hollywood, it is difficult to imagine the nation's most famous intersection, Hollywood and Vine, without The Brown Derby Restaurant and vice versa.

Every organization, when and if it achieves a golden anniversary, tends to remember those events and accomplishments which express the best of what they are. This looking at the record is not, however, just an experience of pleasant nostalgia. In the personal history of every man and every group, there is usually some happening which urges one to make history repeat itself. For us, *The Brown Derby Cookbook* is just such an event. To enrich the celebration of our fiftieth anniversary we could do no better than to reissue what is, for thousands of food lovers, the cookbook.

In this edition, nothing has been omitted. It has not been necessary to add any new material. It seems that a really superb book, like a diamond, is forever. What we have done is enlarge and beautify the format. The size is larger, the cover is new, the art is renovated, but the recipes remain: A treasure for all the generations of gourmets to savor so long as food is more than just "something to eat".

Enjoy! Enjoy!

Affectionately,
/Walter P. Scharfe/
Walter P. Scharfe, President
Brown Derby International Ltd.
Hollywood, California

FOREWORD
to
First Edition

Welcome to *The Brown Derby Cookbook*—may it bring a little of The Brown Derby to your home.

We are happy to share the secrets of the dishes and the methods of our kitchens and bakeshops with you because they reveal that our cuisine is based on the quality of the ingredients and painstaking care. We have always tried to maintain high principles, for we believe that a restaurant is only as good as its last meal.

This is a good place to express our thanks to those who have made *The Brown Derby Cookbook* a reality. First, Leonard L. Levinson, who did the actual writing, has been an enthusiastic Brown Derby patron almost from our beginning and is well qualified both from the historical and gastronomical viewpoints. With him worked Robert Kreis, the supervising chef of The Brown Derby restaurants, a great authority on the preparation of foods and a skilled restaurant kitchen executive, and Rudolf Friedrich, our master pastry chef, who has been responsible for dessert creations which have become national favorites.

We are especially grateful to Marjorie Child Husted, the noted home economics expert and consultant in advertising, public service, and home service of General Mills, who headed their Betty Crocker staff for many years. Mrs. Husted tested and adapted The Brown Derby recipes for practical home use and provided the invaluable link between our professional chefs and you who cook at home.

Lastly, I am indebted to James W. Warren, vice-president and general manager of The Brown Derbys, under whose supervision this book was written. *The Brown Derby Cookbook* has been a favored project of Jim Warren's for many years and I hope you will agree with me that he has brought it to fulfillment with brilliant success.

Robert H. Cobb, President
THE BROWN DERBY CORPORATION

INTRODUCTION

Wonderful food, fine service, and glamorous patrons have brought international fame to The Brown Derby Restaurants. Now more than thirty years of history, with interesting anecdotes of how this mecca of epicures became almost a symbol of the romance of Hollywood itself, is wittily told. And best of all, the backstage secrets of how the superb Brown Derby food is prepared are here revealed.

This is a rarity among cookbooks, one which brings you knowledge of the art of the most skilled professional chefs—men who have devoted their lives to learning everything there is to know about cooking. These men, who prepare a million meals a year, must specialize in turning out food to tempt the palates of the most particular.

The tips on buying, preparing, and serving elegant food they pass on to you in this volume are the results of the most rigorous European training at this time. This is truly international cooking, for it represents the secrets of every cooking culture, not only from Europe but from our own Southwest and the Orient. Now all of this lore has been gathered together and translated into language and procedures familiar to homemakers. It is the first time many of these favorite recipes of Brown Derby patrons have been put on paper. The chefs, as they create a new food treat or as they evolve the tricks and special touches which make some dish taste far more delicious than ever before, usually carry the secret in their heads. But in this book they have been written down, checked, and tested in amounts for home use. And you will be able to follow the recipes as given in their own words, using methods and turning out food with the witchery of master chefs, with the perfect seasoning and that heavenly combination of herbs which lifts a dish into the sublime of eating pleasure.

The special terms that the chefs use—including all the French words and phrases—are explained so that you will know just what they mean by them. A table of weights and measures will answer any question of how much to use. I think you will find the recipes in four of the chapters –"Salads", "Curries", "Barbecues", and "Specialties of the House"—unusually intriguing. As for the meat recipes . . . I believe there is no such marvelous guide to a man's taste anywhere else.

You will see that this is a "deluxe" cookbook. There is no compromise with quality, or with cost, effort, amounts of ingredients . . . or calories. But for those of you who love to go sailing off with saucepan or skillet bound for new culinary adventures, I can say, here is the inspiration . . . and the charts for your course . . . to happy eating!

Marjorie Child Husted

The
BROWN DERBY
Restaurants
1926

THE STORY
OF
THE BROWN DERBYS

irst, take an idea: that good American cooking, using the finest of ingredients will make a restaurant a success.

Mix in a bit of California seasoning . . . and then a dash of the informal comfort of California living.

Add the skill of chefs trained in the finest of European cuisine.

Flavor with a clientele peppered with movie, television, and radio personalities and spiced with renowned visitors from all over the world.

Keep this up for thirty-five years . . . serve quickly and faultlessly . . . and you have The Brown Derby Restaurants.

The Brown Derbys are million-dollar monuments to an idle remark. One night in 1925, Herbert K. Somborn was chatting with Abe Frank, the manager of the Los Angeles Ambassador Hotel, and Sid Grauman of Chinese Theatre fame, and as idle chatter goes remarked, "You could open a restaurant in an alley and call it anything and if the food and service were good, the patrons would come flocking".

The other two agreed, but then anyone with an educated palate in Southern California would have said the same thing, for Los Angeles in 1925 was an epicure's desert. Aside from half a dozen good restaurants, the gawky city dined out at huge assembly-line cafeterias, cottage tearooms, or short-order "cafes".

Somborn elaborated on his theory: a place that served fine American dishes made with the finest and best raw materials obtainable, prepared with skill and experience . . . a place so distinctive that, once seen or heard about, it would never again be forgotten. To achieve the standards he set for his restaurant, Somborn selected a young friend who had been raised in that business. This was Robert H. Cobb, who was the combination food checker, steward, buyer, cashier, and occasional cook when the first Derby opened, and who has been president of The Brown Derby Corporation since Mr. Somborn's death in 1934.

Bob Cobb, whose father was the sheriff and hotelkeeper at Hardin, Big Horn County, Montana, helped in the kitchen and the dining room when the cow hands and ranchers came in for the monthly dances. He played with the Crow and Sioux Indian kids in the fields where their ancestors had cut down General Custer and his men a couple of generations before. He had a boy's-eye-view of the last of the old West, and the walls of his Hollywood office are covered with color prints by Charles Russell, the Western painter, who bought newspapers from Cobb when the latter was a newsboy in Billings.

The Cobb family moved to Billings, where Mrs. Cobb was soon operating the town's favorite boardinghouse. This burgeoned into three restaurants and here young Bob Cobb leaned how to buy and serve food. He went to business school, then was employed in a bank, and followed his family when they moved to California for his mother's health.

In Los Angeles, Cobb first worked in a bank and later returned to the restaurant business. He met Herbert Somborn and Gloria Swanson at the Alexandria Hotel, where Paul Whiteman and his four-piece jazz band played for the Saturday tea dances. Somborn, impressed with Bob's knowledge of the restaurant business, sent for him when he was recruiting a staff for The Original Derby.

"Bob", he said, "we're going to open a new restaurant across the street from the Ambassador and we're going to call it The Brown Derby".

"Yeah?", said Cobb, completely unimpressed.

"Yes", said Somborn. "I want you to come in and manage it."

"I'm not interested", said Cobb. "I've been in the restaurant business since I was a youngster and I never did like it. I'm just going into the real estate game—how would you like to buy a lot in Laurel Canyon?"

But Somborn was extremely per-suasive and infected Cobb with some of his enthusiasm, for the latter abandoned his new career and was soon working a seven-day ninety-hour week.

The Original Brown Derby first tipped its hat in February, 1926. Among its initial patrons were Mary Pickford, Jack Holt, Corinne Griffith, Bebe Dan-iels, Louella O. Parsons and Loretta (then Gretchen) Young. They remained Brown Derby patrons through the years.

The stars who visited the place came at first out of friendship and curios-ity. They kept coming back for several reasons. First, while the menu was short and extremely simple, the food at The

Derby was the best obtainable. Second, the service was swift and flawless. Third, the place was con-veniently located, midway between the downtown theaters and the homes of the stars. Also it stayed open twenty-four hours a day. This meant a great deal to the New Yorkers, such as Harry Ruby,

who once complained about Hollywood that "no matter how hot it gets in the daytime, there is no place to go at night".

The Derby's policy in buying food has always been to pay premium prices for all the merchandise it serves. And in the dear, dead days when ordinary buns cost twelve cents, The Derby paid eighteen for theirs. Their hamburg-er consisted of ninety-five percent top round steak. They paid three cents over the market for coffee—and still do. Their hot dogs were the first skinless frankfurters served in Los An-geles and "built" to their specifications. An old Texan, who did magical things with chili and beans when he wasn't riding imaginary broncos down Main Street, was continually bailed out and put back to work. A Mexican woman in Santa Barbara, who made the finest tamales north of the border, shipped a fresh consignment daily to the restaurant. Cream for coffee was whipping cream. As for the near beer, Cobb merely shudders at the memory and quickly changes the subject.

In the boom times from 1926 to 1929, The Derby flourished and became increasingly popular. Los Angeles was spreading out like civic mumps. It welcomed novel eating places. The screen was learning how to talk and many of the stars, playwrights, and composers imported from New York became steady patrons. The Derby became the Luchow's, Antoine's', the Shanley's of the West, just as during the next decade "21", Toots Shor's, and Lindy's were to become the Eastern counterparts of The Derby.

Tourists and home-grown movie fans followed the stars and came in to gaze at their cinematic idols while munching their meals. This is the only floor show The Derbys have ever offered: the view of the stars.

The Hollywood Brown Derby on Vine Street, half a block below Hollywood Boulevard, is, more than any other single factor, responsible for the designation of that corner as the Time Square of the film capital. Around it grew the theatres, the broadcasting studios, and the business offices which give Hollywood and Vine its reputation and character.

It was opened on St. Valentine's Day, 1929, in a building especially erected by Cecil B. DeMille. It is probably the best-known eating establishment in the world. For over thirty years it has been the foremost restaurant in a town that has at least one newspaper correspondent and one photographer for every star. All three—the star, the reporter, and the cameraman—frequent The Derby, and the last two furnish the newspapers and magazines of the world with a never-ending stream of stories and pictures about the first.

Thus, to movie and television fans throughout the world, The Derby has become the personification of all that is wonderful in restaurants and when they come to Hollywood, it is the place they visit to see their cinema favorites. Scores and sometimes hundreds of them congregate outside for the possibility of a glimpse and an autograph, while the more sophisticated put "Dinner at The Derby" at the top of their Hollywood itinerary.

Two of the first items added to the original menu were a salad and a cake. The salad was almost an accident.

TEA FOR THREE—William Collier Jr., Dorothy Lee and Bert Wheeler lunching together at the famous Brown Derby in Hollywood.

One evening, Bob Cobb found an avocado in the icebox. He chopped it up, along with some lettuce, celery, and tomatoes, plus a strip of bacon and some salad dressing, and had that for dinner. Several days later he tried it again, adding other ingredients which he had purchased on his way to work: breast of chicken, chives, hard-boiled egg, watercress, and a wedge of Roquefort cheese for the dressing. And that's how the Cobb Salad was born. Today, the Cobb Salad, though many restaurants serve it under other names, is a national favorite.

The first dessert The Brown Derby ever served was a cake made by a former bond salesman named Harry Baker. It was a fluffy, golden cake, neither angel food nor sponge, but infinitely lighter and more delicious than either. For almost twenty years, Baker baked these cakes for The Derby, refusing to divulge the secret of its recipe. In 1947, he took it to General Mills in Minneapolis, and they paid him handsomely for the recipe. Launched as "the first new cake idea in a hundred years", this is the famous Chiffon Cake, which differs only slightly from The Brown Derby favorite.

Other dishes were added. A toothsome Corned Beef Hash joined the menu. For three years, without any change at all, Wally Beery occupied the same booth at luncheon and always had the Corned Beef Hash. The luxurious Turkey Derby instantly became a favorite. There were steaks, chops, and chicken and—a radical departure for restaurants catering to smart clienteles—Lamb and Beef stews. But these were stews for an epicure, made of the choicest meats and vegetables, prepared by chefs who never deviated from the savory old-time recipes.

Fine soups were also introduced and in addition to Chicken Soup and French Onion Soup, which are served every day, there are seven featured soups for the seven days of the week.

Dinner Menu

Appetizers

Derby Cocktail:- Avocado Balls, Crab Legs and Diced Celery,
Topped with Thousand Island Dressing 2.50

*Bluepoints on Half Shell 3.25   *Cherrystone Clams 3.25

Chopped Chicken Liver 1.75   Shrimp Cocktail 2.25

Dungeness Crab Cocktail 2.25   *Cracked Crab on Ice 3.25

Jumbo Shrimp on Ice 2.75   Fruit Cocktail Supreme 1.50

*In season

Soups

Chicken Broth with Matzo Ball .60; Bowl .90

French Onion Soup au Gratin .75; Bowl 1.00   Vichyssoise .90

Soup du Jour .50; Bowl .75   Jellied Consomme .90

Chilled Salads

COBB SALAD 3.95
Finely Chopped Lettuce, Romaine, Celery, Chicory, Chives,
Watercress, Avocado, Peeled Tomato, Crisp Bacon, Breast
of Chicken, Hard Cooked Egg and Bleu Cheese. All
tastefully mixed well with Our Special Old-Fashioned
French Dressing.

PALACE COURT SALAD 3.95
A Center of Tomato Slice and Artichoke Bottom filled with Crab
Meat, surrounded with Shrimp, Crab Legs, Lobster, Asparagus
Tips and Pimento Strips arranged on a bed of Shredded Lettuce
and Chopped Hard-Cooked Egg. Topped with Green Pepper Ring,
Capers and Thousand Island Dressing.

CRAB SALAD 3.95

FRUIT SALAD WITH COTTAGE CHEESE 3.50

SHRIMP SALAD 3.95

WHITE MEAT CHICKEN SALAD 3.75

CAESAR SALAD 3.50

MIXED GREEN SALAD 1.95

Choice of Dressing

Charcoal Broiler

Filet Mignon 7.50   Extra Cut French Lamb Chops 6.50

Calf's Liver and Onions 5.25   Half Spring Chicken 4.25

New York Cut Steak 7.50

Vegetables

Julienne String Beans .75   Baby Carrots Glacé .75

Stewed Tomatoes .75   Zucchini Florentine 1.25

Green Peas .75   Creamed Spinach 1.00

Asparagus or Broccoli Hollandaise 1.25

Potatoes

Baked Idaho Russet Potato .90   Cottage Fried Potatoes 1.00

Hashed Browned Potatoes .75   Lyonnaise Potatoes 1.00

Au Gratin Potatoes 1.25
Diced Russet Potato Cooked in Cream,
Topped with Cheddar Cheese

We Proudly Serve Carnation Dairy Products

6% Sales Tax will be added to the price of all food items.

Not responsible for lost or stolen articles.

MARTIN MENU PRINTING CO. LOS ANGELES. DI 9-7924

Served with
COBB SALAD, MIXED GREEN SALAD
or SOUP DU JOUR
————

ROAST PRIME RIBS OF BEEF 6.75
Finest Choice Prime Ribs of Beef Roasted to Peak of
Flavor. Served with Baked Idaho Russet Potato and
Vegetable du Jour.

FILET MIGNON TIDBITS 5.75
Thin Slices of Choice Filet of Beef Marinated in Spices
and Cooked in Wine Sauce with Fresh Mushrooms.
Served with Steamed Rice.

BROILED GROUND SIRLOIN STEAK 5.25
Freshly Ground Sirloin of Beef Broiled to Juicy Perfection
and Smothered with Cooked Onions and Brown Derby
De Luxe Sauce. Served with Baked Idaho Russet Potato
and Vegetable du Jour.

BROILED MINUTE STEAK 6.95
Hickory Charcoal Broiled for Full Flavor. Served with
Baked Idaho Russet Potato and Vegetable du Jour.

CREAMED TURKEY DERBY 5.50
Breast of Turkey in a Creamed Sherry Wine Sauce.
Served on a Toasted Crouton with Cranberry Sauce.

HALF SPRING CHICKEN 4.75
Fresh Half Chicken Saute in Butter or Broiled. Served
with French Fried Potatoes and Vegetable du Jour.

VEAL CUTLET MORNAY 5.75
Breaded Eastern Veal Cutlet with Sharp Cheddar
Mornay Sauce, Glazed, Vegetable du Jour.

SPAGHETTI DERBY 3.95
Italian Spaghetti with Special Brown Derby Meat Sauce,
Topped with Imported Parmesan Cheese.

Seafood

CATALINA SAND DABS SAUTE AMANDINE 5.75
Fresh Catalina Sand Dabs topped with Sliced Almonds,
(Broiled on Request), Served with French Fried Potatoes.

BROILED LOBSTER TAILS 6.95
Baby Lobster Tails with Lemon Butter. Served with
French Fried Potatoes and Vegetable du Jour.

SHRIMP CURRY INDIENNE 5.95
Baja California Shrimp in Curry Sauce with Chutney.
Served with Steamed Rice and Condiment Plate of
Capers, Anchovies and Coconut.

BROILED STEAK AND LOBSTER COMBINATION 7.25

Desserts

Grapefruit Cake .85   Layer Cake .85   Black Bottom Pie .85

Ice Cream or Sherbet .60

Caramel Custard .75   Parfaits 1.00

Rice Pudding .75
(made with Orange Peel, Cinnamon and Raisins)

Beverages

Coffee .40   Tea .40   Sanka .40   Milk .40

Buttermilk .40   Hot Chocolate .40

Michelob Beer on Draught .75

It was only natural that the film stars should begin to offer their favorite dishes to enrich The Derby cuisine. Michael Curtiz, the director, contributed the Veal Paprika recipe which had been in his family for many years and which is now in The Brown Derby repertoire. Pat O'Brien put on a campaign to put Irish Stew on the menu. It became a regular Thursday night dish, and O'Brien became a regular Thursday night customer. Dorothy Lamour not only contributed the recipe for Shrimp Creole but brought her grandmother to The Derby to taste the result and suggest the spices which give it that New Orleans flavor.

The visits of distinguished guests from many foreign lands have resulted in further additions. Prominent among these are Indian curries which have won a permanent spot on The Brown Derby menus.

The Vine Street Derby soon made a vital place for itself in Hollywood. At lunchtime stars in costume and make-up would rush in from the sets to entertain friends or be interviewed by writers. Young and hopeful players would eat frugally on money scrimped for the occasion, hoping to catch the eye of a studio executive looking for "just the type". Other players would drop in for mail addressed to them in care of The Derby, telephone messages, or one of the dozen other services that caravansary offered.

The Brown Derbys can take the credit, or the blame, for the introduction of telephones at tables during mealtimes. They made their appearance when busy executives found it inconvenient to interrupt a luncheon as many as a dozen times to transact business. A loudspeaker system for paging

and phone lines to each table were installed, and today a telephone is as much a part of a busy executive's lunchtime setup as his cup of coffee. The number of times an agent or ad man is paged has come to indicate the degree of his popularity and prosperity, and from time to time there calls have been tabulated and the results circulated as the "Derby Derby".

At dinnertime, the family life and the romances of Hollywood flourished: Tyrone Power, Sr., dining with his seventeen-year-old son, just off the train from Cincinnati . . . Mickey Nielan and Blanche Sweet having a spat in public...long-forgotten romances in their first flame...or their last bash.

Then at midnight, after the theater or the Legion Stadium fights, the place would be humming again, this time with a crowd that laughed, shouted across the room, lingered over light suppers, loath to call it a night.

When they were gone the nighthawks took over The Derby — newspapermen like Mark Kelly, Walter Winchell, Sidney Skolsky, and O. O. McIntire; comedians and nightclub performers like Joe Frisco, Frank Fay, Eddie Cantor, Jimmy Durante, and George Raft; fabulous men like John Barrymore, Wilson Mizner, and Nick the Greek. Will Rogers would join Somborn and Mizner in Booth 50, then Darryl Zanuck, out airing his dog, would drop in for hot cakes and coffee. Soon there

would be eight or ten, all at one table, alone in the big room. And then some of the best stories in the world would get themselves told by some of the best storytellers of the land.

To cover the huge bare walls of The Hollywood Derby, an artist was engaged who made caricatures of the more famous patrons. This was a young Pole whose full name was so long and complicated that no one remembers anything but the last syllable—Vitch. One of the world's finest caricaturists, Vitch displayed an economy of line and sharpness of perception that caught a personality in a few brush strokes.

CARICATURES by EDDIE VITCH

Marlene Dietrich   W. Randolph Hearst   Ed Wynn   Eddie Cantor

As the years passed, the pictures crept up the walls and new Hollywood players used all sorts of stratagems to be included in The Derby collection. When the war began, Vitch was in London. He disappeared and it was not until later that his Hollywood friends learned he was alive. He had fought with the Polish Army and the French underground. Now he is a leading pantomime artist in England.

The collection of caricatures is kept up to date by other artists with the constant addition of new faces and replacement of those who have faded from the public eye, until the décor was changed to its present smart, continental appearance. Adjoining the main dining room is a famous cocktail lounge, The Record Room, which has a sumptuous collection of pastel paintings on its wall, honoring the recording artists who have sold a million or more copies of one record. The Beverly Derby is also styled to flatter and enhance the female stars and other beauties who gather there.

Pastels (above) by Renowned Artist, Nicolaus Volpe, from the Gold Record Room (below)

Gold Record Room Entrance and Bar Area

Almost from their inception, The Derbys have been the scenes of exploitation stunts by film, TV, and radio companies, hilarious pranks by the stars, and the strangest of private luncheons and dinner.

An exotic baroness, accompanied by a butler who served her, helped publicize the picture, *The Baroness and the Butler*. Marie Wilson put on a waitress' uniform and worked for several days to acquire experience for her part in *Boy Meets Girl*. (Derby officials increased their liability insurance for the occasions.) Henry Morgan shaved at his booth with a razor that sponsored his radio program. Pearls have been "found" in Brown Derby oysters and ingénues have been "discovered" in the booths. Dinners have been given in the American Room for Lassie, a lion, and Sir Harry Lauder. There was liver for Lassie, hamburger (rare) for the lion, and bagpipers for Sir Harry.

One young screen couple achieved national publicity by propping upon their table a sign which read "This is *not* a romance". Another couple came back after they were married and measured Booth 22. He had proposed to her there and wanted to build an exact replica in their new home. No. 22 was also the booth John Guedel was sitting in, looking at The Derby scene, when he thought up the idea for *People Are Funny*.

NEW YORK NEWS
Saturday, January 7, 1933

PANTING BRIGADE

(By Wide World)
CAUGHT WEARING TROUSERS, Marlene Dietrich, film star, beats a hasty beeline with her attorney, Ralph Blum, for luncheon at the Brown Derby in Hollywood. Paramount's $200,000 suit against her was halted at conference of lawyers.

One of the most hilarious ribs occurred when Marlene Dietrich shocked Hollywood by appearing at The Derby wearing slacks. This shocked everyone, that is, but Bret Wheeler and Robert Woolsey. The two comics hurriedly adjourned to the Broadway-Hollywood across the street and returned wearing filmy blouses, short skirts, and smoking big cigars.

And long before *Queen for a Day,* a pretty Brown Derby waitress, Jackie Wilmot, was given the Cinderella treatment in a stunt which achieved international attention. After Jackie had been glamorized at Westmore's, Joan Bennett loaned her an evening dress, Marlene Dietrich supplied a car and chauffeur, a hundred thousand dollars' worth of diamonds were draped on her by a local jeweler, and she was studded with orchids from a local florist. Then she was escorted to the opening of *Rebecca* by none other than Prince Michael Romanoff—this was before he opened his own restaurant—and afterward taken to the Clover Club. Next day Jackie was offered several "stock starlet" contracts, but refused them saying, "I make more, with less trouble, at The Derby".

In addition to being the haven for the stars and featured players, The Derby itself has been featured in a dozen pictures, among them *A Star Is Born, Variety Girl, Hollywood Boulevard, Nocturne,* and *Fun and Fancy Free.*

After The Vine Street Derby was firmly established, the people of Beverly Hills wanted one there and The Beverly Derby was built at Wilshire and Rodeo, across from the Beverly-Wilshire Hotel. It soon became, and has ever since remained, one of the most popular gathering places for stars and society people, alike.

During the years he has headed The Derby Corporation, Bob Cobb has surrounded himself with administrative, culinary, and serving experts. James Warren, the vice-president and general manager, joined the staff in 1929 as food buyer and steward when Mr. Cobb left that post to become

Beverly Hills Main Dining Room

general manager and has been associated with Mr. Cobb ever since. Warren undertook the development of food services, the training of new personnel, and the increased scope of operations as The Derbys multiplied and cocktail lounges and food and liquor stores were added. During the war he was given a leave of absence to join the Air Transport Command and brought all of his Brown Derby experience to his work as service officer in the Service Division at Washington, Natal (Brazil), and the Command's "Hotel de Gink" chain which ranged from the Ritz in Paris to basha huts in India.

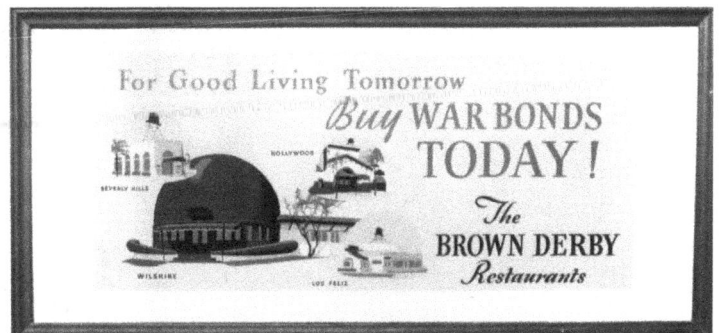

Many of the waiters and other employees of The Derbys have worked for the company for fifteen years. Several have been there for twenty, and one man, Ernest Weigle, was hired by Cobb the day the first Derby was opened. All executive positions in the organization are filled by men who have worked their way up.

Cobb is proud of the many innovations The Derbys have introduced in the restaurant business. In addition to the first phone connections at tables and booths, they inaugurated mobile bars so that customers could prepare their own drinks, as well as cheese and pastry carts which made the rounds of the tables. They replaced the tough range beef of the Western plains with tender Eastern beef. Eastern soft-shelled crabs, lobsters, and other seafood were imported, not as novelties but as year-round items. Irish bacon from Ireland and Canadian bacon from Canada were other pioneering imports. When The Derby brought the first Pascal celery from Colorado, the freight alone was more than local celery would have cost them. Since the war The Derbys have been flying in the heretofore unknown giant Alaska king crab. This is a new variety which is exported in the fresh state and has achieved such a tremendous popularity that the supply has never kept up with the demand.

Cobb and his Derby assistants have never forgotten Herbert Somborn's policy of quality food, well prepared. By adhering to this policy, by searching for the finest and most unusual in eatables and paying well over the market for it, they have built The Brown Derbys into an internationally famous institution.

It would be impossible in one chapter to give more than a glimpse into The Derbys over all the years they have been open. A friend once said to Wilson Mizner, "I'll bet you could write a book about what is seen and heard in The Brown Derby".

"Write a book?" Mizner snorted. "Hell, you could start another war!"

If it's just anyone, any place will do.
If it's someone important, say, "Meet me at The Derby".

The BROWN DERBY
ESTABLISHED – 1926

" Meet me at The Derby."

Enjoy!

SPECIALTIES
OF THE
HOUSE

A fine restaurant will have several dishes which are specialties of the house. In most cases these are exotic and unusual recipes. However, The Brown Derby house specialties are familiar and homelike favorites which have won permanent popularity because of the quality of the materials used and the methods of preparation, and the fact that they are either cooked to order or made fresh daily.

They are all published here for the first time; all, that is, except the recipe for The Brown Derby tamales. These are still made by the Mexican family in Santa Barbara and it is just about impossible to prepare them in any American kitchen.

SPAGHETTI DERBY

Cook spaghetti (allowing 1 lb. for each 3 persons) in boiling salted water, using a very large kettle and plenty of water so that each strand of spaghetti can move about freely. Cook uncovered for 7 minutes. Lift from boiling water (never drain spaghetti) to heated platter or casserole, toss spaghetti in butter and Brown Derby Tomato Sauce, and cover with Brown Derby Meat Sauce. Sprinkle with grated Parmesan cheese to taste.

BROWN DERBY TOMATO SAUCE, 2 qts.

½ cup olive oil
½ large onion, chopped
1 bead garlic, chopped
1 small carrot, diced
2 outside pieces celery, diced
½ tbs. black peppercorns

1 ham bone or shank
½ cup flour
1 No. 2 can tomato puree
1 No. 2 can solid-pack
    tomatoes or 3 lbs.
    fresh tomatoes

¼ tsp. thyme
¼ tsp. basil
¼ tsp. oregano
2 tbs. salt

Heat olive oil in heavy kettle, add onion, garlic, carrot, celery, peppercorns, and ham bone. Allow to smother 8 minutes. Add flour and blend well. Add purée, tomatoes, celery pieces, spices and salt. Cook 1 hour. Strain through fine sieve. Use with spaghetti, meats, fish, poultry.

DERBY MEAT SAUCE (FOR SPAGHETTI), 2 qts.
SERVES 8 – 10

1 lb. ground beef
1 lb. ground veal
½ lb. ground pork
½ cup olive or salad oil
1 large onion, chopped
2 cloves garlic, chopped
    (optional)
½ lb. sliced fresh mushrooms

1 oz. sliced dry mushrooms
1 cup burgundy
1 No. 1 can tomato purée
1 No. 1 can solid-pack tomatoes
    or 2 lbs. fresh tomatoes
2 cups beef stock
½ tsp. orégano

½ tsp. basil
¼ tsp. nutmeg
½ bay leaf
¼ tsp. rosemary
½ tbs. paprika
3 tbs. salt
1 tbs. ground black pepper

Brown meat in oven at 360°[F]. Stir well to get an even brown. Heat oil in heavy kettle; add onion, garlic, and mushrooms. Sauté 5 minutes, stirring well. Add wine, tomato purée, tomatoes, and beef stock; cook 10 minutes and add browned meat. Blend well. Add all spices and salt and pepper. Simmer on slow fire 1½ hours. Skim top several times during each cooking period.

TURKEY DERBY CROUTON

Using a sharp knife, cut a 2½-in.-thick slice of white Pullman or sandwich bread. Cut off crust and trim edges until there is a circle of bread 3 in. in diameter. Leaving a wall ½ in. thick, cut an inside circle, but not all the way through bread. Then insert blade of knife carefully about ½ in. from the bottom of the crouton and cut so that a bread plug can be lifted out and a deep dish of bread remains. Soak that in melted butter and brown in medium hot oven. Fill with Turkey Derby.

TURKEY DERBY

SERVES 3

2 cups heavy cream	*10 oz. cooked and flaked white turkey meat*	*Salt and white pepper*
		3 egg yolks

Bring cream to a boil in top of double boiler. Add the turkey and season to taste. Add egg yolks that have been mixed with a little cream. Let thicken and serve immediately on large bread croutons. Garnish with cranberry jelly.

CHICKEN `A LA KING

SERVES 2

3 oz. butter	*½ cup sherry*	*1 tbs. pimento, cut in*
4 mushrooms, sliced	*1½ cups Cream Sauce*	*diamond shapes*
½ cup pastry cream	*1½ cups pieces of cooked*	*1/8 tsp. cayenne pepper*
2 tbs. green bell pepper,	*chicken (white or dark*	*Salt*
cut in diamond shapes	*meat)*	*2 egg yolks*

Heat butter in heavy skillet. Add mushrooms and green pepper. Sauté about 3 minutes on slow fire. Add sherry and reduce by one third. Add Cream Sauce and pastry cream, mix well, and allow to simmer about 3 minutes. Add chicken, pimento, cayenne pepper, and salt to taste. Simmer about 4 minutes more on slow fire. Thicken with egg yolks that have been mixed with a little cream. Serve on toast, croutons, patty shells, or cornbread.

For Ham, Veal, Lobster, Shrimp or Crab `a la King merely substitute the same amount of cooked meat or shellfish for chicken in the above recipe.

* * *

Ever since The Derbys began serving Corned Beef Hash, it has been the favorite entrée of several male stars including George Montgomery and Dennis O'Keefe.

* * *

PAN-FRIED CORNED BEEF HASH

SERVES 2

1 lb. lean, extra well-done corned beef brisket	*1 tbs. slightly browned onions, chopped*	*Dash of pepper*
1 cup diced boiled potatoes	*finely (optional)*	

Grind or chop corned beef very fine. Place in mixing bowl, add potatoes, onions if desired, pepper, and mix well. Should mixture be too dry, add a small amount of cold water. Mold into 6-oz. patties and brown in butter on both sides. At The Brown Derbys, this dish is served with a poached egg on top.

If it is not practical to use fresh corned beef, a 1-lb. can of corned beef may be substituted.

DERBY DE LUXE ENCHILADAS

This is a celebrated Mexican one-dish meal and consists of special pancakes, a paste filling, and surrounding foods.

ENCHILADA PANCAKES DERBY, 12 PANCAKES

2 cups flour	1 tsp. baking powder	2½ cups milk
1 cup yellow cornmeal	1 tsp. salt	½ cup oil
	6 whole eggs	

Sift together flour, cornmeal, salt, and baking powder. Blend beaten eggs and milk together and add to the dry mixture a small amount at a time to avoid lumping. Beat to a smooth batter. For frying use a 9-in. heavy iron skillet. Rub it with oil and pour batter in evenly. Fry on both sides until light. When pancakes are cool, they may be stacked.

PASTE FILLING, FOR 12 PANCAKES

4 long chili peppers	1 large onion, chopped fine	1 cup cornmeal
4 short chili peppers	1 clove garlic, chopped fine	2 tbs. paprika
6 Japanese chili peppers	1 lb. dark meat chicken,	1½ pts. stock or water
½ cup oil	beef, or veal, cooked	1 cup tomato puree
	and diced small	

Remove all seeds and stems from chili peppers. Put in pot and bring to boil in a little water. Drain and chop very fine. If you cannot obtain chili peppers, you may substitute 5 tbs. good chili powder. Next, smother onion and garlic lightly in oil in hot skillet. Add diced chicken. Smother again about 4 minutes on slow fire. Add cornmeal and mix well. Add paprika and mix again. Add stock, puree, salt, chopped chili peppers. Mix well. Simmer on slow fire for about 15 minutes. Paste should be about the consistency of mush; if too thin, add a little more cornmeal. After cooking, remove from fire and put into pan to cool.

TO MAKE ENCHILADAS

Lay the Enchilada Pancakes out flat. Cover each pancake with ½-in.-thick layer of Enchilada Paste Filling. Roll the pancakes and place in buttered pan, side by side. Cover with julienne of lettuce, ground Cheddar cheese, grated radishes, chopped green onions, and pickled peppers (Mexican or Italian). Place pitted olives on top. Add a little chicken stock to the pan with the enchiladas and bake in medium oven for 20 minutes. Serve with Chili Con Carne and chopped onions.

HAMBURGER STEAK DE LUXE

SERVES 4

2 lbs. lean ground round
    steak*
1 egg
1 tsp. English mustard
2 tbs. Worcestershire
    Sauce

1 tsp. salt (or to taste)
¼ tsp. pepper
1 cup cold chicken broth
    or consommé

2 medium-sized onions,
    sliced thin
2 cups Brown Derby
    De Luxe Sauce

Mix meat, egg, and seasonings thoroughly. Add consommé gradually, blending well. Shape into 8-oz. patties. Sear quickly in a little fat in hot skillet; finish cooking over low heat. Remove hamburgers from pan and keep hot. Add onions to fat remaining in pan. Sauté over low heat until brown. Add sauce, heat thoroughly, and serve with hamburgers.

BROWN DERBY DE LUXE SAUCE, 1 pt.

1 cup Burgundy
1 tsp. peppercorns, crushed
¼ tsp. basil
3 beads shallots, chopped
    fine

1½ cups Brown Sauce
½ cup catsup
½ cup chili sauce
1 tsp. horseradish, grated

1 tsp. English mustard
1 tsp. barbecue spices or
Brown Derby Diable
    Sauce
¼ cup butter

Place wine, peppercorns, basil, and shallots in medium-sized skillet and reduce by two-thirds. Add Brown Sauce, catsup, chili sauce, horseradish, English mustard, barbecue spices or Diable Sauce. Mix well and allow to simmer on slow fire for 20 minutes. Strain through fine sieve. Add butter and mix well. Serve.

FILET MIGNON TIDBITS

SERVES 5

Slice 1 pound of filet of beef thin, cut into 1-in. square tidbits, and cover with a marinade of the following ingredients mixed together:

½ cup olive oil
½ cup wine vinegar
1 cup water
1 tbs. black peppercorns

1 medium-sized onion,
    sliced
2 beads garlic

½ green pepper, sliced
1 cup Burgundy
2 tbs. salt
3 tbs. barbecue spices

Store in refrigcrator for 8-10 hours.

(continued next page)

[*Please observe current health and safety cooking guidelines for the internal temperature of meats.]

Then prepare this finished dish:

1 lb. filet beef pickled *tidbits*	*2 tbs. Burgundy* *1 tsp. brown mustard*	*½ cup Brown Gravy* *2 tbs. Brown Derby Diable*
2 oz. butter	*1 tsp. Worcestershire*	*Sauce or A-1 Sauce®*
6 large mushrooms, sliced	*Sauce*	

Dry tidbits in towel. Heat butter in heavy skillet. Add meat and mushrooms. Sauté quickly until well done. Blend together wine, mustard, Worcestershire, Brown Gravy, and Diable Sauce, and add to tidbits. Bring just to boiling point. Place in heated chafing dish and serve at once.

COBB SALAD   SERVES 4-6

½ cup fine grated imported
Roquefort cheese

½ head of lettuce
½ bunch watercress
1 small bunch chicory
½ head romaine
2 medium-sized tomatoes, peeled
2 breasts of boiled roasting
     chicken
6 strips crisp bacon
1 avocado
3 hard-cooked eggs
2 tbs. chopped chives

1 cup Brown Derby Old-fashioned
     French Dressing

Cut finely lettuce, watercress, chicory, and romaine and arrange in salad bowl, cut tomatoes in half, remove seeds,   dice finely,   and arrange in a strip across the salad. Dice breasts of chicken and arrange over top of chopped greens. Chop bacon finely and sprinkle over the salad. Cut avocado in small pieces and arrange around the edge of the salad. Decorate the salad by sprinkling over the top the chopped eggs, chopped chives, and grated cheese. Just before service, mix the salad thoroughly with Brown Derby Old-fashioned French Dressing.

CHILI CON CARNE BROWN DERBY, 2 qts.

¾ lb. kidney fat, diced	*3 small onions, chopped* *fine*	*8 tbs. chili powder*

3 lbs. lean beef round
     ground or diced small
	4 beads garlic, chopped
	     fine
		1 pt. solid-pack tomatoes
		1 ½ tbs. paprika

1 pt. water		*1 ½ tbs. salt*

Cook kidney fat until melted, then add meat and water and cook 1 hour. Add onions and garlic and cook ½ hour longer. Then add chili powder – the best obtainable – and cook ½ hour longer. Next, add tomatoes and cook 1 hour. Season with paprika and salt and stir well. Serve by itself or with Kidney Beans, Enchiladas, or Tamales.

KIDNEY BEANS FOR CHILI

SERVES 12

2 lbs. dry kidney beans	*1 large onion, chopped fine*	*Salt*
1 ham hock		*Pinch of cayenne pepper*

Cover beans and ham hock with cold water and cook slowly for 30 minutes. Drain, cover with fresh boiling water, and cook 1 hour more. As water boils off, add more boiling water. About 10 minutes before beans are finished, add onion, salt, and cayenne pepper to taste.

Serve in proportion of one-third beans to two-thirds chili.

* * *

For a score of years, The Brown Derbys have served two soups which are so popular that they have appeared on the menu every day.

* * *

BROWN DERBY DOUBLE-STRENGTH CHICKEN SOUP

Make Chicken in the Pot (see "Fowl"), then strain soup and heat again, reducing by one-third.

* * *

When the children of Israel fled into the wilderness, they took with them flour but neglected to bring yeast. So the bread that they made was unleavened, like crackers. In celebrating the Passover today, Jewish people eat a crisp, tasty, modern counterpart of this unleavened bread called matzoths. Matzoth meal, similar to cracker crumbs, is the foundation for light, delicious dumplings—Matzoth Balls—which go as well with Chicken Soup as corned beef does with cabbage.

* * *

MATZOTH BALLS, 25

2 eggs	*3 tbsp. chicken fat or butter*	*1 tbsp. chopped chives*
1 cup Matzoth meal	*1 pinch nutmeg*	*1 tsp. baking powder*
4 tbs. chicken broth	*1 tsp. table salt*	*1 pot chicken broth*

Whip eggs in bowl until foamy. Add Matzoth meal, 4 tbs. chicken broth, chicken fat or butter, nutmeg, salt, chives, baking powder. Mix briskly until well mixed. Let stand 2 or 3 minutes. Roll out Matzoth Ball (with your hand buttered) to the size of a marble. Put in a pot of boiling chicken broth, cook on a slow fire for 12 minutes. Serve immediately. If desired, Matzoth Balls may be kept by putting them in a shallow pan covered with the broth they have been cooked in, covering all with waxed paper. They will keep for 2 or 3 days in a refrigerator.

ONION SOUP BROWN DERBY

SERVES 8

¼ lb. butter or ½ cup oil
2½ lbs. onions, sliced
1 qt. beef stock
1 qt. chicken stock

2 tbsp. Worcestershire Sauce
1 bay leaf
1½ tsp. celery salt
Salt

1 tsp. black pepper or 12 pepper-
*   corns, crushed*
4 French rolls
1 cup Parmesan cheese

Heat butter or oil in heavy kettle. Add sliced onions and brown well, stirring constantly. Add beef and chicken stocks, Worcestershire Sauce, bay leaf, celery salt, and pepper. Allow to simmer 40 minutes. Remove bay leaf and salt to taste.

To serve au gratin: toast very thin slices of French roll on both sides. Float on top of Onion Soup in individual tureen. Sprinkle with cheese. Put under open fire until brown. Serve at once in heated tureen.

For Clear Onion Soup, strain through fine sieve and add 1 tbs. of good dry sherry for each cup or 2 tbs. for each bowl.

SPECIALTIES OF THE DAY

In addition to the Specialties of the House, which are served every day, each day of the week has its own special dish which is available both at luncheon and at dinner.

SUNDAY   **PAPRIKA CHICKEN**

SERVES 2

2½-lb. broiler	Salt and pepper	1 cup pastry cream
3 oz. butter	Flour	1 cup chicken broth
1 tbs. finely chopped onion	1 tsp. paprika	¼ tsp. celery salt

Unjoint chicken in 6 pieces, salt-and-pepper and flour them. Heat butter in heavy skillet and sauté the chicken golden brown on both sides. Add onion and sauté 1 minute more. Add paprika and mix well. Add pastry cream, chicken broth, and celery salt. Cover skillet and allow to simmer 18 minutes on slow fire. Should gravy reduce too fast, add more cream or chicken broth. Care should be taken not to add too much extra cream or chicken broth, as this gravy should thicken by reduction. When chicken is well done, season to taste. Serve with noodles or Spaetzels.

MONDAY   **DERBY BEEF STEW**

SERVES 6

1 cup oil	1 tsp celery salt	1 cup Burgundy
2¼ lbs. beef shoulder clod cut in 1-in. pieces, fat removed	1 tsp. basil	8 cups beef stock
	½ tsp. oregano	1 tbs. peppercorns in bag
	1 tbs. paprika	4 fresh tomatoes or 1 No. 2
½ cup finely chopped onion	4 branches celery, diced	can solid-pack
1 bead garlic, chopped fine	18 small carrots, scraped	tomatoes
1 bay leaf	12 small white onions, peeled	12 potatoes
4 tbs. salt	¾ cup flour	1 cup cooked peas

Heat oil in large heavy skillet. As oil begins to smoke, add meat and sauté until evenly browned. Add chopped onion, garlic, bay leaf, salt, celery salt, basil, oregano, paprika, celery, carrots, onions, and sauté 2 minutes longer. Add flour and blend well. Add wine, beef stock, peppercorns in bag, and tomatoes. Cover kettle securely and cook for 1½ hours on slow fire. Add potatoes and cook until meat is done. Remove peppercorn bag and bay leaf. Serve in heated casserole. Sprinkle heated peas on top.

TUESDAY

OLD-FASHIONED POT ROAST
BROWN DERBY

SERVES 6 - 8

8 lbs. beef shoulder clod	2 branches celery, diced	3 fresh tomatoes, diced
Salt and pepper	1 leek, diced	1 No. 2 can tomato purée
1/3 cup oil	½ cup flour	2 beads garlic
1 medium-sized onion, sliced	2 cups Burgundy	1 tbs. paprika
	¼ tsp. basil	1 tbs. celery salt
3 medium-sized carrots, diced	1 bay leaf	1½ qts. stock

Tie shoulder clod securely with string. Wipe meat with a clean, dry cloth and season with salt and pepper. Place in heavy braising kettle in which oil has been heated smoking hot. Brown meat on all sides. Add onion, carrots, celery, and leek. Continue sautéing until vegetables are brown. Add flour and brown again. Mix together and then add wine, basil, bay leaf, tomatoes, purée, garlic, paprika, celery salt, and stock. Bring to gentle boil. Skim off foam and excess fat. Cover kettle tightly. Place in 375°[F] oven for 2 hours and 40 minutes until meat is well done. Remove from oven. Strain sauce through fine sieve. Serve with sliced meat and Brown Derby Potato Pancakes.

BROWN DERBY POTATO PANCAKES

SERVES 8

2 eggs, well beaten	3 potatoes, grated fine	½ tsp. baking flour
¼ tsp. nutmeg	2 tbs. flour	Salt
1 tsp. chopped parsley		½ cup butter

Beat together eggs, nutmeg, parsley, and potatoes. Add flour, baking powder, and salt to taste. Blend well until smooth. Fry in butter, a tablespoonful of batter for each cake. Keep warm in oven until served.

* * *

Jimmy Durante, practically the most popular man in The Hollywood Derby (his caricature even requires two frames), hops from table to table to greet his friends and fans, and on Tuesdays always ordered the Old-fashioned Pot Roast and Potato Pancakes. And speaking of favorite dishes, this is Betty Grable's also.

* * *

WEDNESDAY   **BRAISED SHORT RIBS WITH VEGETABLES**
SERVES 4

2 tbs. oil	*1 cup tomato sauce*	*4 branches celery, diced*
4 1-lb. short ribs	*Salt and pepper*	*12 small carrots, scraped*
2 tbs. flour	*12 small onions*	*1 bay leaf*
3 cups stock or water		*8 new potatoes*

Heat oil in heavy skillet. Add short ribs and sauté until golden brown on both sides. Add flour and smother for 2 minutes. Add stock and purée, blending well. Salt and pepper to taste. Allow to simmer on slow fire for 1½ - 2 hours. Then add onions, celery, carrots, and bay leaf; cook for 30 minutes. Add potatoes and cook until they are well done (approximately 30 minutes). The higher grade meat use, the shorter the cooking period. The short ribs are cooked when the bone can be removed very easily. Serve with the vegetables but remove bay leaf.

THURSDAY   **BROWN DERBY LAMB STEW**
SERVES 6 - 8

1 cup oil	*1 tbs. celery salt*	*8 cups lamb stock*
2¼ lbs. lean leg of lamb in	*1 tsp. basil*	*4 peeled tomatoes or 1 No. 2*
1½- or 2-in. pieces	*½ tsp. rosemary*	*can solid-pack*
2 beads garlic, chopped	*18 small carrots, scraped*	*tomatoes*
½ cup chopped onion	*12 small, white onions,*	*4 tbs. tomato paste purée*
1 bay leaf	*peeled*	*12 peppercorns in bag*
4 tsp. salt	*4 branches celery, diced*	*12 potatoes, peeled*
1 tsp. orégano	*1 cup flour*	*1 cup cooked peas*
	1 cup white wine	

Heat oil very hot in deep heavy skillet or kettle. Add pieces of lamb from which fat has been remove. Sauté meat until evenly browned on all sides. Add garlic, chopped onion, bay leaf, salt, orégano, celery salt, basil, and rosemary and allow to sauté 2 minutes. Add carrots, onions, and celery and continue to sauté for 2 additional minutes. Add flour and blend well into mixture. Mix together wine, stock, tomatoes, purée, and add to first mixture along with bag of peppercorns. Cover kettle securely and cook for 1½ hours over slow fire. Twenty minutes before serving, add potatoes and cook until they are done.

Remove bay leaf and peppercorn bag. Serve in heated casserole with heated peas sprinkled over the top.

FRIDAY   **CORNED BEEF**

Soak brisket of corned beef overnight in cold water. Remove and place in pot with new cold water, 1 whole onion, 2 or 3 carrots, and 2 branches of celery. Boil over very slow fire until tender (approximately 3½ - 4½ hours). Keep covered with plenty of water at all times. After the brisket is tender (when it can be pierced easily with a fork) – lift out carefully, preferably by placing a pan under it. Place in 300°[F] oven for 25 minutes. Remove to slicing board and trim off excess fat. Serve with steamed cabbage or steamed Idaho russet potatoes.

AND CABBAGE

Cut cabbage into single portions and steam in a steamer; or cover with water, add pinches of salt and crushed pepper, and boil until tender (approximately 10 minutes). Cabbage should never be boiled too long or too far in advance of serving.

* * *

As befits the man who did more than anyone else to popularize the dish, George McManus, the creator of "Jiggs and Maggie", is a Corned Beef and Cabbage gourmet. So were such diverse personalities of pre-Derby days as General Cornelius Vanderbilt, Horatio Alger, Jr., and Stuyvesant Fish.

* * *

SATURDAY   **BAKED HAM BROWN DERBY STYLE**
                                        SERVES 15 - 20

12 lbs. tenderized ham	2 cups white wine	1 orange, quartered
36 cloves	1 small stick cinnamon	1 cup crushed pineapple
1 qt. water	2 medium-sized apples, quartered	1 lb. brown sugar or honey

Use skinned ham from which excess fat has been removed. Score ham with cookie cutter and in each square stick a clove. Place in roaster. Add water, wine, cinnamon, apples, orange, and pineapple. Bake 300°[F] for 2 hours, basting every 20 minutes. Then spread brown sugar or honey on top of ham. Bake 1 hour longer, basting about every 10 minutes so as to glaze ham evenly. If liquid should reduce too fast during baking, keep adding a little hot water. When ham is cooked, liquid should be reduced to a heavy syrup. Serve with Sauce Bigarade.

LITTLE THIN HOT CAKES, 1 qt. batter

1 egg	¾ tsp. vanilla	1 tbs. melted butter or
¼ tsp. salt	1½ pts, milk	salad oil
1 ½ tsp. sugar	1 small pkg. Pancake flour - slightly less than 1 lb.	½ tsp. baking powder

The Brown Derby used a special-formula flour. For the home, any well-known prepared pancake flour may be used.

Beat eggs, salt, sugar, and vanilla well together. Add milk, baking powder, and pancake flour, mixing well together. Then add melted butter or salad oil and blend. This batter is best if it stands overnight. In the morning, if too heavy for thin cakes, add more milk.

* * *

In the days when The Vine Street Derby was open all night, the late John Barrymore would drop in several times a week at 3:00 A.M. for these pancakes with little pork sausages, blanched in milk and fried in butter.

* * *

MELTED CHEESE FOR SANDWICHES
8 - 10 SANDWICHES

1 cup Cream Sauce
2 cups grated Cheddar cheese

1 tbs. Worcestershire Sauce

2 tsp. English mustard
Salt

Put together, bring to a boil, and mix well to eliminate lumps. Serve over toast.

* * *

These are the Specialties of the House which you find at the four Brown Derby restaurants. However, in addition, there are certain intangible specialties which have had their share in building this institution—the cheerful service, scrupulous cleanliness, and skilled teamwork of people who like their work and take pride in their crafts.

Hundreds of individuals contribute to every meal served and a great many of them have been with The Derby for a long time. Scores started with the company when it and they were young. They have married, raised families, built their own homes, and their children until now there is a big Brown Derby family which is another outgrowth of that one Little Hat. And that is a Specialty of the House which fills The Derby with pride.

HORS D'OEUVRES

$\mathcal{J}$n serving buffet appetizers or an hors d'oeuvre tray, the best rule is to break away from the accepted definition (hors d'oeuvre—a sardine sandwich cut forty ways) and use your imagination. Almost any food concoction which has met with success and can be presented interestingly in small servings will do.

Starting with a basically delicious tidbit, you cannot miss if you give it eye appeal. Color combinations, design, and arrangement on trays or in other utensils all help to give your dinner or party a good first impression. Once off to a good start, the rest of the affair can coast merrily along.

Whatever you serve, keep your canapés crisp, your hot dishes piping, and your cold ones well chilled. And don't get in a rut. For each new occasion keep switching and mixing your most popular items.

These are some appetizers which have proven "bestsellers" at Hollywood and Beverly Hills parties catered by The Brown Derby.

FLAMING CABBAGE, 24 portions

1 large head cabbage	24-36 green stuffed olives	Ice cubes
1 can of canned heat	24-36 tiny cocktail	1½ cups cocktail sauce
24-36 cocktail picks	sausages	24-36 tiny finger rolls

Cabbage should be evenly shaped and can be white, green, or purple. Cut bottom so it will set level on large serving compote. Next, hollow out center sufficiently to hold the canned heat firm, with the top rim of can just ½ in. below top of cabbage. Arrange cocktail picks. Insert in cabbage head. On end of each pick, place an olive. Place cabbage in compote. Heap ice cubes all around. Set on large tray with dish of cocktail sauce and tiny finger rolls which have been split and buttered. When ready to serve, remove lid and touch a match to canned heat. The result is a delightful blue flame over which the guests can toast their own "hot dogs", the olive protecting the fingers.

Marshmallows may be substituted for children's parties.

BROWN DERBY CHEESE MIX

1 lb. Cheddar cheese ground fine	1½ tbs. English mustard	1 tbs. salt
	2 tbs. Worcestershire Sauce	1 cup milk

Let cheese get warm and soft. Put in electric mixer and add mustard, Worcestershire Sauce, and salt. Turn mixer to low speed until cheese is smooth. Increase speed and add milk slowly. Keep mixing until cheese is nice and fluffy. Store in refrigerator.

THREE DERBY CHEESE SPREADS

OLD CHEDDAR AND PORT WINE

8 oz. old Cheddar cheese
   (the older the
   Cheddar, the better)

3 oz. California port wine

1 pinch salt
2 tbs. mayonnaise
   (optional)

Put cheese through sieve and grind fine. Place in mixing bowl; add wine, salt (and mayonnaise if a creamier spread is desired), and whip vigorously.

CREAM CHEESE AND AVOCADO

8 oz. cream cheese
1 small ripe avocado
2 oz. soft butter

1 pinch salt
1 tbs. chopped chives

1 pinch celery powder or
   celery salt

Put cheese and avocado through fine sieve. Place in mixing bowl; add butter, salt, celery powder or salt, and chives. Beat slowly until smooth.

BLUE CHEESE WITH BRANDY

8 oz. Blue cheese
2 oz. brandy

2 oz. soft butter or
   sour cream

1 tbs. Worcestershire
   Sauce

Grind cheese fine and put through sieve. Place in mixing bowl; add brandy, butter or sour cream, and Worcestershire Sauce. Whip vigorously.

HOW TO STUFF AN EGG

If hard-cooked eggs are cooked slowly the whites will not be tough. Cut off tips so that they will stand on platter; then with a zigzag motion, cut through center of whites, divide the egg in half. Remove yolks carefully. Stand whites in pan of ice water for a few minutes before filling.

STUFFED EGGS DIABLE, 24 portions

12 hard-boiled eggs	*2 tbs. English mustard*	*2 tbs. Worcestershire Sauce*
½ cup butter	*Salt*	*24 thin slices pimento, 1 ½ in.*
1 cup mayonnaise	*2 tbs. chopped chives*	*long*

Prepare white as above. Put yolks through fine sieve and beat until they become paste. Add butter, mayonnaise, mustard, salt to taste, chives, and Worcestershire Sauce. Beat until very creamy and smooth. Fill egg-white halves generously. Make a ring of a small strip of pimento by rolling around finger tip. Place on top of egg and fill center with either capers, tiny minced onions, chopped salmon, or chopped anchovies. Serve on a bed of crushed ice with parsley under eggs. Garnish with lemon sections.

STUFFED EGGS ANCHOVY, 12 portions

6 hard-cooked eggs	*½ cup mayonnaise*	*Parsley*
	4 tbs. anchovy butter	

Prepare whites as above. Put yolks through fine sieve and blend with mayonnaise and anchovy butter until you have a smooth paste. Fill whites, preferably using pastry bag with star tube. Serve with parsley garnish, placing tiny sprig on top of each egg half.

STUFFED EGGS À LA RUSSE, 24 portions

12 hard-cooked eggs	*½ cup finely chopped onion*	*2 oz. caviar*
½ cup mayonnaise	*24 dime-sized bread*	*25 small, thin strips*
1 cup heavy sour cream or	*croutons*	*pimento*
cream cheese		

Prepare whites as above. Put yolks through fine sieve and blend with mayonnaise, sour cream, and onions until smooth paste is formed. Fill whites, using pastry bag with star tube. Garnish top of each egg half with crouton spread with caviar and bordered with pimento.

STUFFED CELERY ROQUEFORT, BROWN DERBY STYLE, 12 pieces

1 medium bunch celery	*2 oz. soft butter*	*1 tbs. Worcestershire*
1 cup Roquefort cheese	*1 tsp. paprika*	*Sauce*

Cut celery in branches as evenly as possible. No portion should be over 4 inches in length. The little heart with bleached leaves may be left on. Chill in ice water for crispness. Dry thoroughly. Mash Roquefort cheese well, add butter and Worcestershire Sauce; beat until very light and creamy. Place in pastry bag, and with star tube fill in celery cavity, beginning at smaller end. Sprinkle with paprika. Pimento cheese or Philadelphia cream cheese may be substituted for Roquefort for variety. Serve on bed of crushed ice.

STUFFED SALAMI HORNS EN CHEESE
SERVES 12

12 slices Italian salami (sliced paper-thin)	1 pkg. (2½ oz.) 1 tbs. minced chives	2 tbs. sour cream 36 capers

To make horns, fold salami slices around finger to form a cornucopia. Pinch the edges together well. To make sure of sticking, brush with egg white [*Caution: Please observe current health and safety guidelines when using raw eggs*].

Chill the horns in refrigerator at least ½ hour before filling with cheese mixture, which is made by mixing cheese with minced chives; blend in cream until very smooth. Use pastry bag to fill horns. Garnish with capers.

CHICKEN LIVERS ON HORSEBACK,
30-36 pieces

1 lb. chicken livers	1 tbs. celery salt	1 tsp. coriander
15 slices bacon	1 tsp. black pepper	36 cocktail picks
3 tbs. butter	1 tsp. basil	

Blanch and clean livers. Sauté in butter until brown. Add celery salt, pepper, basil, and coriander, blending well. Set aside to cool. Roll each chicken liver with ½ slice of blanched bacon, pinning with cocktail pick. When ready to serve, place on broiler rack, broiling and turning until bacon is crisp. Serve in heated chafing dish or ornamental "porcupine".

STUFFED ARTICHOKE BOTTOMS
SERVES 6

½ medium-size onion, minced very fine	1 tbs. mayonnaise	4 tbs. Caviar
2 hard-cooked egg yolks, sieved	6 artichoke bottoms, freshly cooked or canned, well chilled	1 hard-cooked egg white, cut in diamond shapes 6 lemon-parsley slices

Mix onion, yolk of egg, and mayonnaise into paste. Fill scooped-out portions of artichokes with mixture. Top with caviar. Spread evenly. Garnish each with diamond of egg white. Garnish serving plate with lemon parsley slices.

Fillings may be varied, using deviled ham, chopped livers, Roquefort cheese and chopped olives, or cream cheese.

ANCHOVY CANAPÉS, DERBY STYLE
SERVES 2

1 slice toasted bread	2 oz. anchovy filet	4 large pimento-stuffed green olives (in halves)
1 tbs. butter		

Butter toast well. Arrange filets of anchovy as close together as possible. Using a wide spatula, press firmly down into bread to give an even appearance on top. Cut toast in 8 pieces and garnish each with half an olive.

Toast may be cut in varied and interesting shapes.

Smoked salmon, sardines, sturgeon and roe may be used in the same manner, with varied garnishes for eye appeal and taste.

BROWN DERBY DEVILED HAM, 3 pts.

1 lb. cooked ham trimmings	*½ medium-sized onion, chopped*	*1 tsp. black pepper*
3 tbs. butter or oil	*1 cup white wine or water*	*2 tbs. English mustard*
½ green bell pepper, chopped	*1 cup catsup*	*1 tbs. paprika*

Grind ham in food chopper. Heat oil or butter in skillet. Add pepper and onion; brown lightly. Add ground ham and smother few minutes more. Add water or wine, catsup, pepper, mustard, paprika and cook until well reduced, stirring frequently. If mix should be too solid, add mayonnaise to soften.

CALIFORNIA GARDEN RELISH TRAY

Carrot curls	*Green-pepper fingers*	*Large stuffed olives*
Celery curls	*Radish roses*	*Cooked shrimp*
	Avocado balls with coconut	

Carrot and celery curls are made by cutting into shoe-string strips and tossing into ice water. Scoop out avocado in balls and roll in toasted coconut. Remove pimento from olives and replace with cooked shrimp, garnishing top with the pimento. Arrange all relishes on a deep tray which has been packed with cracked ice. Decorate with garden flowers.

DERBY CHOPPED CHICKEN LIVERS, 1 pt.

1 lb. chicken livers	*1 medium-sized onion, chopped fine*	*1 pinch marjoram*
½ cup milk	*½ green apple, chopped fine*	*½ cup sherry*
1½ cups water	*½ tsp. garlic, chopped fine*	*1 cup stock*
1 cup chicken fat	*1 pinch thyme*	*Salt and pepper*

Blanch chicken livers in milk and water. Heat chicken fat in kettle; add livers and fry until brown; now add onion, apple, garlic, and sauté 10 minutes more. Add sherry and stock, cook 15 minutes in covered casserole. Remove from fire and press through fine sieve or run through fine chopper. Mix well and add salt and pepper to taste.

DERBY HORS D'OEUVRE `A LA RUSSE

SERVES 1

2 leaves lettuce, cup-
    shaped
½ cup Salad Russe
2 anchovy filets
1 tsp. capers

2 slices Italian salami
1 slice baked ham
1 marinated herring
2 quarters hard-cooked eggs
1 slice smoked salmon

1 tbs. antipasto, canned or
    in glass
2 boneless sardines
½ medium-sized tomato
3 slices avocado

Place 2 lettuce leaves on a chilled service plate in cup shape. On this place Salad Russe. Garnish top of salad with anchovy filets and sprinkle with capers. Place salami, rolled ham, rolled herring, egg quarters, rolled smoked salmon, antipasto, sardines, tomato, and avocado around the Salad Russe.

Filet Mignon Tidbits and Chicken à la King make ideal hors d'oeuvres. So do the various Emincés and Stroganoffs (see "Meats") and fine-cut chicken dishes ("Fowl"). Also see the Small Patties ("Curries") and Barbecued Spareribs.

The following dishes are equally suitable as appetizers or first courses.

FIRST COURSES

DERBY MARINATED HERRING

SERVES 4 - 8

1 lb. Bismarck pickled
    herring
½ lb. onions, sliced thin

1 apple, grated fine
2 tsp. sugar

½ pt. sour cream
1 tbs. mixed spices
½ cup water

Filet and skin herrings, removing all bones. Mix sliced onions (which have been dipped in boiling water), apple, and sugar with sour cream. Meanwhile boil mixed spices with ½ cup water for 3 minutes. Strain and allow to cool. Stir sour-cream mixture into spiced liquid. Cover bottom of small jar with mixture, next herring, etc., until used. Cover jar securely and store in refrigerator for 12 days to ripen. Serve on rye or pumpernickel bread.

COLD SALMON, SWEET AND SOUR

SERVES 6

3 lbs. salmon or 6 salmon
    steaks
3 cups fish stock
1 medium-sized onion,
    sliced
1 clove garlic
3 bunches celery, sliced fine

3 medium-sized carrots
    sliced
3 sprigs parsley
½ cup white wine
1 tsp. Worcestershire
    Sauce

12 crushed peppercorns
Salt
12 crushed ginger snaps
1 tbs. finely chopped parsley
1 cup catsup
Lime and lemon slices

Lay the salmon steaks in buttered pan. Add fish stock, onion, garlic, carrots, celery, parsley, vinegar, Worcestershire Sauce, peppercorns, and salt to taste. Cover with oiled paper. Steam on slow fire until well done (approximately 20 minutes). When cooked, remove all bone and skin from steaks. Strain vegetables out of remaining stock. Using cheesecloth, strain the bouillon again. Then add gingersnaps, chopped parsley, and catsup. Pour this mixture over salmon. Store in refrigerator for 24 hours to chill thoroughly and ripen seasonings. Serve on ice, surrounding dish with parsley and lime and lemon slices.

CRAB LORENZO PASTE, 1 qt.

3 oz. butter or oil	1 tsp. Worcestershire Sauce	1 tsp. salt
2 tbs. chopped green pepper	1 tsp. paprika	½ tsp. fine white pepper
1 tbs. chopped onion	2 cups Cream Sauce Brown Derby	½ cup pastry cream
½ cup sherry		2 cups cooked crab meat
		3 egg yolks

Heat butter in heavy skillet. Add green pepper and onions. Sauté about 3 minutes. Add sherry, Worcestershire Sauce, salt, paprika, Cream Sauce, pepper, cream, and mix well. Bring to a boil. Simmer for about 5 minutes. Add crab meat. Mix evenly. Simmer for 5 minutes more on slow fire. Thicken with egg yolks that have been mixed with a little cream. Watch to see that it is cooked gently so that eggs will not curdle. After the mixture is the consistency of mush, remove from fire and put into pan to cool.

This mixture can be used for stuffing artichokes, artichoke bottoms, or mushrooms; or it can be spread on toast or croustades, then sprinkled with grated cheese and reheated in the oven, or to fill empty clam or oyster shells, also sprinkled with cheese and placed under the broiler.

MEDALLIONS OF LOBSTER, PARISIENNE
SERVES 4

1 lb. lobster (medium size), cooked	2 tbs. broth	1 cup mayonnaise
1 tbs. gelatin		1 medium-sized dill pickle sliced

Boil lobster. Remove meat from shell and cut into slivers about the size of a crab leg. Chill very thoroughly. Dissolve gelatin in heated broth, set a bowl in basin of crushed ice and add mayonnaise, stirring constantly until mixture begins to thicken. Dip the lobster slivers in this glace. Then put on draining rack and store in refrigerator until completely set. Arrange on slices of dill pickles, or on toast or croutons garnished with dill pickle.

OYSTERS EN SHELL GRANDMOTHER

24 portions

½ cup white wine
3 cups bread croutons
1 cup sliced toasted
    almonds
1 cup Fish Sauce Suprême*
½ tsp. basil
2 tbs. Worcestershire Sauce
    Sauce

1 tbs. celery salt
1 tbs. parsley
¼ lb. butter
½ cup chopped green
    onions
6 sliced crisp bacon
4 egg yolks

½ cup pastry cream
Salt and pepper
24 oysters in half shell
1 cup chopped Cheddar
    cheese
Dash paprika
Lemon slices

Mix together wine, croutons, almonds, Sauce Suprême, basil, Worcestershire Sauce, celery salt, and parsley. Blend well. Heat butter in heavy skillet. Add onions and bacon, sautéing for 3 minutes over a very slow fire. Add egg yolks and pastry cream. Simmer until thick. Add first mixture, blending well. Salt and pepper to taste. Put oysters in half shell on bed of rock salt. Cover each oyster with 2 heaping tbs. of mixture, taking care to smooth top. Sprinkle cheese over each one. Then top with dash of paprika. Bake in 350°[F] oven for 8 minutes. Serve with paprika and lemon slices as garnish.

*To prepare Fish Sauce Suprême, use fish stock instead of chicken stock in Sauce Suprême recipe.

SEAFOOD COCKTAIL

SERVES 1

1/3 cup Derby Seafood
    Cocktail Sauce
2 medium-sized crab legs

2 small pieces boiled
    lobster
6 Olympic oysters
1 tbs. crab meat

2 shrimp, cooked and sliced
Paprika
Lemon slices

In the bottom of ice-cold cocktail glass place a little Cocktail Sauce. Then fill with alternate pieces of various seafood. Over all add the remainder of sauce. Garnish with parsley and paprika-sprinkled lemon slices, crab legs, and choice bit of lobster.

DERBY SEAFOOD COCKTAIL SAUCE

SERVES 6

1 cup chili sauce
1 cup catsup
1 tsp. grated horseradish

1 tbs. olive oil
1 tsp. Worcestershire Sauce
Salt

½ tsp. English mustard
¼ tsp. crushed black
    pepper

Mix all ingredients together in bowl. Stir to a nice, smooth consistency. Chill in refrigerator and serve with any seafood cocktail or with fried shrimp.

DERBY COCKTAIL

SERVES 1

1 tbs. diced celery
6 avocado balls

4 crab legs

3 tbs. strained Thousand
Island Dressing

Place celery in cocktail glass, topped by avocado balls (or diced avocado) and crab legs. Cover with dressing.

ICED CRAB LEGS DERBY

Marinate cooked crab legs and large shrimp in Brown Derby Old-fashioned French Dressing overnight in refrigerator. Serve 3 of each for each guest, arranging on a mound of cracked ice in bowl edged with parsley. On the side, arrange a small bowl of mayonnaise and another of Thousand Island Dressing, some cocktail picks and napkins.

DUNGENESS CRAB LEGS GLACÉED

12 portions

12 cooked crab legs
(about 6 oz.)
1 tbs. gelatin
2 tbs. broth

1 cup Thousand islands
Dressing
12 croutons, size of crab
legs

6 anchovy filets, split
lengthwise
48 capers

Lay crab legs on a rack and chill in refrigerator for 30 minutes. In small bowl soak gelatin in broth. Then add to Thousand Island Dressing and mix well. Place bowl in basin of cracked ice, stirring all the time until it begins to set. Cover crab legs with mixture, taking care to spread evenly. Return to refrigerator to become solid. Trim off any extra dressing. Serve on croutons. Garnish with rings of anchovy and capers just before service.

MELON SUPRÊME AU VIN

SERVES 1

4 balls each of watermelon,
Persian, honeydew
cantaloupe

½ cup sweet white wine
4 frosted mint leaves
Powdered sugar (optional)

Soak melon ball in wine for 1 hour in refrigerator. Frost mint leaves by dipping first in egg white , then in very fine granulated sugar, allowing to dry for a few minutes before using *[raw egg may contain bacteria which may be harmful to your health]* powdered sugar. Arrange melon balls in an ice-cold cocktail glass. Pour remaining wine over all, then garnish with frosted mint leaves.

CRAB COCKTAIL DERBY STYLE

SERVES 1

2 tbs. crab meat   1/3 cup Derby Seafood   4 large crab legs
                                   Cocktail Sauce

In bottom of ice-cold cocktail glass, place part of Cocktail Sauce, then fill with crab meat. Cover with remainder of sauce. Garnish top with crab legs and serve.

The same procedure and portions may be used for lobster, oysters, or shrimp.

STUFFED CANTALOUPE SURPRISE

SERVES 2

1 cup Derby Fruit Salad   1 medium cantaloupe, cut   1 cup watermelon balls
½ cup sweet white wine   in half zigzag   1 cup honeydew melon balls
                                 8 mint leaves

Allow Fruit Salad to marinate in wine in refrigerator for several hours. Fill halves of very cold cantaloupe with fruit salad. Garnish with mint leaves and watermelon and honeydew balls. Serve on iced plates.

Other suggestions: Derby Fruit Supreme and Brown Derby Shrimp Louie (see "Salads and Dressings").

SOUP

S O U P S

se plenty of fresh vegetables and good stock in your soups, says The Brown Derby chef. And don't skimp on cooking time, for too little cooking can spoil the broth. Stir occasionally while soup simmers, especially if it is a heavy one, where the solid ingredients can sink to the bottom and burn.

All but the cream soups will improve if, after cooking, they stand awhile—anywhere from 1 to 3 hours. Then, depending on the soup, serve either piping hot or ice-cold, in pre-warmed or well-chilled plates or cups (or bowls).

DERBY SPLIT PEA SOUP

SERVES 8

1 lb. green split peas
¼ cup butter
1 medium-sized onion, sliced
2 small pieces of celery, sliced

1 ham hock or whole ham bone
3 pts. chicken or beef stock
½ bay leaf

½ tsp. black peppercorns
Salt
1 cup pastry cream
½ cup croutons

The peas should be the quick-cooking kind, otherwise soak them overnight in water. Heat butter in heavy kettle. Add onion and celery. Allow to simmer 4 minutes. Add peas, ham bone, stock, bay leaf, peppercorns and salt. Cook 1 ½ hours on slow fire. Strain through fine sieve and add heated cream. Taste for salt. Serve in heated tureen with croutons floating on top.

DERBY VEGETABLE SOUP

SERVES 10 – 15

¼ lb. butter
½ cup diced onion
1 head garlic, diced
½ cup diced celery
1 cup diced white cabbage
1/3 cup diced leeks
1 cup diced carrots

1 gal. chicken or beef stock
Spice bag containing 12 peppercorns, 1 bay leaf, 1 tsp. basil, 1 sprig rosemary
Salt and pepper

1/3 cup raw rice, washed
1 cup raw potatoes, diced
1½ cup tomatoes
½ cup peas
½ cup string beans
1 tbs. parsley, chopped
Cheese croutons

Heat butter in heavy kettle. Add onion, garlic, celery, cabbage, leeks, and carrots. Smother 8 minutes. Add stock gradually; then add spice bag and small amount of salt. Cook 40 minutes on slow fire. Next add rice, potatoes, tomatoes, peas, beans, and cook 30 minutes more. Taste for salt and pepper. Sprinkle with parsley. Serve with cheese croutons.

DERBY SCOTCH LAMB BROTH WITH BARLEY
10 cups; 5 bowls

¼ cup butter	½ clove garlic, chopped fine	½ bay leaf and 9 peppercorns
½ cup finely diced onion	½ cup barley	in bag
1 large carrot, diced small	3 level tbs. flour	Salt and pepper
½ cup finely diced celery	2 qts. strong lamb stock	1 cup pastry cream

Melt butter in heavy kettle. Add onion, carrot, celery, garlic. Braise without allowing to change color for 5 minutes. Add barley and flour. Continue to braise 2 minutes longer. Add hot lamb stock and mix well. Add bay leaf and peppercorns in bag. Allow to simmer slowly for 1½ hours. Remove spice bag; salt and pepper to taste. Add cream and allow to simmer few minutes more before serving.

OLD-FASHIONED POTATO AND LEEK SOUP WITH FRANKFURTERS
SERVES 10

¾ cup butter	3 qts. chicken broth	8 frankfurters, cooked,
1 cup finely chopped onion	½ tsp. nutmeg	skinned and sliced
2 cups finely chopped leeks	1 ham hock or bone	Salt and pepper
5 lbs. potatoes, cut shoe-string	1 cup pastry cream	1 cup bread croutons
	Salt and pepper	
	1 cup bread croutons	

Heat butter in medium-sized heavy kettle. Add onion and leeks and smother without allowing to change color for 4 minutes. Add potatoes, chicken broth, nutmeg, and ham hock. Bring to boil and allow to simmer 1¼ hours. Remove ham hock and strain soup through fine sieve, pressing as much of the solids as possible through sieve. Pour back into kettle. Add cream and bring to a boil. Season with salt and pepper. Serve with bread croutons and frankfurters.

DERBY CLAM CHOWDER
SERVES 10

1 lb. Eastern clams	1 bead garlic, chopped	¼ tsp. celery salt
½ cup butter	½ cup diced bell pepper	Salt and pepper
½ cup finely diced salt port	4 tbs. flour	3 medium-sized tomatoes, diced
1 cup diced onion	¼ tsp. thyme	2 cups raw, diced potatoes
1 cup julienne leeks	1 medium-sized bay leaf	1 tbs. minced parsley
2 cups celery	3 qts. chicken stock	

Remove clams from shells, saving liquor. If clams are large they may be cut. Heat butter in large heavy kettle. Add salt pork and braise 3 minutes. Then add onion, leeks, celery, garlic, and pepper. Continue to sauté over slow fire 5 minutes. Care must be taken not to permit vegetables to brown. Add flour, thyme, and bay leaf. Continue sautéing 2 minutes longer. Add chicken stock and clam liquor which have been heated, bringing mixture to a boil. Skim off all foam. Add clams, celery salt, salt and pepper to taste. Cook 1 hour on slow fire. Add tomatoes, potatoes, and parsley. Cook 15 minutes more. Serve in heated tureen.

OLD-FASHIONED BEAN SOUP DERBY
SERVES 8

1 cup dried beans
¼ cup butter
½ cup diced carrots
½ cup diced celery

½ cup diced onion
¼ cup julienne leeks
(optional)
2 qts. chicken or beef stock

1 ham hock or bone
2 medium tomatoes, peeled
and diced
1 tbs. chopped parsley

Soak beans 8 hours in cold water. Heat butter in large kettle. Add carrots, celery, onion, leeks, and braise 5 minutes without browning. Add beans, stock, ham hock and cook 1½ hours. Add tomatoes and parsley. Allow to simmer 10 minutes more. Remove ham before serving. Meat may be trimmed from ham hock, diced fine, and put back in soup.

CREAM OF CHICKEN À LA REINE
SERVES 8

½ cup butter or chicken fat
¾ cup flour
3 pts. chicken broth

1 pt. pastry cream
½ cup finely diced mushrooms
Salt and pepper
Juice of ½ lemon

½ cup cooked diced chicken
meat (white or dark)
½ cup croutons

Heat butter in heavy kettle. Add flour. Cook gently 4 minutes, without browning. Add hot chicken broth and blend well. Add hot cream and mushrooms. Simmer 40 minutes on slow fire. Season with salt and pepper to taste. Add lemon juice and diced chicken. Serve with croutons.

ASPARAGUS SOUP À LA DERBY

Complete the Cream of Chicken à la Reine recipe and then add ½ lb. raw green asparagus, cut in pieces. Cook well 30 minutes more; then press through a fine sieve.

CREAM OF TOMATO SOUP DERBY
SERVES 8

2 cups or 2 7-oz. cans
tomato purée
1 tsp. sugar

1 cup Cream Sauce
Brown Derby

1 cup pastry cream
¼ cup butter
Salt and pepper

Add Cream Sauce and sugar to purée and heat to boiling point in top of double boiler. In another container, heat cream to boiling point. Combine the two and whip in the butter vigorously. Season to taste.

CREAM OF MUSHROOM SOUP

SERVES 6

½ cup butter	½ cup white wine	½ tsp. nutmeg
½ lb. mushrooms, chopped	1 qt. chicken broth	Salt and pepper
½ cup flour	1 pt. pastry cream	1 tbs. minced chives

Heat butter in heavy kettle; add mushrooms and sauté until lightly colored. Add flour, mix well; smother for 1 or 2 minutes more without browning. Add wine and chicken broth and mix well to dissolve any lumps of flour. Add cream. Allow to simmer 30 minutes. Season with nutmeg; salt and pepper to taste. Serve with sprinkle of minced chives.

CLEAR CONSOMMÉ, 2 qts.

2 lbs. ground beef shank	5 eggshells or ¼ cup egg	2 cups crushed ice
½ onion, sliced	whites	2 qts. beef stock, cold, no fat
2 branches celery, sliced	12 black peppercorns	1 tomato, chopped
½ leek, sliced	1 bay leaf	Salt
2 medium carrots		

In a medium-sized heavy kettle, place meat, onion, celery, leek, carrots, eggshells, peppercorns, bay leaf, and crushed ice. Mix well. Add ice-cold beef stock, tomato, and mix again. Place on fire, bring to a very slow boil, and allow to simmer for 1½ hours. Strain, a ladle at a time, through fine cloth, and season with salt.

To make Beef Aspic, soak 9 sheets or 9 heaping tbs. of powdered gelatin in water, then press water out and add to the hot consommé after it has been strained. Bring to a boil, cool, and allow to set in refrigerator.

For Chicken Aspic, prepare as above, with two exceptions: Use chicken broth instead of beef stock and eliminate the tomatoes.

JELLIED TOMATO BOUILLON MADRILÈNE

SERVES 8

2 lbs. ground lean beef shank	½ leek, sliced (optional)	1 bay leaf
2½ lbs. tomatoes, chopped	2 medium-sized carrots, sliced	1 gal. chicken stock
Juice of ½ lemon	6 eggshells or ¼ cup egg	9 sheets gelatin or
½ medium-sized onion, sliced	whites	9 heaping tbs. powdered gelatin
2 branches celery, sliced	12 peppercorns	Salt

Place in a medium-sized heavy kettle beef, tomatoes, lemon juice, onion, celery, leek, carrots, eggshells, peppercorns, bay leaf, and stock. Cover and bring to a slow boil. Allow to simmer for 2 hours. Add gelatin. Strain, a ladle at a time, through fine cloth. Season to taste. Put in refrigerator to cool; then pour in molds or serving cups.

COLD VICHYSSOISE, 2 qts.

½ cup butter
½ cup finely chopped onion
½ cup finely chopped carrots
½ cup finely chopped celery

2 cups dried navy beans,
        soaked overnight
6 sorrel leaves (optional)

1 qt. pastry cream
1 qt. chicken broth
Salt and pepper
4 tbs. finely chopped chives

Heat butter in heavy kettle. Add onion, carrots, celery; smother without allowing them to take color for 4 minutes. Add soaked beans, sorrel, pastry cream, chicken broth; simmer slowly for 1½ hours. Strain through fine sieve, pressing through all the beans and as much of the vegetables as possible. Mix well and allow to cool. Before serving, place container in bed of shaved ice. Should soup be too thick, thin down to desired consistency with ice-cold pastry cream. Season to taste and serve in ice-cold soup cup, sprinkling with chives.

While known principally as a cold soup, this Vichyssoise is also excellent when served hot.

CREAM OF AVODELLO

SERVES 4

8 medium-sized carrots, diced
1 medium-sized apple, diced
½ large onion, diced
1 tbs. curry powder

1 small bay leaf
2 cups heavy cream
1 qt. chicken stock
1 large avocado, seeded
        and peeled

1 cup flour
½ cup melted butter
Salt and pepper

GARNISH: Diced, fresh pineapple, whipped cream, and shredded coconut.

Cook carrots, apple, onions, curry powder, and bay leaf in chicken stock until vegetables are tender. Add avocado and allow to cook 5 minutes more. Thicken with flour and butter which has been rubbed to a paste. Cook 10 minutes. Strain all through a fine sieve, pressing the vegetables into purée. Chill thoroughly. This mixture will become very heavy when chilled. Before serving, blend in cream, whipping slowly. Add salt and pepper to taste. *Serve in chilled soup plates.* In bottom of chilled soup plate, place 2 tbs. diced, fresh pineapple and add 1 cup chilled soup. Garnish with whipped cream topped with coconut.

COLD RUSSIAN BORSCHT, 1 qt.

1½ cups jellied consommé
        or cold chicken broth
1 cup sour cream

1½ cups finely chopped beets.
        with juice

1 tbs. finely chopped chives
Salt and pepper
1 tbs. finely chopped chives

Blend together in a medium-sized mixing bowl the consommé or broth with beets, sour cream; salt and pepper to taste. Mix well with a French whip; then serve with chives sprinkled on top. Canned consommé can be used if more convenient.

CALIFORNIA COLD SOUP

SERVES 8 – 10

1 qt. tomato juice
½ onion, chopped fine
Juice of 1 lemon
2 tbs. finely chopped green
*   pepper*
¾ tsp. Tabasco sauce

1 tsp. Worcestershire Sauce
1 cucumber, peeled
*   seeded, chopped fine*
1 pt. chicken broth, no fat,
*   ice-cold*

1 medium avocado, diced fine
2 tbs. olive oil
Celery salt
Pepper
12 cheese croutons
Rye bread

Blend together in a medium-sized mixing bowl tomato juice, onion, lemon juice, green pepper, Tabasco, Worcestershire Sauce, cucumber, and chicken broth. Add avocado, olive oil, mix lightly again. Season with celery salt and pepper to taste. Cool. Serve ice-cold with cheese croutons and rye bread.

OLD-FASHIONED LENTIL SOUP

SERVES 8

½ cup butter
½ cup finely chopped onion
¼ cup finely chopped leeks
¼ cup finely chopped carrots

4 slices bacon, chopped fine
½ lb. lentils, soaked 8 hours
3 pts. chicken broth

1 ham bone
Salt and pepper
4 frankfurters, skinned
*   and sliced*

Heat butter in heavy kettle. Add onion, leeks, carrots, and bacon and smother, without browning, for 4 minutes. Add lentils, chicken broth, ham bone, and simmer on slow fire for 1½ hours. Remove half of the lentils and press through fine sieve. Add the purée of lentils to soup and mix well. Simmer for 10 minutes more. Remove ham bone; season with salt and pepper to taste. Serve with sliced frankfurters in soup.

LOUISIANA BLACK BEAN SOUP

SERVES 8

8 slices bacon, chopped fine
1 cup finely chopped onion
½ cup finely chopped leeks
½ cup chopped carrots
1 cup butter

1 lb. black beans, soaked
*   8 hours*
1 ham bone
3 qts. chicken broth

2 cups chopped mustard
*   greens*
8 frankfurters, skinned and
*   sliced*
Salt and pepper

Fry bacon bits in heavy kettle. Add onion, leeks, and carrots. Allow to smother for 10 minutes. As it becomes dry, add butter to avoid burning. Add black beans which have been pre-cooked to point of tenderness, along with ham bone and broth. Cook 1 hour. Then add mustard greens. Cook for 1½ hours more. Divide the soup in half. Press half through sieve. Then mix both together again. Remove ham bone and cut any meat on the bone into very fine pieces. Add meat to the soup. If insufficient, then add thinly sliced frankfurters. Season lightly with salt and pepper to taste. Serve in a heated soup tureen with buttered croutons.

BLACK BEAN POT

SERVES 6

1½ lbs. black beans
½ lb. salt pork, sliced
1 small ham bone
1 qt. water
1 onion, minced

½ clove garlic, chopped fine
½ carrot, diced
5 tbs. fat
1 bay leaf, crushed

Pinch thyme
¼ tsp. nutmeg
2 tbs. brown sugar, warned
½ cup Jamaica rum
Salt and pepper

Soak the beans 2 hours, drain, and place in a large cast-iron pot with salt pork, ham bone, and water. Bring to a boil. Sauté the onion, garlic, and carrot in the fat in a separate skillet. Then add to pot. Add the bay leaf, thyme, and nutmeg. Cook slowly for 3 hours. Add sugar and rum and season to taste. Mix well and serve.

CHICKEN OKRA SOUP DERBY, 2 qts.

3 oz. butter
½ cup onion
¼ cup diced celery
½ cup diced bell pepper
½ bead garlic, chopped fine

1 cup sliced and washed
fresh okra
1 cup seeded, diced tomatoes
¼ cup raw rice, washed
1½ qt. chicken broth

½ tsp. celery salt
1 small ham hock or bone
Herb bag - 1 bay leaf, 10
peppercorns, sprig thyme
½ tsp. Gumbo Filé
Salt and pepper

Heat butter in heavy kettle. Add onion, celery, bell pepper, and smother without browning vegetables for about 4 minutes. Add garlic, okra, tomatoes, rice, and chicken broth. Then add celery salt, ham hock, and herb bag. Boil on slow fire for 1 hour. Add Gumbo Filé and salt and pepper to taste.

BISQUE OF LOBSTER

SERVES 4

¼ cup butter
1 medium-sized carrot, diced
¼ medium-sized onion, minced
1 sprig parsley
¼ tsp. thyme
1 bay leaf

3 lbs. lobster (raw,
if available)
3 tsp. brandy
½ cup white wine
½ cup consommé

Salt and pepper
½ cup raw rice
4 cups chicken broth or
consommé
4 tbs. whipped cream
¼ tsp. cayenne pepper

Heat butter in heavy, deep saucepan; add carrot, onion, parsley, thyme, and bay leaf. Sauté until golden brown. Add all of lobster, cut in small pieces, except some tail meat, cut in thin slices, which will be used as garnish. Sauté until meat turns very red. Sprinkle with brandy. Add wine, consommé, and season with salt and pepper. Cover and simmer gently for 15 minutes. In a separate saucepan, cook rice in 3 of the cups of broth until very soft (approximately 30 minutes). Then rub rice through fine sieve. Drain lobster and vegetables, saving slices of lobster for garnish and any remaining liquid, but removing bay leaf. Pound lobster and vegetables into paste an put through sieve. Add puréed rice and remaining liquor. Blend well and place in top of double boiler. Add remaining cup consommé while beating. Allow to reach boiling point and keep over hot water until served. Several small lumps of butter may be added to prevent skim forming. Add 1 tbs. of whipped cream with a dash of cayenne pepper to each plate. Garnish with lobster meat saved for this purpose.

BEEF STOCK

5 lbs. beef bones in 3-in. pieces	*3 branches celery*	*15 black peppercorns*
1 onion	*1 bay leaf*	*3 tbs. salt*
4 carrots		*1 sprig parsley*

Blanch bones, then wash thoroughly. Put bones back into pot, cover with water, add remainder of ingredients, and bring to boil. Skim, then simmer for 2½ - 3 hours. Strain and use wherever stock is called for.

To give color to stock, cut onion in two and burn cut edge over open flame until black.

DERBY OXTAIL AND VEGETABLE SOUP
10 bowls; 20 cups

2 oxtails (4 lbs.), unjointed	*2 cups diced celery*	*12 medium-sized carrots,*
4 lbs. neck meat of beef (bones)	*4 medium-sized onions, sliced*	*scraped*
1 gal. water or light beef stock	*3 beads garlic, chopped fine*	*1 cup diced leeks (optional)*
1 medium-sized cabbage, diced	*1 bay leaf and 24 peppercorns*	*Salt and pepper*
4 medium-sized tomatoes, diced	*in bag*	*2 tbs. finely chopped chives*

Place oxtails and beef in a heavy kettle. Cover with cold water and bring to boil. Drain off liquid and wash oxtails and meat well. Return to kettle. Add water or stock, cabbage, tomatoes, celery, onions, garlic, bay leaf and peppercorns, carrots, leeks, salt and pepper. Allow to simmer until meat is well done. Remove tails and meat. Allow to cool. Remove spice bag. Remove meat from tails and neck bones. Dice and add to soup; then bring to a boil. Serve with chives.

Also see Beef and Chicken Petite Marmites ("Meats" and Fowl") and the Onion Soups and Chicken Soup recipes ("Specialties of the House").

SALADS

SALADS
AND
DRESSINGS

$\mathcal{I}$t has long been a Western custom to follow the soup course with a salad and this custom has been slowly spreading eastward. The year-round availability of fresh fruits and vegetables in Hollywood has led The Derby restaurants to specialize in a wide variety of salad dishes and many of the stars, because of diet or choice, order a salad as their main or only dish at lunchtime.

As with appetizers, salads should have a strong appeal to the eye. This is the hostess' opportunity to blend, in an artistic manner, foods which complement each other in taste, color, and texture. The vegetables and fruits should be crisp and fresh, looking as if they just came out of the garden. And when using the Old-fashioned French Dressing, which is the pride of The Derby, make sure that the oil and vinegar are well-mixed.

Listed first is the Brown Derby Mixed Green Salad, an overwhelming favorite with roasts or steaks. Though simple, the patrons never tire of it. The Caliente Salad and its variation, the Gourmet, came north from Agua Caliente Hotel in Mexico and are mixed at the table with just a bit of pomp and ceremony.

[Caution: Current health safety guidelines recommend caution when using raw eggs. These following recipes are included just as presented in the 1ˢᵗ edition.]

BROWN DERBY MIXED GREEN SALAD
SERVES 4

½ head romaine cut in 1-in. pieces	½ head chicory	½ cup Brown Derby
½ head (medium size) lettuce, pulled	2 tomatoes, peeled and	Old-fashioned
½ bunch watercress	quartered	French Dressing
	½ cup chopped celery	

Toss the greens in a large, cold salad bowl and mix lightly. Garnish with the tomatoes. Sprinkle chopped celery on top. Just before serving, add French Dressing and toss lightly.

CALIENTE SALAD

SERVES **4**

*1 large head romaine, cut in
1-in. pieces
1 cup French-bread croutons
2 eggs coddled 1 minute*

*4 chopped anchovies
1 tsp. crushed black pepper
2 heaping tbs. Parmesan Cheese
1 tbs. Worcestershire Sauce*

*½ tsp. English mustard
½ cup Brown Derby
Old-fashioned
French Dressing*

Place the crisp, clean romaine in mixing bowl. Prepare croutons by frying ½ –inch cubes of French bread crisp in garlic oil or butter, made by combining a little chopped fresh garlic with oil or butter. Sprinkle the croutons over the romaine. Break the coddled eggs into a smaller mixing bowl, taking care to scoop out the whites from the shells. *[Be sure to follow health guidelines when cooking raw eggs.]* Add chopped anchovies, crushed pepper (preferably put through pepper mill), cheese, Worcestershire Sauce, and mustard, and mix. Slowly add the French Dressing into this mixture. Pour the dressing over the romaine and croutons. Toss the salad and serve.

BROWN DERBY POTATO SALAD

SERVES **4**

*3 Idaho russets, large
1 tbs. parsley
2 tbs. chives
4 slices crisp bacon, chopped fine*

*1 tsp. celery salt
½ cup hot chicken broth
½ cup Brown Derby
Mayonnaise*

*1/3 cup Brown Derby
Old-fashioned
French Dressing
2 tbs. wine vinegar*

Boil potatoes until well done. While still slightly warm, slice into a medium-sized salad bowl. Add chives, bacon, chicken broth, celery salt, Mayonnaise, French Dressing, wine vinegar, and parsley. Mix well; allow to stand for 1 hour and serve.

GOURMET SALAD

SERVES **4**

*½ head romaine lettuce cut in
1-in. pieces
½ head (medium size) lettuce,
pulled
½ bunch watercress*

*2 tomatoes, quartered
2 tbs. crisp chopped bacon
12 cheese croutons
2 coddled eggs*

*1 tbs. garlic oil or pinch
of chopped fresh garlic
½ cup Brown Derby
Old-fashioned
French Dressing*

Place greens in large salad bowl. Garnish with tomatoes. Sprinkle with bacon. Garnish with cheese croutons, made from thin slices of French-bread rolls which are toasted with garlic butter and Parmesan cheese. Take smaller bowl and break coddled eggs into it, taking care to scoop out the whites. Add garlic and French Dressing and mix well. Pour over salad, toss and serve.

BEVERLY SALAD BOWL

SERVES 4

1 medium-sized head romaine	*2 cups shredded coleslaw*	*4 oz. white meat of chicken*
¼ medium-sized head lettuce	*¾ cup Brown Derby Old-fashioned*	* julienne*
¼ bunch watercress	* French Dressing*	*2 hard-cooked eggs, sliced*
½ bunch chicory	*4 oz. lean baked ham julienne*	*2 tbs. chopped chives*
	4 oz. Swiss cheese julienne	

Cut romaine, lettuce, watercress, and chicory in 1-in. pieces and toss together in a chilled salad bowl with the coleslaw and French Dressing. Arrange the ham, cheese, and chicken on top in wedge style. Garnish with sliced eggs, sprinkle with chopped chives.

COLESLAW FOR SANDWICHES

SERVES 10

2 cups shredded cabbage	*½ cup Thousand Island*
	* Dressing*

In a medium-sized bowl, place cabbage and dressing and toss well.

CHICKEN SALAD DERBY

SERVES 2

½ cup Brown Derby Mayonnaise	*1 cup diced cooked chicken,*	*1 cup Pascal celery, diced very*
½ cup lemon juice	* white or dark meat*	* small*
½ tsp. Worcestershire Sauce	*2 lettuce leaves*	*Salt and pepper*

GARNISH:

1 tomato in quarters, peeled	*1 hard-cooked egg, sliced*	*1½ cups julienne chicken,*
2 rings bell pepper		* white meat*

Blend together Mayonnaise, lemon juice, and Worcestershire Sauce. In a chilled bowl, using fork, toss together chicken and celery. Add dressing mixture and toss again. Season to taste with salt and pepper. Heap in lettuce cup on chilled service plates. Garnish each plate with tomato quarters on each side, pepper ring in center with egg slices inside. Then sprinkle all with chicken julienne.

DERBY CHEF SALAD

SERVES 2

*4 cups mixed greens (lettuce,
    romaine, chicory,
    watercress)
½ cup diced celery*

*½ cup diced baked ham
1 hard-cooked egg, chopped fine
1 tbs. finely chopped parsley*

*1½ tomatoes, cut in quarters
½ cup Brown Derby
    Old-fashioned
    French Dressing*

Toss mixed greens in a medium-sized, ice-cold salad bowl. On top of them, sprinkle celery, ham, egg, and parsley. On sides of bowl, lay quartered tomatoes. Serve in the bowl with French Dressing.

* * *

Heading the list of seafood salads is Crab and Avocado Rodeo, which was created for the opening of the Beverly Hills Brown Derby, located at Rodeo Drive and Wilshire Boulevard.

* * *

CRAB AND AVOCADO RODEO

SERVES 2

*1 cup shredded cabbage
½ cup Thousand Island Dressing
1 cup cooked crab legs
½ avocado, peeled and sliced*

*4 anchovy filets, split lengthwise
4 hard-cooked eggs, sliced
2 rings bell pepper
1 tbs. capers*

*1 medium-sized tomato,
    peeled and sliced
4 asparagus tips, cooked
1 lemon, cut in half*

In a band across center of cold plate and from rim to rim, arrange shredded cabbage that has been mixed with a small amount of the Thousand Island Dressing. On top of cabbage arrange crab legs and meat as neatly as possible. Cover with remainder of the dressing. Arrange sliced avocado in neat line on this. On top of avocado, place filets of anchovy, ring of pepper, and a few capers. On both long sides, place sliced tomato, asparagus tips, and egg slices. Garnish with lemon.

Shrimp or lobster may be used in place of crab legs.

CRAB SALAD DERBY

SERVES 2

*1 cup cooked crab meat and legs
1 cup finely diced Pascal celery*

*½ cup mayonnaise
2 lettuce leaves [cup-shaped]
Juice of ½ lemon*

*½ tsp. Worcestershire Sauce
Salt and pepper*

GARNISH:

*2 rings bell pepper
2 large crab legs*

*1 tomato, peeled and
    quartered*

*1 hard-cooked egg, sliced or
    quartered*

In a medium-sized, ice-cold salad bowl, place crab meat and legs, celery, half of mayonnaise, lemon juice, Worcestershire Sauce, salt and pepper to taste. Mix well. On two ice-cold plates arrange lettuce cups. Place half the salad in each lettuce cup, cover with remainder of mayonnaise. Garnish each top with 1 ring of bell pepper and a large crab leg. Around the sides, place quarters of tomato and egg.

PALACE COURT SALAD

SERVES 1

1 cup shredded lettuce	*1 large artichoke bottom*	*1 tsp. capers*
4 crab legs, cooked	*4 lobster medallions, cooked*	*4 shrimp, split and cooked*
2 hard-cooked eggs, chopped fine	*2 tbs. Thousand Island*	*4 cooked asparagus tips*
1 large slice tomato	*Dressing*	*8 pimento strips*
	1 ring green pepper	

Arrange a round bed of shredded lettuce in the center of an ice-cold plate. Over lettuce sprinkle chopped hard-cooked eggs. Press the egg into the lettuce with a cloth until you have around platform. In the center of platform, place a slice of tomato. On top of tomato, place an artichoke bottom. Fill artichoke bottom with lobster and crab legs. Cover with dressing. On top, place the pepper ring. Sprinkle capers in center of ring. Around the base of the platform, arrange the shrimp, asparagus tips, and strips of pimento in equal distances.

AVOCADO NEPTUNE DERBY

SERVES 2

1 large avocado	*½ cup Tartar Sauce*	*1 shrimp, split in half*
1 cup seafood salad (either shrimp,	*2 rings bell pepper*	*1 tsp. capers*
crab, lobster, or a	*2 crab legs*	*2 lettuce leaves*
combination	*2 slices lobster*	*1 lemon, cut in half*

Cut avocado in half lengthwise and remove stone. Fill with seafood salad and mold to the side of the avocado. Cover with Tartar Sauce. Place 1 ring of pepper in middle of avocado. Decorate with crab leg, sliced lobster, and ½ shrimp. Sprinkle a few capers over top. Serve on a bed of lettuce with lemon as garnish.

DERBY FRUIT SUPREME

SERVES 1

2/3 cup Derby Fruit Salad Mixture	*4 grapefruit sections*	*1 fresh strawberry (or cherry)*
4 orange sections	*1 slice fresh fig (if available)*	*2 mint leaves*

Place Derby Fruit Salad Mixture in ice-cold cocktail glass. Garnish with sections of orange and grapefruit. Decorate with mint leaves held down by a slice of fresh fig; on top of fig, place a strawberry.

SHRIMP SALAD DERBY

SERVES 2

½ cup mayonnaise
½ tsp. Worcestershire Sauce
Juice of ½ lemon
1 cup shrimp, split, cleaned,
     cooked

1 cup finely diced Pascal
     celery
Salt and pepper
2 lettuce leaves [cup-shaped]

1 tomato, peeled and
     quartered
1 hard-cooked egg, sliced
2 rings bell pepper
2 large shrimp, split, cooked

Blend together mayonnaise, Worcestershire Sauce, and lemon juice. In a chilled salad bowl, toss together shrimp and celery. Add first mixture and toss again. Season with salt and pepper to taste. Heap in lettuce cups on chilled service plate. Garnish with tomato quarters. Top with egg slices, pepper ring, and crown with large shrimp.

SEAFOOD GOURMET

Escarole
Chicory
Celery
Lobster

Crab
Shrimp
Artichoke hearts

Pickled mushrooms
Hard-cooked egg
Brown Derby Old-fashioned
     French Dressing

Cut escarole and chicory in 1-in. square pieces. Place in ice-cold salad bowl. On top sprinkle with celery, lobster, crab, and shrimp. Garnish with artichoke hearts, mushrooms, sliced or quartered hard-cooked egg, and serve with French Dressing.

CALIFORNIA QUEEN SALAD

SERVES 1

Shredded lettuce
3 stewed pear halves
Bits of ripe olives

Pimento strips
Cottage cheese
Cream cheese

Avocado balls
Sliced stuffed olives
Lemon

Place a mound of finely shredded lettuce on chilled salad plate. Arrange pears evenly spaced with smaller ends toward center. Make a face on each pear half by using bits of ripe olives for eyes and nose and strip of pimento for mouth. Next, place a scoop of cottage and cream cheese, mixed, in center of place where pears meet. Garnish cheese with avocado balls and sliced olives. Serve with lemon for dressing.

* * *

If Mae West ever comes up to see you, serve her this salad. It is what she always orders at The Derby at lunchtime.

* * *

LOUISE SALAD

Lettuce slice   Pineapple slice   Brown Derby Mayonnaise
                                   Celery curls

On a slice of lettuce, arrange slice of pineapple. Sprinkle with celery julienne which has been soaked in ice water to make it curl. Serve with Mayonnaise.

DERBY FRUIT SALAD MIXTURE

SERVES 6

2 oranges, in sections   2 medium apples, peeled,   1 cup diced cantaloupe
2 grapefruit, in sections   cored, diced   1 cup canned or fresh sliced
1 cup strawberries, quartered   1 cup canned or fresh grapes   pineapple
6 peach halves (fresh or canned)   1 cup diced watermelon   Orange juice, if canned fruit
    diced   not used

In a medium-sized salad bowl, place sections of oranges and grapefruit, strawberries, peaches, apples, grapes, watermelon, cantaloupe, pineapple, and just enough of the canned fruit juice for mixing. If canned fruit is not used, add orange juice for moisture. Toss lightly. Serve in lettuce cups. A Princess Dressing may accompany.

This mixture is the basis for the two following recipes, which are similar, except that the first is served in a dish and the second in a cocktail glass.

DERBY FRUIT SALAD

SERVES 1

1 leaf lettuce, cup-shaped   6 orange sections   1 fig
1 cup Derby Fruit Salad   6 grapefruit sections   1 strawberry (or cherry)
    Mixture   2 mint leaves

Place cup-shaped lettuce leaf in bottom of ice-cold deep glass dish. Fill cup with Derby Fruit Mixture. Around the Fruit Mixture, arrange sections of orange and grapefruit alternately. On top, place peeled fresh fig in star shape*. In middle of star, place strawberry. Garnish with mint leaves. Preserved figs, although difficult to cut, may be used if fresh figs are not available.

*Make two cuts at right angles down through the fig, almost all the way through, and open into star shape.

AVOCADO IMPERIAL SALAD

SERVES 2

1 avocado   1 cup Derby Fruit Salad   12 grapefruit sections
2 leaves lettuce, cup-shaped   Mixture   2 ripe strawberries
1 cup shredded lettuce   12 orange sections   ½ cup Princess Dressing

Use a medium-sized ripe avocado. Split lengthwise, remove stone, and peel off shell. Place avocado in lettuce cup; balance with shredded lettuce; stuff with Derby Fruit Salad Mixture. Garnish with orange and grapefruit. On top of each stuffed avocado, place strawberry. Serve with Princess Dressing.

DERBY SALAD BOWL

SERVES 4

½ cup Brown Derby Old-fashioned Dressing	1 lb. cabbage julienne ¾ cup cooked chicken, white, julienne	¾ cup smoked beef tongue julienne 3 hard-cooked eggs, sliced

Toss cabbage and French Dressing in an ice-cold salad bowl. On top of this coleslaw, arrange chicken and tongue, each covering half of the bowl. Through the center, arrange sliced eggs. Chill thoroughly.

OLYMPUS SALAD

ERVES 1

1 medium tomato, peeled ½ cup shredded lettuce Salt and pepper ½ cup cottage cheese	1 tbs. cook peas 1 tbs. chicken white meat, julienne 2 strips pimento	8 cooked asparagus tips 3 tbs. Brown Derby Old-fashioned French Dressing

Make the ripe peeled tomato into a rosette by 4 cuts across the center, taking care not to cut all the way through; tomato will open like a flower. Arrange shredded lettuce neatly on ice-cold salad plate. On this, place the flower-shaped tomato. Salt and pepper lightly. In middle of tomato, place a round ball of cottage cheese. Sprinkle on top with peas and chicken. Criss-cross with pimento strips. Stand an asparagus tip between each section of tomato. Serve with French Dressing.

BROWN DERBY SHRIMP LOUIE

SERVES 2

1 cup finely shredded lettuce 1 cup cooked shrimp, cleaned, split ½ cup Thousand Island Dressing	1 tbs. capers 1 medium tomato, peeled and sliced	1 hard-cooked egg, sliced 4 asparagus tips 2 rings bell pepper 1 lemon, cut in half

Place shredded lettuce in middle of cold plate. Arrange shrimp on top in a neat line. Over the shrimp, put 4 tbs. Thousand Island Dressing, covering all shrimp. On each side, place ½ slice tomato. On top of tomato, arrange a slice hard-cooked egg. Place asparagus tip at each end. In center of shrimp, place 1 pepper ring. Sprinkle few capers in center of ring. Serve with parsley-lemon slices or halves as desired.

SALAD VICTOR

Diced chicken meat
Boiled rice
Diced tomato

Sliced string beans
Tarragon Dressing
Lettuce leaves [cup-shaped[
Chives

Paprika
½ Lemon
Parsley

In a chilled salad bowl, mix chicken, boiled rice, tomato, and string beans. Toss with Tarragon Dressing.

Place in cup of lettuce leaves and sprinkle with chives and paprika. Serve with lemon and spring of parsley.

MOUNT VERNON SALAD

Heart of romaine
Raw Virginia ham, diced

Fresh boiled mushrooms
Red and green pepper

Brown Derby Old-fashioned
French Dressing

Cut romaine in 1-in.-long pieces and place in chilled salad bowl. On romaine, sprinkle diced ham. Garnish with mushrooms and pepper. Toss with French Dressing.

HOLLYWOOD SALAD

SERVES 1

1 cooked carrot, diced
1 tbs. cooked peas
2 tbs. cooked string beans
2 tbs. cooked potatoes, diced

Salt and pepper
3 tbs. Brown Derby
    Old-fashioned
    French Dressing

2 lettuce leaves [cup-shaped]
3 slices tongue julienne
3 slices chicken julienne
2 quarters tomato

In a small bowl, mix carrots, peas, string beans, potatoes, salt and pepper to taste, and French Dressing. Place in refrigerator to chill thoroughly.

In center of ice-cold salad place, place 2 lettuce leaves in cup shape. In middle of lettuce cup, arrange the vegetable mixture in as high a shape as possible. Sprinkle tongue and chicken on top of vegetable mixture. Garnish with tomatoes and serve very cold.

HOW TO WILT LETTUCE

4 strips bacon, fully chopped
2 tbs. vinegar
1 dash celery salt

1 tbs. chopped chives
Juice of 1 lemon

1 tsp. sugar
½ head medium-sized lettuce
    pulled

Sauté bacon in pan until brown and crisp. "Stop" the sautéing with vinegar. Keep over heat, add celery salt, chives, lemon juice, and sugar; stir well and bring to boil. Then pour over lettuce which has been placed in bowl. Cover with plate and allow to steam for 5 or 6 minutes. Remove cover, toss lettuce and serve.

RAW VEGETABLES IN SOUR CREAM

SERVES 2

2 medium-sized cucumbers   *8 radishes*   *Juice of ½ lemon*
6 medium-sized carrots   *1½ cups sour cream*   *Salt and pepper*

Peel cucumbers, split lengthwise; remove seeds with small spoon, slice as thin as possible. Shred carrots through fine shredder. Slice radishes as thin as possible. Place vegetables in chilled salad bowl. Add sour cream, lemon juice, salt and pepper to taste, and mix well.

RAW VEGETABLES WITH SOUR CREAM

In a chilled salad bowl, toss together a combination of chopped radishes, green onions, cucumbers julienne, lettuce, and carrots. Serve with a liberal portion of sour cream.

COTTAGE CHEESE DERBY

SERVES 2

1 cup cottage cheese   *1 cup sour cream*   *1 tbs. caraway seed*
    2 tbs. finely chopped chives

Place 2 heaping tbs. of cottage cheese on ice-cold salad plate. Add 2 tbs. sour cream and serve with chives and caraway seeds on side.

LENTEN SALAD

SERVES 1

Lettuce [cup-shaped]   *Watercress*   *Brown Derby Old-fashioned*
Cream cheese   *Unsweetened whipped cream*   *French Dressing*
    Chopped nuts

In a cup of lettuce leaves, place a large scoop of cream cheese. Around the cream cheese, arrange leaves of watercress. On top of cheese, place a large spoon of whipped cream. Sprinkle with chopped nuts. Serve with French Dressing.

CALIFORNIA GREEN GODDESS SALAD

SERVES 3

½ lb. raw spinach   *1 cup Green Goddess or*   *1 cup bread croutons*
    Chef Robert Dressing

Toss well-washed and slightly cut spinach in a medium-sized salad bowl. Serve with Green Goddess Salad Dressing or Chef Robert Dressing. Just before serving, toss in croutons.

GREEN GODDESS SALAD DRESSING

SERVES 6

½ cup heavy cream	1 rounding tbs. anchovy paste	2 tbs. shallot vinegar
1 tbs. lemon juice	2 tbs. tarragon vinegar	¼ cup finely chopped onion
1 cup Brown Derby Mayonnaise	2 tbs. garlic vinegar	1/3 cup finely chopped parsley

Add lemon juice to cream, then mix with other ingredients. Serve with green salad.

* * *

The Green Goddess Salad Dressing originated more than thirty [now ninety] years ago. It was named for the play in which George Arliss was starring and was first served at a testimonial dinner given him the opening night in San Francisco. Delicately flavored, its smooth consistency causes this dressing to fully coat each leaf in bowl.

* * *

SHREDDED CUCUMBER AND CARROTS WITH SOUR CREAM

SERVES 2

2 lettuce cups	1 cup shredded baby carrots	4 tbs. sour cream
	1 cucumber, shredded	

On a chilled salad plate, arrange in lettuce cup a nest of shredded carrots. On this, place shredded cucumber. Salt to taste and top with sour cream.

ROBERT SALAD

SERVES 2

1 medium-sized head romaine	1 cup Parmesan cheese	1 clove garlic
1 French roll in ¼-in. slices		½ cup Chef Robert Dressing

Place romaine, cut in 1½-in. pieces, in a medium-sized, ice-cold salad bowl. Rub the French roll slices in garlic on both sides. Butter them well and brown under open fire. When brown on both sides, sprinkle Parmesan cheese on each slice. Put the croutons on top of romaine. Serve with Chef Robert Dressing.

DERBY TOMATO STUFFED WITH CHICKEN

SERVES 2

¾ cup chicken salad	2 large tomatoes, peeled, bottom slightly scooped	2 tbs. mayonnaise
2 hard-cooked eggs, put through sieve		2 small sliced chicken white meat julienne
2 lettuce leaves [cup-shaped]	2 rings bell pepper	2 pimento strips

Divide the chicken salad in equal portions. Roll into balls, then roll in egg until covered. Place the ball into the scooped-out tomatoes. Arrange the tomato in a cup of lettuce. On top of chicken salad, put one pepper ring, a little dab of mayonnaise in center. On top of mayonnaise, arrange chicken in neat pile. Over chicken, place 1 strip of pimento.

Variations: Stuff with crab salad and use a crab leg for garnish; with lobster salad and garnish with a lobster slice; or try shrimp salad and decorate with a half shrimp.

DERBY SALAD PLATE

SERVES 2

6 lettuce leave, [cup-shaped]	*2 avocado slices*	*2 crab legs*
2 pimento strips	*1 small slice chicken julienne*	*2 tbs. whipped cream*
1 cup chicken salad	*2 tbs. Thousand Island*	*1 cherry cut in half*
1 cup fruit salad	*Dressing*	*1 medium tomato, peeled*
1 cup crab salad	*2 small rings bell pepper*	*cut in 6 pieces*
2 tbs. mayonnaise		*2 sprigs*

Place 3 cup-shaped lettuce leaves on chilled plate. In 1 cup, arrange chicken salad; in second, fruit salad; and in third, crab salad. Over the chicken salad, place 1 tbs. of mayonnaise. Put a slice of avocado on top of mayonnaise. Over avocado, arrange chicken julienne and 1 strip of pimento. Place 1 tbs. of Thousand Island Dressing over the crab salad, then 1 ring of green pepper. In center of ring, place a crab leg. Decorate top of fruit salad with 1 tbs. of whipped cream and garnish with ½ cherry. Divide the three salads with tomato sections. Place sprig of watercress in center of plate.

SALAD RUSSE

SERVES 1

2 medium-sized cooked carrots, diced	*1 small cooked potato, diced*	*Juice of ½ lemon*
½ cup cooked string beans, diced	*½ cup cooked peas*	*Salt and pepper*
	½ cup mayonnaise	

Use a medium-sized salad bowl. Mix carrots, string beans, potatoes, peas, mayonnaise and lemon juice thoroughly. Add salt and pepper to taste.

FRESH STRING BEAN SALAD

SERVES 2

1 lb. cooked string beans julienne	*2 lettuce leaves, cup-shaped*	*4 tbs. Brown Derby*
½ bead garlic, finely chopped	*4 slices bacon, crisp and*	*Old-fashioned*
4 tbs. chopped onion	*finely cut*	*French Dressing*

In a small ice-cold mixing bowl, place string beans, garlic, onion and French Dressing. Toss lightly. Place in lettuce leaves; sprinkle with bacon and serve.

ASSORTED COLD CUTS DERBY

SERVES 1

1 slice roast turkey (white meat)   *1 slice baked ham, horse*   *½ cup potato salad*
1 slice smoked beef tongue   *shoe cut*   *1 quarter tomato*
1 slice Swiss cheese   *1 slice rack of roasted lamb*   *2 slices hard-cooked egg*
1 slice corned beef   *1 small leaf lettuce, cup-shaped*   *1 kosher pickle*

Arrange sliced meat and cheese in fan-shape on chilled service plate. In center of fan, place potato salad in cup of lettuce. Garnish with tomato, hard-cooked egg slices and kosher pickle, cut fin-shaped.

CHICKEN AND HAM JULIENNE
WITH VEGETABLES IN ASPIC

SERVES 2

1½ cups beef or chicken aspic   *2 medium-sized cooked carrots, diced*   *4 tbs. Brown Derby*
2 slices hard-cooked egg   *4 tbs. cooked string beans*   *Old-fashioned*
1 cup chicken julienne   *4 tbs. cooked peas*   *French Dressing*
1 cup ham julienne   *8 cooked asparagus tips*   *1 lemon cut in half*
                        2 lettuce leaves

Place two ½-pt. molds on a tray. Fill ¼-in. with cool aspic. Put in refrigerator to set. Take out and in middle of mold, place 1 slice of hard-cooked egg. Surround with half of chicken and ham. Cover with aspic [reserve some aspic for top]; put back in refrigerator to set.

Mix together carrots, beans and peas. Fill the molds two-thirds full of vegetable mixture and place 4 asparagus tips lightly against side of mold, spaced evenly. Fill molds with aspic even with top of vegetables. Put back in refrigerator. As soon as aspic is set, fill mold completely full with remaining aspic and place back into refrigerator until solid.

To remove aspic, dip molds in warm water for a few seconds, then turn upside down on lettuce leaf. Serve with French Dressing and lemon. See Clear Consommé ("Soups") for Aspic recipe.

BROWN DERBY LENTIL SALAD

SERVES 2

1½ cups cooked lentils, well   *2 lettuce leaves, nice and crisp*   *½ medium-sized tomato,*
     drained   *2 tbs. finely chopped chives*   *peeled and diced fine*
1/3 cup Brown Derby Old-fashioned   *2 hard-cooked eggs, finely*   *6 bacon slices, crisp and finely*
     French Dressing   *chopped*   *chopped*

In a medium-sized, ice-cold salad bowl, marinate cooked lentils in French Dressing. Line sides of bowl with lettuce. Arrange 4 equal strips across lentils: 1 consisting of chives; another, eggs; third, diced tomato; lastly, chopped bacon. Serve in bowl.

More salads in "Barbecues".

SALAD DRESSINGS

There are two basic salad dressings, French and Mayonnaise. Practically all others require one of these as a foundation.

BROWN DERBY OLD-FASHIONED FRENCH DRESSING, 1½ qts.

This is the French Dressing which became so popular among the stars that The Brown Derby was prevailed upon to bottle it for home use. The cup of water is optional, depending upon the degree of oiliness desired in this dressing.

1 cup water
1 cup red wine vinegar
1 tsp. sugar
Juice of ½ lemon

2½ tbs. salt
1 tbs. ground black pepper
1 tbs. Worcestershire Sauce

1 tsp. English mustard
1 bead garlic, chopped
1 cup olive oil
3 cups salad oil

Blend together all ingredients except oils. Then add olive and salad oils and mix well again. Chill. Shake before serving.

This dressing keeps well in the refrigerator. Can be made and stored in a 2 qt. Mason jar.

TARRAGON DRESSING

1 cup Brown Derby Old-fashioned French Dressing

1 tsp. chopped fresh tarragon

Mix well.

ANCHOVY DRESSING, 1 pt.

24 filets anchovy, finely chopped
2 tbs. finely chopped chives

1 pt. Brown Derby Old-fashioned French Dressing

Blend together chopped anchovies and chives. Add French Dressing and mix well. Chill before serving. Keeps in excellent condition in sealed glass in refrigerator.

CHEF ROBERT DRESSING, 1 pt.

6 eggs, boiled 1 minute
½ cup Parmesan cheese
1 tbs. celery salt

6 slices crisp bacon, finely chopped
4 tbs. finely chopped chives

1 pt. Brown Derby Old-fashioned French Dressing

Scoop out the eggs *[please follow health safety guidelines for cooking eggs]* into a medium-sized mixing bowl. Add cheese, celery salt, bacon, chives, and mix to a smooth paste. Add French Dressing slowly while mixing sharply. Chill thoroughly.

CAESAR DRESSING

SERVES 2

1 egg, coddled 1 minute
1 heaping the grated Parmesan cheese

½ cup Brown Derby Old-fashioned French Dressing
4 tbs. pastry cream

Place coddled egg in a mixing bowl; add cheese and pastry cream. Blend well. Slowly whip in French Dressing. Any salad mixed with this dressing should be garnished with garlic-French-bread croutons.

ROQUEFORT CHEESE DRESSING, 1 pt.

1 cup Roquefort cheese
½ cup pastry cream
1 tsp. Worcestershire Sauce

1 tbs. finely chopped chives
1 tsp. celery salt

1 pt. Brow Derby Old-fashioned French Dressing

Using a fork and a medium-sized mixing bowl, blend cheese and cream to a smooth paste. Add Worcestershire Sauce, chives, celery salt and mix again. While mixing sharply add French Dressing slowly. Chill thoroughly.

VINAIGRETTE DRESSING, 1 pt.

3 medium-sized dill pickles
12 green olives, pitted
⅓ cup capers

4 tbs. chives
1 tbs. tarragon
2 tbs. bell pepper
3 hard-cooked eggs

1 pt. Brown Derby Old-fashioned French Dressing

Chop the following ingredients fine: dill pickles, green olives, capers, tarragon, bell pepper and eggs. Place in medium-sized bowl and blend together with French Dressing. Mix well and chill thoroughly.

LORENZO DRESSING, 1 pt.

4 tbs. watercress
2 tbs. chives

1 tbs. parsley
½ cup chili sauce

1½ cups Brown Derby
Old-fashioned
French Dressing

Chop finely watercress, chives, parsley and place together with chili sauce and French Dressing in a 1-qt. Mason jar with tight cover and mix. Chill and serve.

PAPRIKA-TOMATO FRENCH DRESSING, 1 pt.

1/3 cup tomato purée
1 tbs. paprika

1 tsp. horseradish

1 pt. Brown Derby
Old-fashioned
French Dressing

Place purée, paprika and horseradish in a 1-qt. glass jar with tight cover and mix well. Be sure to dissolve all paprika. Add French Dressing, shake vigorously, store in refrigerator.

CALIFORNIA FRENCH DRESSING, 1 qt.

3 egg yolks*
1 tbs. paprika

1½ tsp. salt
½ tsp. black pepper
1 pt. olive or salad oil

¼ pt. vinegar
1½ tsp. sugar

Mix egg yolks with paprika, salt, and pepper. Whip until fluffy; then add oil slowly. Thin down with vinegar as mixture thickens during process and add sugar.

BROWN DERBY MAYONNAISE, 1 qt.

6 egg yolks*
2 tsp. salt
1 tsp. English mustard

1 tsp. Worcestershire Sauce
4 tbs. mild vinegar

3 cups salad oil
Juice of 1 lemon
2 tbs. boiling water

Beat egg yolks with electric beater or French whip. Add salt, mustard, Worcestershire Sauce, and 2 tbs. vinegar. Mix well. Add oil in fine stream, whipping fast to absorb oil. Stop adding oil if it is not absorbed. As mixture becomes thick, add remaining vinegar and lemon [juice]. Continue whipping until all oil, vinegar and lemon juice have been used. If mixed correctly, all ingredients should be absorbed. Finally whip in the boiling water. Keep in cool place, but not under 45°[F]. Never allow to freeze.

*[Caution: Current health safety guidelines recommend caution when using raw eggs. This recipe is included only as presented in 1st edition.]

MUSTARD MAYONNAISE

1 cup Brown Derby Mayonnaise   Juice of ½ lemon
1 tsp. English mustard   1 tsp. Worcestershire Sauce

Blend well.

PRINCESS DRESSING, 1 pt.

1½ cups Brown Derby   3 maraschino cherries,   2 tbs. maraschino syrup
    Mayonnaise   chopped fine   ½ cup whipped cream

Blend together Mayonnaise, maraschino syrup and chopped cherries. Mix well. Fold in whipped cream. Serve with fruit salad, stewed pears, stewed pineapple, prune or date salad.

LEMON CREAM DRESSING, 1 ½ pts.

1 cup Brown Derby Mayonnaise   Juice of 2 lemons
    1 cup sour cream

Blend well and serve.

TARTAR SAUCE, 1 qt.

4 large dill pickles, chopped   ½ small onion, minced   2 tbs. parsley
    very fine   3 tbs. chives   1 qt. Brown Derby
½ cup capers, chopped fine   4 hard-cooked eggs, sieved   Mayonnaise
    Juice of 1 lemon

Use a medium-sized mixing bowl; add chopped pickles, capers, onion, chives, eggs, lemon juice, parsley and Mayonnaise. Blend well.

SAUCE RAVIGOTE DRESSING, 1 qt.

1 tbs. tarragon   Juice of 1 lemon   1 tsp. crushed black pepper
1 tbs. chervil   4 tbs. tarragon vinegar   1 qt. Tartar Sauce
    1 qt. Tartar Sauce

Blend together tarragon, chervil, lemon juice, tarragon vinegar and pepper. Add to Tartar Sauce and blend well again.

SOUR CREAM DRESSING HUSSARD, 1 pt.

1 cup sour cream
1 cup Brown Derby Mayonnaise

1 tbs. horseradish
Juice of 1 lemon

2 tbs. finely chopped chives
3 tbs. finely chopped capers

Mix sour cream, Mayonnaise and horseradish in a medium-sized bowl. Add lemon juice, chives, capers and mix well. Chill thoroughly.

THOUSAND ISLAND DRESSING, 1 qt.

3 cups Brown Derby Mayonnaise
1 cup chili sauce
1 large bell pepper, seeded
    chopped fine

½ cup finely chopped pimento
4 tbs. finely chopped chives
½ cup finely chopped capers

6 hard-cooked eggs,
    chopped fine
Juice of ½ lemon

Blend well together in a medium-sized mixing bowl Mayonnaise, chili sauce, bell pepper, pimento, chives, capers, eggs and lemon juice. Chill thoroughly.

MIGNONETTE DRESSING, 1 pt.

1/3 cup white wine
1 tbs. crushed white pepper
2 tbs. salt
2/3 cup red wine vinegar

1 tbs. Worcestershire Sauce
Juice of 1 lemon
3 tbs. chives
2 sprigs chervil

1 cup olive oil
1 medium-sized head yellow
    romaine julienne
¼ tsp. celery salt

Blend together in a medium-sized bowl wine, pepper, salt, vinegar, Worcestershire Sauce, lemon juice, celery salt; mix well. Add chives and chervil; mix again. Add olive oil while mixing sharply. Add romaine last. Chill thoroughly.

SOUR CREAM DRESSING DERBY, 1 pt.

1 cup sour cream

1 cup Brown Derby Mayonnaise
2 tbs. finely chopped chives

¼ tsp. black pepper

Blend together in a small mixing bowl sour cream, Mayonnaise, chives and black pepper. Mix well. Chill thoroughly.

Also: Mayonnaise Bengal ("Curries"), and Barbecue French Dressing and Barbecue Mayonnaise ("Barbecues").

Photograph of some caricatures as they appeared on
"The Great Wall at The Hollywood Brown Derby"

Photograph of some caricatures as they appeared on
"The Great Wall at The Hollywood Brown Derby"

FISH
AND
SEAFOOD

The most important factor in this chapter is that the fish or seafood must be fresh.
In selection of the larger fish, observe the scales. They should be solidly set, even and firm. Trout should still be shiny. Also judge trout, sand dabs and other small fish by their eyes—they should be clear. If the head is off and the fish is cleaned, let your nose be your guide. If filleted, the flesh should be firm, not flabby or soft.

If using frozen fish, it should be cooked immediately after it is thawed out. Frozen fish is usually better with batter (egg, milk, flour) to preserve the juices. Butter the pan before baking to prevent sticking, or dip in butter and bread crumbs.

When broiling, dip in some marinade or Paprika Butter (soft butter mixed with paprika). Broil small fish fast. With big ones, broil fast at the start; then reduce flame.

The safest way to insure freshness in lobsters is to purchase them alive and cook them yourself. If this is not practical be careful when purchasing cooked lobster. It should feel heavy, the color should be deep red and the tail curled and solid under the lobster—not stretched out. Crabs should also have good color and a shiny shell, and should be heavy. Shrimp, if purchased frozen, should be cooked as soon as they are thawed out. They should be very light in color.

Oysters and clams must have well-closed shells, never opened. Knock two of the shells together. If you get a solid sound, that indicates that they are still alive and edible. When opened, a good oyster will fill the shell well, be surrounded with plenty of liquor, and have a fresh color.

BROILED COLUMBIA RIVER SALMON BALOISE
SERVES 2

¼ tsp. paprika	2 salmon steaks (about	2 oz. butter (¼ cup)
½ tsp. celery salt	5 oz. each)	4 medium-sized boiled
Salt and pepper	18 French-fried onion rings	potatoes
2 tbs. salad oil	Juice of ½ lemon	1 tsp. minced parsley

First, blend paprika, celery salt, salt and pepper with oil; then dip slices of fish in mixture, turning from side to side before placing on broiler rack. Broil until salmon steaks seem done, length of time depending on thickness of the steaks. If bone can be removed easily, fish is done. Place on heated platter. Cover with onion rings. Sprinkle lemon juice over the steaks. Cover all with butter, which has been browned. Serve with boiled potatoes with parsley sprinkled over all.

PLANKED HALIBUT DERBY

SERVES 4

12 small white onions
12 small carrots
4 large mushrooms, sautéed
3 cups Duchesse Potatoes

1 ½ lbs, halibut (in 4 pieces)
4 small tomatoes (baked with
    Parmesan cheese
4 small pieces boiled
    cauliflower

½ cup cooked peas
½ cup corn, sautéed in butter
½ cup Flank Butter Sauce
[Sugar]

Prepare vegetables separately as follows: boil onions until three-fourths done. Glaze lightly in skillet with butter and small sprinkle of sugar. Boil carrots until tender. Then glaze lightly in skillet with butter and sugar. Sauté mushrooms in butter. Bake tomatoes with Parmesan cheese. Keep all vegetables in separate heated dishes.

Prepare Duchesse Potatoes. Place in pastry bag and then dress the border of heated plank neatly with potatoes.

Broil halibut three-forth done. Place in center of each plank 1 portion of halibut. Arrange hot vegetables in little bouquets around fish. Place mushroom cap on top of each piece of fish. Cover fish with Plank Butter Sauce. Place in 375°[F] oven for 10 minutes. Serve immediately.

BROILED SHAD ROE WITH BACON

1 lb. shad roe
4 tbs. oil
½ tsp. paprika

1 tsp. salt
¼ tsp. celery salt
½ cup bred crumbs

8 slices bacon, fried crisp
½ cup Sauce Diable
1 lemon, quartered

Dip raw roe in oil, paprika, salt, and celery salt; then in bread crumbs. Broil on both sides under broiler until golden brown. Arrange on heated plate. Place 2 slices of crisp bacon on each serving. Serve with Sauce Diable and lemon.

BROILED CALIFORNIA SWORDFISH STEAK

SERVES 4

4 tbs. salad oil
1 tsp. paprika
1 tsp. celery salt

1 tsp. Worcestershire Sauce
1 ½ lbs. swordfish in
    ½-in. steaks

½ cup melted butter
1 tbs. chives
Juice of ½ lemon

Make an oil mixture consisting of salad oil, paprika, celery salt, and Worcestershire Sauce. Dip fish steaks in mixture. Broil on both sides 5 minutes to a side. Before serving on heated platter, pour a butter mixture made of butter, chives and lemon juice over the fish. Serve with French-fried potatoes or boiled potatoes sprinkled with parsley.

Recipes for fried fish frequently call for burned butter in three different shades. Whole butter browned while shaking the pan over a hot fire until the butter foams and breaks down is called beurre meunière when it reaches a light brown color, beurre noisette when it is a deeper brown, and beurre noir when it is burned black.

Beurre manié, which is used as a thickening agent, is a mixture of slightly more melted butter (4/7) than flour (3/7).

FILET OF RAINBOW TROUT MEUNIÈRE
SERVES 2

1-lb. trout filet, boned	*½ cup flour*	*1 tsp. finely chopped parsley*
Salt and pepper	*½ cup oil*	*Juice of ½ lemon*
½ cup milk	*½ cup butter*	*Beurre meuniére*

Season trout with salt and pepper; then dip in milk and roll in flour. Fry in mixture of oil and butter in heavy iron skillet until golden brown. Place on heated platter; sprinkle with parsley and lemon juice. Prepare beurre meunière and pour over fish. Serve with boiled parsley potatoes.

Filet of Rainbow Trout Belle Meunière is prepared the same way with the addition of a slice of breaded, fried tomato and a large, sautéed mushroom button before garnishing and adding beurre meunière.

Filet of Rainbow Trout Amandine is the same as the Trout Meunière with the addition of 2 tbs. toasted, shaved almonds.

CATALINA SAND DABS SAUTÉ MEUNIÈRE
SERVES 4

3 lbs. sand dabs	*4 oz. butter*	*Juice of ½ lemon*
½ cup milk	*1 tsp. finely chopped parsley*	*Beurre noisette (optional)*
½ cup flour		*Salt*

Filet sand dabs and wash carefully. Dip filets in milk, roll in flour and salt lightly. Fry in butter in heavy skillet until golden brown. Arrange on heated plate. Sprinkle with parsley and lemon juice. Pour beurre noisette over filets or use butter in which fish has been fried.

This recipe becomes Sand Dabs Amandine by sprinkling the sautéed fish with toasted shaved almonds.

FILET OF SOLE SAUTÉ AMANDINE
SERVES 4

6 pieces (1 lb.) filet of sole	*3 tbs. flour*	*1 tsp. parsley*
Salt and pepper	*½ cup oil*	*3 tbs. toasted almonds*
½ cup milk	*Juice of ½ lemon*	*2 tbs. whole butter*

Clean and bone sole; salt and pepper to taste; dip in milk and roll in flour. Fry in heavy skillet with hot oil until golden brown on both sides. Remove from skillet and arrange on heated plate. Sprinkle with lemon juice, parsley and toasted almonds. Make beurre noisette from the whole butter and pour over fish. Serve with French-fried potatoes or boiled parsley potatoes.

ABALONE STEAKS SAUTÉ AMANDINE
SERVES 2

10 oz. abalone steaks	1 cup egg batter	Sauce Beurre Amandine
1 cup flour	1 tsp. minced parsley	4 oz. butter
	Juice of ½ lemon	

Dip abalone steaks in flour; then in egg batter and again in flour. Fry in heavy skillet in which butter has been heated but not burned. Fry quickly, about 2 minutes on each side. Do not turn more than once. Remove from skillet, arrange on very hot plate, sprinkle quickly with minced parsley; then squeeze the juice of ½ lemon over the steaks. Cover with Sauce Beurre Amandine*. Serve at once with either new potatoes in parsley or French-fried potatoes.

Without the almonds, this is Abalone Steaks Sauté Meunière.

LAKE SUPERIOR WHITEFISH BEURRE MAÎTRE D'HÔTEL
SERVES 2

12-oz. filet of whitefish, boned, scaled, halved	4 tbs. Sauce au Beurre Maître d'hôtel	Salt and pepper [Oil or butter]

Season filets with salt and pepper. Brush with sweet oil and butter. Broil either over charcoal or under broiler. Remove to heated platter and surround with lemon slices. Pour sauce over fish. Serve with parsley new potatoes or steamed rice.

SAUCE AU BEURRE MAÎTRE D'HÔTEL
1 cup

6 oz. butter, melted (¾ cup)	1 tbs. Worcestershire Sauce	2 tbs. minced chives
Juice of 1 lemon	¼ tsp. celery salt	1 tbs. minced parsley

Use small heated mixing bowl. Pour melted butter in bowl; add lemon juice, Worcestershire Sauce, celery salt, chives and parsley. Beat very well. Use for any broiled fish.

BAKED FILET OF SOLE FLORENTINE
SERVES 3

2 oz. melted butter (¼ cup)	Juice of ½ lemon	1 cup purée of spinach
12 oz. boned filet of sole	¼ tsp. celery salt	1 cup thick Sauce Mornay
½ cup white wine	Salt	2 tbs. Parmesan cheese
½ cup fish stock or water		½ tsp. paprika

*For Sauce Amandine, use Sauce Beurre Noisette in which 2 tbs. of toasted slivered almonds have been heated.

Pour butter in heavy skillet. Fold filets in half and arrange in skillet. Add wine, fish stock, lemon juice, celery salt, and salt to taste. Cover and steam 8 minutes over slow heat. Remove sole, arrange in heated casserole on bed of hot purée of spinach. Return broth to heat and reduce by two-thirds.* Then add Sauce Mornay. Blend well. Pour over sole in casserole. Sprinkle with cheese and paprika. Brown under broiler.

*When a recipe called for the broth or liquids to be reduced, use salt sparingly if added before the reduction process. Once the liquid is concentrated, it may taste saltier.

BAKED FILET OF SOLE MARGUERY
SERVES 4 – 6

2 lbs. (12 boned filets) sole	1 tbs. chopped shallots	1 cup heavy cream
8 large shrimp, cleaned, cooked	½ cup Sauce Hollandaise	3 oz. butter
4 – 6 large mushrooms	½ cup sherry	4 tbs. flour
8 large shucked oysters	1 pt. fish stock or water	1 tbs. salt

Butter flat pan well. Fold filets in half and lay in pan. On top of fish place shrimp, mushrooms, oysters and shallots. Add wine, stock and salt. Cover and allow to simmer for 15 minutes. Remove sole to heated casserole. Arrange shrimp, mushrooms and oysters neatly on top. Reduce remaining stock by one-third. Add cream, butter and flour which have been mixed together. Blend sharply. Cook for 5 minutes, stirring constantly. Strain sauce through fine sieve. Add Sauce Hollandaise and blend well. Pour over contents of casserole. Brown gently under broiler.

BAKED FILET OF SOLE PORTUGUESE
SERVES 2

12 oz. filet of sole	½ cup sliced mushrooms	Juice of ½ lemon
¼ cup butter	Salt	1 tbs. finely chopped celery
½ cup white wine	1 medium-sized tomato	1 tsp. beurre manié
½ cup fish stock	peeled and diced	1½ cups rice (cooked
2 tbs. finely chopped green onion		20 minutes)

Clean and bone sole and fold in half. Place in buttered skillet. Add wine, fish stock, onion, mushroom, tomato, lemon juice, celery and salt to taste. Cover and steam 8 minutes. Remove sole and arrange on heated plate or in casserole. Heat stock very hot. Reduce by one-third and thicken with beurre manié. Pour sauce over filet and serve with steamed rice.

* * *

Traditionally, white wine is always used in cooking fish. But to be different, The Brown Derby created a new way to prepare sole—with a red wine. This not only colors the fish but gives it a different flavor which won immediate favor with Derby patrons. It was named Baked Filet of Sole Beaulieu in honor of the vineyards which supply The Brown Derbys with their vintage wines.

* * *

BAKED FILET OF SOLE BEAULIEU

SERVES 2

12 oz. filet of sole	*2 beads shallots*	*¼ tsp. celery salt*
2 oz. whole butter	*½ cup Brown Sauce*	*1 tbs. finely chopped chives*
1 cup burgundy	*Juice of ½ lemon*	*Salt*

Arrange filet, which has been cleaned, boned and folded in half, in heavy skillet using half of butter. Add wine, shallots, Brown Sauce, lemon juice, celery salt and salt to taste. Cover and simmer 10 minutes. Remove fish to heated plate. Reduce sauce by one-third. Add remaining butter to sauce while mixing sharply; then add chives. Pour sauce over filet and serve at once.

POACHED RAINBOW TROUT AU BLEU

SERVES 2

1 lb. very fresh trout, whole and cleaned	*1 qt. Court Bouillon*

For this recipe, use 2 tbs. wine vinegar in place of lemon in making the Court Bouillon to give the fish the blue color which make the dish distinctive.

Submerge trout in hot bouillon and simmer 12 minutes. Remove to heated casserole and add some of the strained bouillon. Serve with new boiled potatoes and Sauce Hollandaise or melted butter.

BAKED FILET OF LAKE SUPERIOR WHITEFISH CALIFORNIA

SERVES 2

12 oz. filet of whitefish, cut in two	*2 beads shallots, chopped*	*½ cup fish stock or water*
¼ cup butter	*¼ tsp. celery salt*	*½ cup heavy cream*
½ medium-sized ripe avocado,	*½ cup white wine*	*1 tsp. beurre manié*
peeled		*Salt and pepper*

Arrange fish in buttered heavy skillet. On top of each, place quarter slice of avocado and spread slightly. Add shallots, celery salt, wine, and fish stock. Cover and simmer 10 minutes over slow fire. Remove whitefish to heated plate. Care must be taken that avocado slices do not fall off.

Heat remaining liquid. Add cream and reduce by one-third. Thicken with beurre manié. Salt and pepper to taste. Pour sauce over fish and serve at once.

BAKED HALIBUT PRINCESS

SERVES 2

2 oz. butter	*½ cup fish stock*	*2 egg yolks*
2 - 6-oz. pieces filet of halibut	*2 oz mushrooms, sliced*	*1 tbs. chopped chives*
½ cup white wine	*Salt*	*10 asparagus tips*
	1 cup pastry cream	

Place halibut in buttered, heavy skillet. Mix white wine, fish stock, mushrooms and salt to taste. Cover halibut with this mixture. Cover skillet and simmer gently for 12 minutes. Remove fish to heated platter. Reduce stock by one-third; then add 12 tbs. cream. Thicken with egg yolks which have been mixed with remaining 4 tbs. cream. Care must be taken not to get this too hot. On top of each piece of halibut, arrange chopped chives and 5 asparagus tips which have been heated. Cover with the sauce. Garnish with lemon slices and watercress. Serve at once with steamed rice.

BAKED FILET OF WHITEFISH PIÉMONTAIS
SERVES 2

12 oz. filet of whitefish, scaled, boned, halved	¼ tsp. basil ,	3 tbs. tomato purée
¼ cup butter	½ bead garlic	4 tbs. bread croutons
½ cup white wine	1 medium-sized tomato, peeled and diced	1 tsp. finely chopped parsley
		Salt

Arrange 2 pieces filet in buttered, heavy skillet. Add salt to taste, wine, basil, garlic, tomato and purée. Cover and simmer slowly 10 minutes. Remove fish to heated plate. Reduce sauce by one-third on slow fire. Pour sauce over fish. Sprinkle bread croutons and parsley over top.

BAKED SEA BASS À LA DERBY
SERVES 2

2 oz. butter	3 tbs. Virginia ham, finely chopped	1 cup white wine
2 – 6-oz. filets of sea bass, boned	Salt	½ cup fish stock or water
2 beads shallots, chopped fine	2 oz. mushrooms, chopped	1 tsp. beurre manié
2 tbs. finely chopped green onion	1 medium-sized tomato, chopped fine	½ cup bread crumbs, sautéed in butter

Place bass in buttered skillet. Add shallots, onion, ham, mushrooms, tomato, wine, fish stock and salt to taste. Cover skillet and simmer for 12 minutes. Remove fish to heated plate. Reduce sauce by one-third. Thicken with beurre manié; pour over fish. Sprinkle bread crumbs over the sauce and serve at once.

POACHED SALMON STEAK WITH CAPERSAUCE
SERVES 2

2 salmon steaks (about 6 oz. each)	2 tbs. capers	1 tbs. chives
3 cups Court Bouillon	1 tsp. beurre manié	1½ cups cooked rice
1 cup pastry cream		(20 minutes}

Poach salmon in bouillon until tender. Remove to heated plate. Add cream and capers to ½ cup of the strained bouillon. Bring to a gentle boil. Thicken with beurre manié. Add chives. Cover salmon, which has been boned and skinned, with this sauce. Serve with steamed rice.

A quickly made substitute for Court Bouillon to be used with this recipe is 2 cups water, salted with 1 tbs. chopped onion, ½ carrot, chopped, 1 bay leaf and 1 slice of lemon.

POACHED SALMON WITH CAVIAR SAUCE

SERVES 2

¼ cup butter	¼ cup white wine	2 tbs. caviar
2 salmon steaks, about 6 oz. each	1 cup pastry cream	2 egg yolks
2 tbs. finely chopped onion	¼ tsp. celery salt	Salt and pepper

Arrange salmon steaks in heavy, buttered skillet. Add onion, wine, cream (saving out 4 tbs.), celery salt and season to taste. Cover and simmer 12 minutes. After salmon has been boned and skinned, place in heated casserole. Return stock or liquid back to heat and add caviar. Reduce by one-third. Thicken with egg yolks which have been mixed with 4 tbs. of cream. Pour over salmon and serve at once.

STEAMED OR BOILED FINNAN HADDIE

SERVES 2

1 qt. water	1 lb. finnan haddie, boned	4 oz. butter
1 cup milk	and skimmed	1 tbs. minced parsley
	1 lemon, cut in half	
	6 new potatoes, steamed	

In a heavy kettle, heat water and milk; add finnan haddie. Cover and cook until well done, about 20 minutes. Remove to napkin, bone and remove skin. Serve on heated dish with lemon garnish and steamed potatoes in parsley butter sauce. Serve at once.

CREAMED FINNAN HADDIE DERBY

SERVES 4

1½ cups finnan haddie, boiled	1 cup pastry cream	2 oz. butter
1 cup Cream Sauce Brown Derby	¼ tsp. celery salt (or to taste)	1 tbs. minced parsley
	8 new potatoes, steamed	

Flake cooked finnan haddie, first making certain all bones and skin have been removed. Heat Cream Sauce and add cream and celery salt. Add finnan haddie and simmer gently 4 minutes. Serve at once, with new potatoes covered with parsley butter sauce.

COURT BOUILLON, 1 qt.

3 cups fish stock	1 bay leaf	1 sprig parsley
1 cup white wine	12 black peppercorns	1 small carrot, sliced
½ cup white vinegar	½ onion, sliced	1 tbs. salt

Boil all ingredients sharply for 5 minutes. Used for poaching fish.

A glamorous and eye-filling way to serve trout or shad roe is *en papillote*—in paper. Large paper balloons are brought to the table, slit open, and the savory entrée lifted out, ready to be eaten.

For each serving, take a sheet of Patapar paper 28 by 20 in. and cut it into a heart 28 in. wide and 20 in. high. Butter well on both sides.,

After individual portions of fish, sauce and vegetables are ready, place them on right half of heart and fold left half of paper over at center. Now you have a half heart with the fish inside. Next make the paper as airtight as possible. This is done by folding the two cut edges over, beginning just below the top left and going right, crimping or pleating the paper over in folds ½ in. wide and about 3 -5 in. long, continuing right around the top and down the curved side of the half heart, making from 16—20 folds, rolling the edge under and winding up with a tail extending out beyond the folded left side of the half heart at the bottom.

Place in buttered baking dish in oven until the paper puffs like a balloon. Serve at once, slitting paper and lifting contents out at table.

FILET OF RAINBOW TROUT EN PAPILLOTE
SERVES 2

1 lb. trout
2 tbs. milk
3 tbs. flour
4 tbs. salad oil
2 large sheets Patapar paper
2 oz. butter
2 tbs. Virginia ham,
    finely chopped

2 tbs. mushrooms, finely
    chopped
1 head shallot, chopped fine
¼ tsp. basil
1 tsp. finely chopped chives
1 medium-sized tomato,
    peeled, chopped fine

½ cup white wine
1 tsp. Worcestershire Sauce
Juice of ½ lemon
1 tsp. beurre manié
4 new potatoes, boiled
2 slices peeled lemon
Salt

Filet and bone trout; then dip filets of trout in milk, roll in flour and fry in salad oil until golden brown. Place each serving of trout on right half of paper. Heat butter in skillet; add ham, mushrooms, shallots if available, basil and chives. Sauté until lightly browned. Add wine and reduce by one-third. Add tomato, Worcestershire Sauce and lemon juice. Salt to taste and bring to gentle boil for 4 minutes more. Thicken with beurre manié and divide sauce over the portions of fish. Place a boiled potato at each end of trout. In middle of fish, on top of sauce, place a slice of peeled lemon. Fold paper as instructed above and bake in 300°[F] oven for 5 minutes.

FRESH SHAD ROE EN PAPILLOTE
SERVES 2

1 lb. shad roe
¼ cup butter
¼ cup sliced mushrooms
¼ cup fish stock or water

¼ cup white wine
Salt and pepper
Patapar paper
¼ cup pastry cream
2 tbs. capers

2 tbs. beurre manié
4 medium-sized new potatoes,
    boiled
1 tsp. finely chopped parsley

Place shad roe in buttered skillet and add mushrooms, fish stock, wine, salt and pepper to taste. Cover skillet and steam for 12 minutes. Remove roe and divide between 2 paper hearts. Return stock to heat. Add cream and reduce by one-third. Add capers and thicken with beurre manié. Pour over shad roe. Place a boiled potato at top and bottom and sprinkle with parsley. Fold paper as instructed above and bake in 350°[F] oven for 6 minutes.

STUFFED SWORDFISH DERBY

SERVES 4

4 - 6-oz. swordfish steaks
1 cup Brown Derby Avocado
    Mushroom Stuffing*

Salt and pepper
½ cup flour

1 beaten egg, with a little milk
1 cup bread crumbs
¼ cup oil or butter

Cut steaks in book form—splitting lengthwise but keeping attached at one end. Stuff steaks with Avocado Mushroom Stuffing. Salt and pepper to taste. Dip in flour, egg, bread crumbs and shape the steaks individually. Sauté the stuffed and breaded steaks in butter or oil for 10 minutes on each side. Serve with melted butter or lemon butter.

*For Avocado Mushroom Stuffing, see Stuffed Veal Cutlets St. Galle ("Meats").

GEFÜLLTE FISH

SERVES 12

6 oz. filet of halibut
6 oz. sea bass
6 oz. filet of carp
6 oz. whitefish
6 oz. barracuda
1 medium-sized onion, chopped

3 pieces tender celery, chopped
3 beads garlic, chopped
¼ tsp. marjoram
Salt and pepper
2 eggs, well-beaten
4 tbs. finely chopped parsley

2 cups matzoth meal or
    white bread crumbs
2 cups pastry cream
2 carrots, sliced
3 lemons, peeled and sliced
2 qts. fish stock

In a large bowl, place filet of halibut, sea bass, filet of carp, whitefish and barracuda. All these fish should be cut in small strips. Add chopped onion, celery, garlic, marjoram, salt and pepper to taste. Mix well. Put through fine grinder twice. Put back in large bowl and add well-beaten eggs, parsley, matzoth meal and mix well. Add cream slowly until all cream is absorbed. Mold fish paste into oblong pieces about 2 oz. in weight. Arrange in buttered pan; add sliced carrots. On each piece of fish, put 1 slice of peeled lemon. Add fish stock and simmer on slow fire 25 minutes. Remove from fire; cool and put into ice-box [refrigerator] until jellied. Serve with red horseradish sauce, made by mixing horseradish with finely chopped beets.

FRESH FROG LEGS SAUTÉ MEUNIÈRE

SERVES 2

Take the legs of 4 skinned frogs. Salt and pepper to taste. Dip in flour. Place in heated skillet with butter and fry slowly until golden brown. Remove from skillet and place on platter. Squeeze the juice of ½ lemon over the cooked frog legs and cover with beurre meunière. Sprinkle with chopped parsley and serve with rice or French-fried potatoes.

FROG LEGS À LA DERBY

SERVES 2

1/3 cup butter
1 lb. unjointed frog legs
2 oz. mushrooms
¼ tsp. celery salt
Salt and pepper

2 tbs. green onions, finely
    chopped
¼ tsp. basil
½ cup white wine

1 garlic clove
2/3 cup Brown Gravy
1 tbs. chives
1½ cups steamed rice
    (cooked 20 minutes)

Heat butter in heavy skillet. Add frog legs which have been dipped in milk and then in flour. Sauté gently. Add mushrooms and celery salt; salt and pepper to taste. Sauté until frog legs are golden brown. Add onion and basil. Continue to sauté 2 minutes more. Add wine and allow to reduce by one-third. Finally add chives and serve with steamed rice in very hot serving dish.

STEAMED CLAMS À LA BORDELAISE

SERVES 2

36 Coo-Coo clams*
4 beads shallots, chopped
    fine (optional)

2 tbs. chopped celery
1 cup white wine
1 tsp. celery salt
1 tbs. parsley

4 oz. butter (½ cup), melted
1 lemon, cut in half
½ cup fish stock or water

Put well-cleaned clams into heavy kettle; add shallots, celery, white wine, fish stock, celery salt and parsley. Cover pot securely; allow to steam until all clams are open. Remove clams to very hot deep dish. Then strain broth through cloth or fine sieve. Serve broth in heated tureen or cup. Serve clams on side with melted butter and lemon.

*If Coo-Coo clams are not available, razor clams or any good medium-sized steaming clams may be used.

EASTERN SCALLOPS SAUTÉ AMANDINE

SERVES 4

3 oz. butter
1 lb. scallops, split
½ cup milk

½ cup flour
Salt and pepper
4 tbs. toasted, shaved almonds

Juice of ½ lemon
1 tsp. chopped parsley
Beurre meunière

Heat butter in heavy skillet. One by one place scallops, that have been salted and peppered to taste and dipped in milk and flour, into the hot butter. Sauté until brown. Care should be taken to cook the scallops on a fast fire only. Otherwise they will not brown quickly. They should be cooked about 3 minutes on each side.

Remove from skillet and put on serving platter. Sprinkle the scallops with toasted almonds. Squeeze the lemon juice over the scallops. Sprinkle with parsley. Cover with beurre meunière and serve with French-fried potatoes.

BAKED OYSTERS KIRKPATRICK

SERVES 1

6 large oysters	1 tsp. bell pepper, finely chopped	3 slices bacon, blanched
6 tbs. chili sauce	¼ tsp. celery salt	3 tbs. grated Parmesan cheese
	1 tsp. Worcestershire Sauce	

Open oysters and leave in the deeper shell. Loosen oyster from shell but don't take out. Arrange shell on pan of rock salt. Mix together in a small bowl chili sauce, bell pepper, celery salt and Worcestershire Sauce. Cover oysters with mixture. On top of each, place ½ slice of blanched bacon. Sprinkle with Parmesan cheese and bake in 375°[F] oven for 10 minutes.

BAKED OYSTERS IN SHELL HASHAMAMOOK

SERVES 2

12 large Lynnhaven oysters in shell	3 bacon strips, crisp, chopped fine	1 tbs. Worchestershire Sauce
1/3 cup butter	1 tsp. celery salt	2 egg yolks
2 tbs. green onion, finely chopped	2 tbs. toasted almonds, shaved	1 cup heavy cream
	1 cup toasted bread cubes	½ cup grated American cheese
	½ cup white wine	

Remove oysters from shells; clean deep halves of shells, set them on a bed of rock salt, and heat in 450°[F] oven for 4 minutes. Heat butter in large, heavy skillet. Add oysters and sauté 3 minutes. Return oysters to half shells. Add onion, bacon, celery salt, almonds, bread cubes and sauté 2 minutes more. Add wine and Worcestershire Sauce. Mix egg yolks with cream and add to skillet. Allow to thicken. Cover oysters in the shell with the above paste, heaping shells full. Sprinkle American cheese on top and bake in oven until golden brown. Serve immediately with lemon garnish.

BAKED OYSTERS IN SHELL ROBERT

SERVES 1

6 large oysters in shell	6 large crab legs	1/3 cup heavy cream
¼ cup butter	1/3 cup white wine	6 tsp. Cheddar cheese
¼ medium bell pepper, chopped fine	1/3 cup Sauce Diable	1 tsp. paprika
1 tbs. finely chopped chives	1 egg yolk	½ lemon

Open shells and remove oysters and liquid to bowl. Heat empty deep halves of shells on bed of rock salt in a pan by placing in 450°[F] oven for 5 minutes; then removing. Heat butter in heavy skillet; then add oysters and liquid, bell pepper and chives. Sauté until oysters are curled at edges; then remove oysters and return to shells in pan. Now add crab legs to skillet and sauté for 2 minutes. Remove and place a crab leg on each oyster. Next add wine to skillet and reduce by one-third. Add Sauce Diable and egg yolk [mixture], which has previously been mixed with cream. Allow to thicken. Using a large spoon, cover each oyster with this sauce. Sprinkle 1 tsp. of cheese on each oyster; then a little paprika. Place under broiler until cheese is melted. Garnish with lemon and serve.

BAKED OYSTERS IN SHELL FLORENTINE

SERVES 1

6 large oysters
½ cup spinach, cooked,
    finely chopped

6 tbs. Sauce Mornay
¼ cup butter

2 tbs. Parmesan cheese
1 tsp. paprika

Open shells and remove oysters. Clean deep halves of shells, place on rock salt and heat in 450°[F] oven 5 minutes. Heat spinach. Heat Sauce Mornay. Heat butter in heavy skillet. Add oysters and sauté until they curl at the edges. Remove and keep hot. Put spinach in skillet and mix well to absorb all oyster liquid. Place 1 tbs. of spinach in each shell. Press down evenly. Then place 1 oyster on spinach. Cover oyster and spinach with Sauce Mornay. Sprinkle Parmesan cheese and a little paprika on each oyster. Brown under broiler.

FANCY OYSTER PEPPER ROAST

SERVES 2

2 tbs. green onion
2 slices bacon, fried crisp
2 tbs. bell pepper
2 tbs. pimento

2 oz butter
12 large New York count oysters
½ cup white wine
Juice of ½ lemon

Salt
1 tbs. parsley, finely chopped
6 boiled new potatoes

Chop fine the onions, bacon, bell pepper and pimento. Heat butter in heavy skillet. Add oysters and the chopped mixture. Sauté until oysters curl at edges. Add wine and lemon juice and salt to taste. Cook 3 minutes more. Decorate with parsley and serve in casserole with new potatoes.

FRIED EASTERN OYSTERS

SERVES 3

18 large New York count oysters
1 cup flour

1 cup egg batter
2 cups bread crumbs
½ cup salad oil or butter

1 lemon
6 tbs. Tartar Sauce

Dry oysters lightly with towel or napkin. Dip in flour, then in egg batter. Roll in bread crumbs, pressing them down on crumbs very lightly. Fry in hot oil or butter in heavy skillet. Serve with lemon garnish and Tartar Sauce.

OYSTERS POULETTE

SERVES 2

2 oz. butter
18 oysters, fresh or New York count
1 bead shallot, chopped fine
2 tsp. finely chopped chives

½ cup mushrooms
½ cup white wine
Juice of 1 lemon

1 cup Sauce Suprême
½ cup pastry cream
¼ tsp. cayenne pepper
2 egg yolks

Heat butter in heavy skillet. Add oysters, shallot (optional), chives and mushrooms. Sauté until oysters curl on edges. Add wine and lemon juice. Add Sauce Suprême, half of cream and cayenne pepper. Simmer 3 minutes. Add egg yolks, which have been mixed with remaining cream, to thicken. Serve in heated casserole lined with mashed potatoes.

Milk may be used in place of Sauce Suprême. Then add 1 tbs. of flour while sautéing oysters.

CHINESE SHRIMP BATTER

2 eggs   *1 cup water*   *Salt*
1 cup rice or pastry flour   *1 tbs. soy sauce*

Beat eggs in bowl; add rice flour, water, soy sauce; salt to taste. Beat vigorously until smooth. This makes sufficient batter to fry 1-lb. of shrimp.

CHINESE SHRIMP
SERVES 4

1 lb. raw shrimp   *½ cup flour*   *Chinese Shrimp Batter*

Peel shrimp, split through middle lengthwise and wash thoroughly, being sure to remove intestinal tract. Dry well. Roll in flour and dip in Chinese Shrimp Batter. Shake excess batter from shrimp and fry in oil at 350°[F] for 12 minutes. Serve with Special Shrimp Sauce.

SPECIAL SHRIMP SAUCE FOR CHINESE SHRIMP
SERVES 4

1 cup chili sauce   *½ green pepper, chopped fine*   *Dash of Lea and Perrin's*
2 tbs. English mustard   *Oil*   *Worcestershire Sauce*
                                3 sprigs parsley, chipped fine

Place chili sauce in small bowl. Add English mustard which has been mixed with enough oil to give it a creamy consistency, dash of Worcestershire, green pepper, parsley and mix well. Serve in separate dish with Fried Shrimp.

SHRIMP CREOLE WITH RICE
SERVES 4

2 oz. butter   *½ cup white wine*   *2 cups Spanish or Creole Sauce*
1 lb. shrimp   *3 cups cooked rice*

Heat butter in heavy skillet. Add shrimp, which have been split, cleaned and boiled, and brown lightly. Add white wine and reduce by two-thirds. Add sauce. Cook for 5 minutes over slow heat. Serve with rice which has been steamed 20 minutes.

Another method is to cook the shrimp along with the sauce in one operation. Brown the shrimp for 5 minutes, then add:

2 tbs. green pepper julienne	1 medium-sized tomato, in small	1 pinch basil
2 tbs. onion julienne	pieces, seeds removed	½ tsp. black pepper, crushed
2 tbs. celery julienne	¼ bead garlic, chopped fine	Salt

Sauté all for 10 minutes; add ½ cup white wine. Reduce to a half. Add ½ cup Brown Derby Tomato Sauce. Simmer for 10 minutes more and serve with rice.

FRESH SHRIMP HAWAIIAN

SERVES 2

2 oz. butter	1 medium-sized tomato, seeds	½ cup brown stock or
1 lb. raw shrimp, split, cleaned	removed, cut is pieces	consommé
3 slices canned pineapple,	1/3 cup white wine	Dash celery salt
cut in small pieces	3 tbs. soy sauce	3 cups cooked rice
1 pinch basil	3 tbs. shaved toasted almonds	Salt and pepper

Heat butter in heavy skillet. Add raw, split shrimp. Sauté on medium heat 8 minutes. Add pineapple, tomato and basil; sauté 2 minutes. Add wine. Reduce by two-thirds. Add soy sauce, almonds, brown stock or consommé and celery salt. Simmer for 10 minutes. Salt and pepper to taste. Serve in casserole with boiled rice.

FRESH SHRIMP SAUTÉ BROWN DERBY

SERVES 3

4 oz. butter	1 bead garlic chopped fine	½ cup Brown Gravy or
1 lb. raw shrimp, peeled,	2 tbs. finely chopped green onion	chicken broth
split and cleaned	½ tsp. basil	1 tsp. celery salt
½ lb. mushrooms, sliced	½ cup white wine	2 cups steamed rice
		1 tsp. Worcestershire Sauce

Heat butter in heavy skillet. Add shrimp and sauté on medium heat for 8 minutes. Add mushrooms, garlic, green onion and basil. Sauté 2 minutes more. Add wine and reduce by two-thirds. Add Brown Gravy, celery salt and Worcestershire Sauce. Cook 8 minutes longer. Serve with rice which has been cooked 20 minutes.

FRESH SHRIMP À LA NEWBURG

SERVES 3

2 oz. butter	1 tbs. paprika	1 cup pastry cream
1 lb. shrimp, cooked and split	¼ cup sherry	Pinch cayenne pepper
1 bead shallot, chopped fine	1 cup Sauce Suprême	3 egg yolks
		Salt

Heat butter in heavy skillet. Add cooked shrimp and sauté until lightly browned. Add shallot and paprika. Sauté 1 minute longer. Add wine and reduce by two-thirds. Add Sauce Suprême, 10 tbs. cream and cayenne pepper; cook 8 minutes longer. Salt to taste. Thicken with egg yolks* which have been mixed with 6 tbs. cream.

In place of Sauce Suprême, milk or chicken broth may be used. If so, add 1 tbs. flour to the shrimp while sautéing.

*1 tbs. beurre manié may be used in place of egg yolks.

FRESH CRAB LEGS AND MUSHROOMS DIABLE
SERVES 2

2 oz. butter	2 oz. dry sherry	½ cup Cream Sauce Brown
8 oz. crab legs	1 tsp. English mustard	Derby
4 mushrooms, quartered	2 tbs. Brown Derby Diable	½ cup heavy cream
1 tbs. green pepper, chopped	Sauce	Salt and pepper
very fine		

Oregon, Alaska or Eastern crab may be used, and if these are not available, use canned crab. Heat butter in skillet. Add crab, mushrooms and green pepper. Sauté about 6 minutes. Add sherry. Reduce by two-thirds. Add mustard, Diable Sauce, Cream Sauce and cream; simmer for 10 minutes on slow fire. Salt and pepper to taste. Serve on toast.

If Diable Sauce is not available, Escoffier Sauce or A-1 Sauce may be substituted.

OYSTERS, SHRIMP, AND MUSHROOMS DIABLE

Made the same as Crab Legs and Mushrooms Diable except that 8 New York count oysters and 12 shrimp (halved) are substituted for crab legs.

CRAB MEAT BALTIMORE OR À LA MARYLAND

At first glance, these would appear to be quite similar recipes but since they are prepared differently and are both favorites with Derby patrons, it was decided to include both of them. Crab Meat Baltimore is a "dry mix" recipe and is served in shell. À la Maryland is a continuous-cooking recipe which eventually finds its way into a casserole.

CRAB MEAT BALTIMORE
SERVES 4

1½ cups fresh crab meat	2 tbs. chives	1 cup grated American Cheese
½ cup mayonnaise	1 tbs. English mustard	1 tsp. paprika
½ cup Cream Sauce Brown	1 tsp. Worcestershire Sauce	½ cup bread crumbs
Derby or heavy cream	4 clean crab shells	Salt
	[Lemon]	

Mix well together the crab meat, mayonnaise, Cream Sauce, chives, bread crumbs, mustard, and Worcestershire Sauce; salt to taste. Fill the crab shells heaping full of this mixture, sprinkle with cheese and top with a dash of paprika. Bake in 350°[F] oven for 15 minutes. Serve with lemon garnish.

CRAB MEAT À LA MARYLAND
SERVES 2

2 oz. butter	½ cup pastry cream	2 egg yolks
1 tbs. finely chopped bell pepper	1½ cups fresh crab meat	1 hard-cooked egg, sliced
1/3 cup sherry	½ cup yellow corn, steamed	Salt and pepper
½ cup Cream Sauce Brown Derby		

Heat butter in a heavy skillet; then sauté bell pepper for 1½ minutes. Add sherry and reduce by one-third. Next, add Cream Sauce and cream [hold back a little cream for egg yolks] and mix all well. Bring just up to gentle boil; then add crab meat and corn kernels. Simmer gently for 5 minutes; then thicken with egg yolks that have previously been mixed with a little of the cream. Season with salt and pepper; place in heated casserole, garnish with slices of hard-cooked egg and serve at once.

BROILED CALIFORNIA LOBSTER
SERVES 2

2-lb. live lobster	1 lemon	½ cup melted butte
2 tbs. butter	1 tsp. paprika	Dash salt and black pepper

Plunge live lobster into vigorously boiling water for 4 minutes. Remove, allow to cool sufficiently to handle, split through the middle [length-wise], rinse out entrails. Arrange on heavy broiler pan, meat side up. Make a mixture of butter, salt, pepper and paprika and spread over all of meat. Broil, using 550°[F] heat, for 20 minutes. Serve at once with melted butter and lemon garnishes.

For charcoal-broiled lobster: Spread only half the butter mixture on meat side of lobster. Place over charcoal broiler, meat side down, for 6 minutes. Turn lobster, pour on remainder of butter mixture and finish broiling (approx. 10 minutes). Garnish with lemon and watercress. Serve at once with melted butter.

CALIFORNIA LOBSTER THERMIDOR
SERVES 2

2-lb. cooked lobster in shell	6 tbs. sherry	1 tsp. chopped chives
2 oz. butter	½ cup heavy cream	2 tbs. Sauce Hollandaise
½ cup diced mushrooms	1 tsp. Worcestershire Sauce	(or 2 egg yolks)
1 bead shallot, chopped fine	½ cup Cream Sauce Brown	2 tbs. whipped cream
1 tsp. English mustard	Derby or milk	Salt

Split lobster length-wise; take out meat, then wash and clean shell for serving and place on bed of rock salt in 325°[F] oven to dry for 10 minutes. Cut meat in ½-in. pieces. Using a heavy skillet, heat butter gently; add lobster and mushrooms. Sauté, stirring constantly until light brown. Add shallot and mustard, sauté 1 minute more. Next, add wine. Reduce for 2 minutes; then add Worcestershire Sauce, cream and Cream Sauce along with chives. Blend well and cook until a good degree of thickness is reached. Remove from fire; salt to taste and blend well. Fill heated shells with mixture. Top lobster with mixture of the Sauce Hollandaise and whipped cream. Brown under open flame. Constant care must be given since this topping browns extremely fast. Serve at once.

If milk is used instead of Cream Sauce, 1 tbs. flour must be added while sautéing lobster. And in place of Hollandaise and whipped cream, you may sprinkle with paprika and brown lightly.

LOBSTER IN SHELL CARDINAL
SERVES 2

2-lb. cooked lobster	*1 tsp. paprika*	*1 tsp. celery salt*
2 oz. butter	*3 oz. sherry*	*2 egg yolks*
1 bead shallot, chopped fine	*1 cup Sauce Suprême or milk*	*Dash cayenne pepper*
2 oz., mushrooms, quartered	*½ cup pastry cream*	*Salt*

Split lobster [length-wise]; remove and dice meat. Heat butter in heavy skillet; add lobster meat, browning lightly. Add shallot, if obtainable, with quartered mushrooms and sauté for 2 minutes more. Add paprika; cover all with sherry and reduce by two-thirds. Mix together Sauce Suprême, cream, celery salt, and cayenne pepper; add to skillet mixture. (If milk is used, add 1 tbs. flour while sautéing lobster.) Cook over very slow fire 8 minutes. Add egg yolks, blending well; allow to thicken, then remove from fire immediately and salt to taste. Pour into shells which have been cleaned and heated on a bed of rock salt. Sprinkle with dash of paprika; brown lightly under broiler flame; serve at once.

LOBSTER À LA L'AMÉRICAINE
SERVES 2

2-lb. live lobster	*½ cup white wine (Chablis)*	*4 tbs. fish stock or chicken*
½ cup olive oil	*½ cup brandy*	*broth*
1 bead shallot, chopped fine	*2 medium-sized fresh tomatoes*	*4 tbs. Brown Gravy*
½ clove garlic, chopped fine	*seeded and diced*	*½ cup sweet butter*
½ cup quartered mushrooms		*2 tbs. chives, chopped fine*

Plunge lobster into boiling water for 4 minutes, remove and pull off tail, wash and cut into ½-in. pieces, leaving shell on. Heat olive oil in heavy skillet; add lobster, sautéing until lightly browned (about 3 minutes). Add shallot, garlic, mushrooms and continue to sauté 2 minutes more, using a very slow fire. Drain off oil; then add wine and reduce by two-thirds. Next add brandy and light immediately with match. As soon as fire dies down, add tomatoes, fish stock and Brown Gravy, which have all been blended together. Continue to cook gently, reducing by one-third. Add butter, cut in small pieces; add chives, stirring briskly. Serve at once on heated platter, surrounding with steamed rice.

MÉDAILLONS OF LOBSTER ROBERT
SERVES 2

2-lb. cooked lobster

Carefully break off tail or edible parts of lobster, wrap it in a towel and break shell into small pieces, being careful not to break meat. Remove shell and slice meat into ¼-in.-thick slices. These are known as medallions. Make a batter of the following:

1 egg	*1/3 cup milk*
½ cup flour	*Salt*

Beat the egg well. Add flour and small amount of milk, mixing to a smooth paste. Add remainder of milk and season with salt.

Heat 1/3 cup salad oil in heavy skillet. Dip medallions into the batter and fry. Arrange on heated deep platter.

2 oz. butter	*1 tbs. finely chopped chives*
2 artichoke bottoms, diced	*2 tbs. capers*

Prepare sauce by heating butter slowly in skillet until browned but not burned. Add artichokes, chives and capers and sauté 2 minutes. Pour sauce over medallions. Serve at once, garnished with parsley and minute potatoes.

LOBSTER CREOLE WITH RICE

Made the same as Shrimp Creole, substituting cooked lobster meat, diced, for the shrimp.

LOBSTER NEWBURG
SERVES 2

2 oz. butter	*½ cup sherry*	*1 tsp. Worcestershire Sauce*
2-lb. cooked lobster, diced	*1 tbs. paprika*	*2 egg yolks**
1 tbs. flour	*Dash cayenne pepper*	*2 slices toast*
1 bead shallot (if obtainable)	*½ cup Sauce Suprême*	*Salt*
	1 cup pastry cream	

Heat butter gently in heavy skillet. Then add lobster, browning lightly. Add flour. Next, add shallot and sauté ½ minute more. Add sherry and gently reduce by two-thirds. Mix together paprika, cayenne pepper, Sauce Suprême, cream and Worcestershire Sauce. Add this mixture to lobster mixture. Add salt to taste and reduce by one-fourth over a very slow fire. Remove from fire and thicken with egg yolks which have been beaten with a small portion of the pastry cream. Blend very well. Serve at once on heated plates with slices of toast. Garnish with watercress or parsley.

*[*Please observe current health and safety cooking guidelines for the preparation of eggs in these recipes — safety first.]*

LOBSTER BROCHETTE, SAUCE DIABLE

SERVES 2

2-lb. live lobster
1 cup Sauce Diable

10 slices blanched bacon
4 large button mushrooms
½ cup bread crumbs

¼ cup butter
1 lemon, quartered

Cook live lobster in shell by plunging into boiling water for 20 minutes. Remove. When sufficiently cool to handle, remove from shell and cut in 1-in. squares.

In small bowl, mix Sauce Diable: 1 tbs. prepared dark mustard, 1 tbs. catsup, 1 tbs. Worcestershire Sauce.

Dip lobster squares in sauce. Cut blanched bacon in 1-in. pieces. Using 2 broiling skewers or brochette needles, place mushroom button on each; add a square of lobster, then a piece of bacon, then lobster and bacon, continuing until needle is almost filled. On the end of needle place another mushroom. Gently sprinkle or roll in bread crumbs. Place on generously buttered broiler pan. Place under 550°[F] flame for 4 minutes on each side. Constant attention is required to prevent burning. Serve at once with lemon and hot Sauce Diable

This may also be made using raw shrimp or oysters.

* * *

Carleton Morse, the creator and author of One Man's Family, *is equally well-known among gourmets as a trencherman, authority on food and writer on the subject. Need we say that The Hollywood Brown Derby is like a second home to Mr. Morse? Of all his favorite dishes, his latest enthusiasm is for the Derby Seafood Pot Pie.*

* * *

BROWN DERBY SEAFOOD POT PIE

SERVES 4

8 New York count oysters
8 raw shrimp, split
4 pieces scallop
8 crab legs
4 small pieces of filet of
     sole, folded in half
4 small pieces lobster

1 tsp. chives
1 cup white wine
Pinch celery salt
½ cup water
1 medium-sized tomato,
     chopped and diced
Juice of 1 lemon

4 mushrooms
3 oz. butter
2 tbs. flour
½ cup light cream
4 pie dough covers
Salt and pepper

Take heavy skillet and butter lightly. Place all the seafood in the skillet. Add chives, celery salt, wine, water, tomato, lemon juice and mushrooms. Cover the skillet and cook on slow fire for 20 minutes. Remove seafood and place in 4 deep pot-pie dishes. Divide the mushrooms, 1 to each dish. Keep the remaining liquid hot. Take smaller skillet and melt the butter. Add flour. Sauté lightly. Add liquid and cream. Stir well. If too thick, add a little more white wine or if too thin, thicken with 1 or 2 egg yolks. If egg yolks are added, do not boil any more. Remove from fire and test for salt and pepper. Divide the sauce into the pot-pie dishes. Cover with pie dough covers that have been baked in advance and serve boiling hot.

For pie dough covers, use Brown Derby Pastry for Covered Pies ("Desserts").

SEAFOOD NEW ORLEANS STYLE

SERVES 4

3 oz. butter
4 oysters
8 small scallops
8 shrimp, split
½ cup crab meat

6 small pieces cooked lobster
2 tbs. chopped green onion
Dash celery salt
4 medium-sized mushrooms,
    sliced
½ cup white wine

2 dashes Tabasco sauce
1 cup Sauce Suprême
1 tsp. Worcestershire Sauce
Juice of 1 lemon
Salt and pepper

Heat butter in heavy skillet. Add all seafood. Sauté 5 minutes. Add green onion and mushrooms. Sauté 5 minutes more. Add wine, Tabasco sauce, Sauce Suprême, Worcestershire Sauce, celery salt. Simmer on slow fire 10 minutes. Add lemon juice; salt and pepper to taste. Serve with cooked rice.

In place of Sauce Suprême, milk may be used. Add 3 tbs. flour while sautéing seafood.

PLANK BUTTER SAUCE

½ cup Brown Sauce
3 oz. butter, melted

Juice of ½ lemon
1 tsp. Worcestershire Sauce

¼ tsp. celery salt
1 tbs. finely chopped chives

Heat Brown Sauce in heavy skillet. Add butter, lemon juice, Worcestershire Sauce, celery salt and chives. Bring to a gentle boil. Pour over fish steaks just before serving. This amount will serve 3 small planks or 1 large one.

For other fish and seafood recipes, turn to "Hors d'Oeuvres", "Curries", and "Barbecues".

MEATS

The best advice on the selection of meats is to buy from a reliable butcher who carries top-quality merchandise. In the recipes which follow, the proper cuts are indicated and the same results will not be achieved if cheaper meats are substituted.

BEEF

Good beef is an attractive light red in color and has "marble" lines of fat running through. The fat covering should be white, medium thick, even and not bumpy. Do not buy steaks cut too thin. They should be at least ½ in. thick.

ROAST PRIME RIBS OF BEEF IN ROCK SALT
SERVES 20 - 24

18 lbs. prime ribs   30 lbs. or more rock salt

Use only choice prime ribs. Trim and tie securely with string. Cover the bottom of roasting pan with 2-in. rock salt. Place the ribs in center; cover completely with rock salt and press lightly all over meat. Sprinkle with a little cold water. Place in 500°[F] oven. Roast 11 minutes to the pound. To remove ribs, break the crust of rock salt with mallet. Allow meat to rest in warm place for about 1 hour before serving. This will make slicing much easier. Serve with its own thin clear brown juice.

FILET MIGNON OF BEEF
SERVES 4

2 lbs. filet of beef   Salt   2 tbs. salad oil
                                  1 tsp. crushed black pepper

Use enough filet of beef to have 2 lbs. clean filet after fat and skin have been removed. Cut crosswise in 4 equal steaks. Season with salt and pepper and dip in oil. Broil over charcoal or under broiler. The time of broiling must be ascertained by thickness of meat and preference for rare, medium, or well done. Mignon steak weighing about 8 oz. will require 8—10 minutes for rare and 12 minutes for medium and 20 for well-done meat.

[Caution: Please review current health and safety guidelines on the recommended internal temperature of meats.]

ROAST FILET OF BEEF, BRILLAT

SERVES 8

4 lbs. filet of beef	1 branch celery, diced	2 cups Brown Sauce
8 strips bacon	12 black peppercorns	1 tbs. truffle (optional)
1/8 lb. butter	¼ tsp. basil	8 large button mushrooms
½ onion, diced	1 cup sherry	8 Stuffed Tomatoes Soubise
2 carrots, diced		Salt and pepper

Remove all fat and skin from filet. Wrap bacon around filet and tie securely with string. Place in roasting pan with butter, onion, carrots, celery, peppercorns and basil. Roast in 400°[F] oven 30 minutes (for rare). Remove and drain off excess fat. Add sherry and Brown Sauce and simmer 8 minutes. Season with salt and pepper to taste. Strain through fine sieve. Add truffle. Remove strings from filet and place on heated platter and glaze with gravy. On top of filet, place mushrooms which have been sautéed in butter. Garnish with Stuffed Tomatoes Soubise.

TOURNEDOS AND GRENADINES

The most tender beef is the tenderloin section. The large end is used for tenderloin steaks, the middle for filet mignons and the small end is utilized for tournedos or grenadines. The only difference between the last two is that tournedos are sliced 1—1½ in. thick, 2½ in. diameter, weigh from 3 to 4 oz., and are served 2 to the order while grenadines are ¼—1/3 in. thick and come 3 to the order.

TOURNEDOS OF FILET OF BEEF NATUREL

SERVES 4

8 tournedos, 3-4 oz.	Salt and pepper	2 tbs. olive oil or butter
	8 slices blanched bacon	

Season each tournedos with salt and pepper to taste, roll in circle with bacon strip, secure with toothpick, dip in oil and either sauté in skillet with desired fat, olive oil or butter, or broil over charcoal. In either case use brisk heat, being careful to turn only once during cooking. Time: 3—4 minutes for rare, 6 for medium, and 8 for well done. Remove toothpicks before serving.

TOURNEDOS OF BEEF FILET ON PLANK GARNI

SERVES 4

8 tournedos from above recipe	8 small onions, boiled	4 tbs. sautéed corn
4 cups Duchesse Potatoes	4 small tomatoes, baked	8 small glazed carrots
8 button mushrooms	4 small cauliflower bouquets	8 tbs. Sauce Bordelaise
	4 tbs. cooked peas	

Using 4 walnut planks, place 2 tournedos on each. Around edge make a border of Duchesse Potatoes. Arrange all vegetables in neat bouquets around tournedos. Cook tournedos with Sauce Bordelaise and serve.

TOURNEDOS OF BEEF FILET, DERBY HOUSE
SERVES 4

8 tournedos from Naturel recipe
1 large tomato, sliced
4 tbs. Sauce Béarnaise

2 tsp. chopped truffle
2 cups potatoes julienne,
    fried crisp

8 artichoke bottoms
8 tbs. cooked peas

Remove toothpicks and arrange tournedos on heated platter. On top of each, place 1 slice of tomato brushed lightly with melted butter. Place under broiler for 1 minute to heat tomato. Remove and on each tomato slice, place 1 tbs. Sauce Béarnaise. Sprinkle chopped truffle over sauce. Garnish around sides of tournedos with crisp potatoes and hot artichoke bottoms filled with cooked peas and serve.

TOURNEDOS OF BEEF FILET CALIFORNIA
SERVES 4

8 tournedos from Naturel recipe
4 medium-sized tomatoes
16 avocado balls

Salt and pepper
½ cup grated Cheddar
    cheese

1 cup Sauce Bordelaise
8 button mushrooms

Scoop out tomatoes, salt and pepper lightly; fill with avocado balls and top with cheese. Bake in 350°[F] oven until done. Sauté mushrooms in butter. When they are done, add Sauce Bordelaise. Place 1 mushroom on each tournedos and glaze with the sauce. Serve 2 tournedos with 1 stuffed baked tomato to each guest.

GRENADINES OF BEEF FILET WITH SAUCE BÉARNAISE
SERVES 4

1½ lbs. trimmed filet of beef

1/8 lb. butter

4 tbs. Sauce Béarnaise

Cut filet lengthwise into slices 1/3 in. thick. These are the grenadines. Salt, pepper and flour. Heat butter in heavy skillet; add grenadines; brown on hot fire until done as desired. Remove to heated platter and serve with Sauce Béarnaise.

GRENADINES OF BEEF FILET CHASSUER
SERVES 4

1½ lbs. filet of beef
1/8 lb. butter
8 chicken livers, split and blanched
4 button mushrooms, quartered

¼ tsp. basil
½ cup burgundy
1 small tomato, peeled and
    diced

½ cup Brown Sauce
2 cups cooked Risotto
Salt and pepper

Prepare grenadines as in recipe above, except for sauce. Remove to heated platter, then add chicken livers and mushrooms to pan and sauté until brown. Add basil and wine and reduce half. Add tomato and Brown Sauce; simmer for 4 minutes. Season with salt and pepper to taste and pour sauce over grenadines. Serve with Risotto which has been cooked 20 minutes.

GRENADINES OF BEEF FILET ALEXANDRIA
SERVES 4

Similar to Grenadine Chasseur, but substitute 8 baby artichoke hearts for the chicken livers.

STEAKS

Salt and pepper, season with barbecue spices or rub with garlic, according to taste. Always dip in oil before broiling to prevent sticking to grill or grate.

Steaks should be cooked as quickly as possible. First, sear on both sides to keep juices in; then, turn only once more for each side.

BUTTERFLY MINUTE STEAK
SERVES 1

12-oz. New York sirloin steak, well-trimmed

To butterfly the steak, you split it from the lean side. Care should be taken not to cut all the way through. It should be split to resemble an open book. Flatten out with mallet. Salt, pepper and flour the steak and sauté on fast fire or very hot charcoal. This steak usually cooks medium in about1½ minutes on each side.

NEW YORK SIRLOIN STEAK SAUTÉ À LA MINUTE
SERVES 1

12 oz. New York sirloin	*Salt and pepper*	*¼ cup butter*
Salt and pepper		

Hammer meat thin. Season with salt and pepper; sauté in butter melted in heavy skillet. Use brisk heat, sauté 1 minute, turning only once. Serve on heated platter surrounded with minute-fried potatoes.

MINUTE STEAM SAUTÉ BALOISE
SERVES 1

10 oz. New York sirloin, pounded thin	*1 tbs. butter* *French-fried onion rings*	*1/3 cup minute potatoes sautéed in butter*

Pound steak thin, trim fat, salt and pepper and flour well. Sauté in butter on hot fire to desired doneness: 4 minutes for rare, 6 minutes for medium, 8 minutes for well done. Garnish with French-fried onion rings and minute potatoes.

CALIFORNIA PEPPER STEAK

SERVES 4

2 lbs. round steak
1/3 cup oil
½ lb. onion, sliced
2 medium-sized green
    peppers, diced

¼ tsp. basil
[Flour]
1 tsp. paprika
1 bead garlic, chopped fine

½ cup burgundy
1 cup tomato purée
1 cup Brown Sauce
1 cup clear stock

Use lean round steak and cut in 4 pieces. Pound with wooden mallet. Season with salt and pepper and dust heavily with flour. Heat oil in braising kettle or deep, heavy skillet. Add steaks and brown well on both sides. Add onions and green pepper and smother until lightly browned. Add basil, paprika and garlic. Continue smothering for 3 minutes longer. Add wine, tomato purée, Brown Sauce and stock, which have all been blended together. Braise over slow fire until tender (approximately 1 hour).

PAN-FRIED ROUND STEAK

SERVES 4

4 ½-lb. round steaks
1/8 lb. butter

1 tbs. green peppers
    finely chopped
2 strips bacon, chopped fine

1 tbs. flour
1 cup pastry cream
Salt and pepper

Use lean round steak. Pound with wooden mallet as thin as possible. Season with salt and pepper and dust with flour. Place in skillet with heated butter. Brown on both sides as fast as possible. Remove from skillet to heated platter. Put onion and bacon in skillet and sauté until lightly browned. Add flour and blend well. Smother a minute or two more. Add cream and salt and pepper to taste. Bring to a gentle boil. Serve gravy with steaks.

MINUTE STEAK SAUTÉ BORDELAISE

SERVES 4

4 ½-lb. New York sirloin steaks   *¼ cup butter*   *1 cup Sauce Bordelaise*

Pound steaks lightly; season with salt and pepper and flour; place in skillet with heated butter and sauté to desired turn. Serve with Sauce Bordelaise.

SWISS STEAKS

SERVES 4 - 6

2 lbs. round steak   *¼ tsp. basil*   *1 cup tomato purée*
1/3 cup oil   *1 tsp. paprika*   *1 cup Brown Sauce*
1 lb. onions, sliced   *1 bead garlic, chopped fine*   *1 cup stock*
                               ½ cup burgundy

Use lean round meat. Cut in 4 equal steaks. Pound the steaks, salt and pepper, and flour heavily. Heat oil in braising kettle. Add the steaks and brown on both sides. Add onions and smother until lightly browned. Add basil, paprika, garlic and smother a few minutes longer. Add wine, tomato purée, Brown Sauce and stock (which have been mixed together) and braise on slow fire until done (approximately 2 hours).

BRAISED BRISKET OF BEEF WITH BRUSSELS SPROUTS

SERVES 8

6 lbs. brisket of beef   *1 leek, diced*   *1 tbs. paprika*
*   (fat removed)*   *2 cups burgundy*   *½ cup flour*
1/3 cup oil   *½ tsp. basil*   *1½ qts. clear stock*
1 medium-sized onion,   *Salt and pepper*   *1 tbs. celery salt*
*   sliced*   *1 bay leaf*   *2½ lbs. Brussels sprouts*
3 medium-sized carrots,   *2 beads garlic*   *   steamed*
*   sliced*   *3 fresh tomatoes, diced*   *¼ cup butter*
2 branches celery, diced   *1 No. 2 can tomato purée*   *1/8 tsp. nutmeg (for sprouts)*

Wipe meat clean with dry cloth.. Season with salt and pepper. Place in heavy braising kettle in which oil has been heated smoking hot. Brown and sear meat on all sides. Add onions, carrots, celery, leeks and continue sautéing until all vegetables are brown. Mix together wine, basil, bay leaf, garlic, tomatoes, tomato purée, paprika, flour, celery salt and stock; add to kettle and bring to gentle boil. Skim off foam and excess fat. Cover kettle tightly; place in 375°[F] oven for 2 ½ hours or until meat is well done. Remove and strain sauce through fine sieve. Serve sliced meat covered with gravy and Brussels sprouts that have been sautéed in butter and nutmeg.

STUFFED GROUND STEAK WITH CHEDDAR CHEESE
SERVES 2

12 oz. lean ground round steak   *Salt and pepper*   *Brown Derby De Luxe Sauce*
4 oz. chopped Cheddar cheese

Salt and pepper the ground round to taste. Mold in 4 equal patties. On 2 of the patties divide the cheese. Use the 2 remaining patties to cover the cheese and mold together. Fry in butter to the desired turn (about 20 minutes). Cover with De Luxe Sauce and serve with mashed or baked potatoes.

The recipe for Derby De Luxe Sauce will be found in the "Specialties of the House" chapter.

BEEF PETITE MARMITE   SERVES 8

8 lbs. brisket of beef   *4 medium-sized tomatoes,*   *6 sprigs parsley*
2 lbs. marrow bones   *peeled, cut in squares*   *½ head cabbage*
2 onions, split and burned   *1 bay leaf*   *1 cup noodles*
16 medium-sized carrots   *15 black peppercorns*   *2 leeks*
8 branches celery, diced   *Salt and pepper*

Choose lean brisket of beef. Place in heavy kettle with marrow bones. Cover with cold water and bring to quick boil. Remove water and wash brisket. Return to kettle. Add onions that have been split crosswise and burned on cut side under open flame. Also carrots, leeks, celery, tomatoes, bay leaf, peppercorns, parsley, and salt and pepper to taste. Cover with water and simmer 3 hours. Add cabbage and cook 5 minutes more. Then add noodles and continue simmering until brisket is well done. To serve: cut brisket in thick slices, arrange in casserole. For each serving, place 1 or 2 marrow bones in casserole. Also add all vegetables and noodles that have been cooking with brisket. Cover with the broth and serve with horseradish.

This may also be served separately as soup and meat, the soup as a broth, or with the noodles, or the vegetables, chopped; the meat as brisket with Horseradish or Mustard Sauce.

SAUERBRATEN
SERVES 6 - 8

8 lbs. shoulder clod of beef   *¼ tsp. basil*   *2 cups burgundy*
½ onion, diced   *1 bay leaf*   *2 cups water*
3 carrots, diced   *½ cup oil*   *1½ qts. Brown Gravy*
2 branches celery, diced   *1 cup wine vinegar*   *12 peppercorns*
2 beads garlic, chopped   *Salt*

Make marinade of all ingredients except meat, oil and Brown Gravy. Tie shoulder clod securely with string and soak 36 hours. After completing marinating, heat oil in heavy kettle. Add meat and brown deep golden brown on all sides. Add vegetables from marinade, 1 cup of marinade liquid and Brown Gravy. Simmer gently on slow heat for 4 hours or until meat is very tender. Should gravy reduce too fast, add a little water. Serve with gravy, which may be thickened as desired.

BRAISED OX JOINTS À LA BOURGEOISE

SERVES 6

1 cup oil or lard
6 lbs. ox joints, cut in the
     joints
1 cup flour
1 small clover garlic,
     chopped fine
2 bay leaves

Rind of 1 lemon, chopped
     fines
1 large tbs. black pepper-
     corns
1 pt. burgundy
3 pts. beef stock
1 No. 2 can tomato purée
3 tbs. salt

4 tbs. butter or lard
24 baby onions
2 bunches baby carrots
1 bunch celery, cut in 1-in.
     pieces
2 lbs. small new potatoes
1 cup fresh-cooked peas

In a large iron skillet, place oil or lard and bring to the smoking point. Add ox joints and fry until nice and brown. Add flour, garlic, lemon rind (yellow part only, chopped fine), bay leaves and peppercorns. Smother for approximately 2 minutes. Add wine, beef stock, tomato purée and bring to boil; then add salt. Let this mixture simmer very slowly for 2 ½—3 hours. Skim grease from top periodically.

While this is cooking, in another skillet put butter or lard and add onions, carrots, celery and smother for about 5—6 minutes, or until vegetables take color. Then all this mixture to ox joints. (You may keep potatoes out until about ½ hour before finished, if desired.)

Serve ox joints en casserole and sprinkle cooked peas on top.

BEEF À LA STROGANOFF

SERVES 6

4 oz. butter
1½ lbs. filet of beef cut in
     small pieces
1 tbs. finely chopped onion
3 large mushrooms julienne

1 medium-sized truffle
     julienne (optional)
½ tsp. salt
¼ tsp. pepper
2 tbs. flour
½ cup dry sherry

1 cup sour cream
1 cup heavy cream
½ cup Brown Gravy
½ doz. chives, cut fine
1½ tbs. horseradish

In large frying pan, heat butter very hot. Add meat, onion, truffle, mushrooms, salt and pepper; sauté 3 minutes over hot fire. Add flour and blend well. Sauté 1 minutes more. Mix sherry, sour cream, sweet cream, Brown Gravy, chives and horseradish. Add to meat mixture. Mix well and allow to reach a full boil. Remove from fire as soon as boiling or meat will be tough. Serve with noodles or rice.

This recipe may also be made with pork, veal and veal kidneys.

EMINCÉ OF BEEF À LA SWISS   SERVES 4

¼ cup butter
1 lb. beef filet julienne
¼ lb. mushrooms, sliced
½ medium-sized onion,
     chopped fine

Salt and pepper
1 tsp. flour
1 medium-sized tomato,
     peeled and sliced

½ cup burgundy
1 cup Brown Sauce
1 cup cooked string beans
½ cup grated Swiss cheese
1 tbs. chives

Heat butter in heavy skillet. Add beef julienne, mushrooms and onion; season with salt and pepper to taste. Sauté until golden brown. Add flour and sauté 1 minute longer, blending well. Add burgundy, tomato, Brown Sauce, string beans and bring to quick boil. Put in heated casserole, sprinkle with grated Swiss cheese, brown under broiler; then sprinkle with chives.

EMINCÉ OF BEEF À LA DUTCH EN CASSEROLE
SERVES 4

1 lb. filet of beef, cut in small pieces	1 onion, chopped	½ cup sherry
1 veal kidney, sliced	1 green pepper, cut in 1-in. diamond-shaped pieces	1 cup Brown Sauce
4 oz. butter		Fried potatoes in dollar-size slices
8 mushrooms		Stewed tomatoes

Sauté beef and kidney slices in butter over brisk fire. Add mushrooms, onion and pepper, sautéing 1 minute longer. Add wine and Brown Sauce. Bring to a boil. Serve in heated casserole or deep platter in circle, garnished with fried potatoes and stewed tomatoes over all.

BOILED OX TONGUE

1 ox tongue	1 leek, diced	4 cloves
½ onion, diced	2 carrots, diced	Salt an pepper
	1 bay leaf	

Blanch tongue by placing in heavy kettle, covering with cold water, bringing to a brisk boil, draining and washing. Return tongue to kettle and add onion, leek, carrots, bay leaf, and cloves; salt and pepper to taste. Cover with water and cook until done. The best way to determine is to test the tip of the tongue for tenderness. When done, allow to cool slightly before peeling.

If tongue is salted and smoked, cook in plenty of water. No vegetables are necessary.

TONGUE WITH CAPER SAUCE
SERVES 6 - 8

3 lbs. cooked tongue	2 cups Caper Sauce	8 Potato Dumplings

Slice boiled fresh tongue and arrange on heated plate. Cover with hot Caper Sauce. Serve with Potato Dumplings.

TONGUE AND RAISIN SAUCE
SERVES 6

3 lbs. cooked tongue	1½ cups California Raisin Sauce	2 cups mashed potatoes
		1 tsp. minced chives

Slice tongue in fairly thick slices. Arrange on heated platter and cover with California Raisin Sauce. Serve with mashed potatoes into which chives have been blended.

DEVILED SMOKED BEEF TONGUE
SERVES 4

12 slices smoked tongue   1½ cups Sauce Diable   8 rice timbales
  (center cut)   1 tbs. chopped chives

Arrange slices of tongue in a heated casserole; cover with Sauce Diable. Arrange rice timbales around edge; sprinkle all with chopped chives.

CREAMED CHIPPED BEEF MESA
SERVES 4

½ lb. chipped beef   1½ cups pastry cream   16 avocado balls
1½ cups Cream Sauce   12 pitted, ripe olives, sliced 4 English muffins
  Brown Derby   in rings

Cut chipped beef into small pieces. Cover with water and bring to brisk boil. Drain. Place beef in hot Cream Sauce; add cream and ripe olives. Allow to simmer 3 minutes. Add avocado balls and simmer a minute longer. Serve on split, toasted English muffins.

HOW TO PREPARE TRIPE

The honeycomb-type tripe is the best tripe to use. It is already precooked when you purchase it in the meat market, but is still tough and needs more cooking. Wash it well with a stiff vegetable brush in plenty of cold water and place in a heavy kettle. For 3 lbs. of tripe, cover with 1 gal. cold water and the following vegetables and seasonings:

1 medium-sized onion   Salt   12 black peppercorns
2 carrots, diced   1 large leek   1 bay leaf
2 branches celery, diced   1 small bead garlic

Bring to a boil and simmer for from 3 ½ to 4 hours. Then cut into either dices or julienne. For a small family, cut recipe in half.

TRIPE À LA CREOLE
SERVES 4

1/8 lb. butter   1 lb. tripe julienne, well done 1½ cups Creole Sauce

Heat butter in heavy skillet. Add thinly sliced tripe; brown lightly, stirring constantly; then add Creole Sauce; allow to come to gentle oil for 2 minutes. Serve with rice.

TRIPE À LA MODE DE CAEN

SERVES 6 - 8

3 lbs. honeycomb tripe
3 marrow bones, cracked
    and blanched
2 cups sliced carrots
½ cup sliced onions

2 whole leeks
1 sprig thyme
1 bay leaf
2 cloves
1 tsp. salt

2 cups cider
3 cups white wine
3 cups water
3 oz. brandy
1 cup flour

This is a favorite French dish and the tripe is used as it comes from the butcher. Wash tripe well and cut into 2-in. squares. Butter generously with either butter or bacon fat. Place the marrow bones in heavy casserole, then half the tripe. Cover this with half the carrots, onions and 1 leek. Repeat the layers. Add the seasonings with the cider, wine, brandy and water. Cover with heavy lid which is sealed airtight with heavy paste, made by mixing 1 cup flour with just enough water to make thick paste. Cook in 300°[F] oven for at least 8 hours—the longer the better. Then, if mixture looks dry, add a little hot cider and serve.

BROWN DERBY MIXED GRILLE

SERVES 4

½ lb. cooked sweetbreads
4 slices calf's liver
4 slices tongue
4 button mushrooms

4 slices kidney
4 peeled slices eggplant
4 pieces zucchini, cut
    lengthwise

¼ cup oil
½ cup butter
1 tbs. parsley or chives
Salt and pepper

Brush oil over all ingredients and season with salt and pepper to taste. Place under broiler, turning to cook on both sides. Arrange artistically on hot platter. Season with melted butter in which chives have marinated. Serve with Duchesse Potatoes.

BEEF AND KIDNEY PIE DERBY

SERVES 8

2 lbs. top sirloin
2 lbs. kidneys
¼ cup butter
1 medium-sized onion,
    sliced

16 small carrots, peeled
8 button mushrooms
½ cup burgundy
1 tbs. English mustard
1 bay leaf
6 peppercorns

2 cups Brown Sauce
¼ tsp. nutmeg
1 bead garlic
1 lb. Brown Derby Pastry for
    Covered Pies
[Egg yolk and milk]

Use enough top sirloin of beef to have 2 lbs. of meat after fat has been removed. Divide into 8 steaks. Season with salt and pepper and dust with flour. Split, skin and blanch kidneys in water. Heat butter in a heavy braising kettle. Add steaks and kidneys. Sauté on both sides until brown. Add onion, carrots and mushrooms, continuing to sauté until vegetables and mushrooms are brown. Blend together wine, mustard, bay leaf, peppercorns, Brown Sauce nutmeg and garlic. Add to meat and vegetables. Cover and braise until steaks are tender. Should gravy be used up too fast, add small amount of hot water as needed. When meat is tender, place steaks, kidneys and vegetables in heavy casserole. Cover with gravy. Cover casserole with rich pastry cover. Brush lightly with yolk of egg and milk. Bake in 425°[F] oven until brown, about 10 minutes.

More beef dishes: Corned Beef Hash, Hamburger Steak De Luxe, Filet Mignon tidbits, Derby Beef Stew, Pot Roast, Braised Short ribs and Corned Beef and Cabbage in "Specialties of the House" and Barbecued Beef Mexican Style and Barbecued Hamburger Steaks in "Barbecues" chapters.

VEAL

Veal should not be aged, but used while fresh, with a good pinkish color. In buying, the best cutlets are those cut from a young leg or made from chops which have been boned and trimmed. For goulash, use shoulder, chuck or shank. All veal is improved if hammered a little before using. Dampen cutlets before pounding with mallet. The thinner they are, the better they taste.

A good calf's liver weighs from 3 ½ to 4 ½ lbs. and is not too dark in color. It should have a fresh, shiny appearance. Have the butcher remove skin and arteries.

ROAST SADDLE OF VEAL SANTA ANITA
SERVES 8 - 10

8-lb. saddle of veal	*1 cup diced celery*	*1 cup white wine*
3 veal kidneys	*Salt and pepper*	*3 medium-sized tomatoes,*
½ cup oil	*2 cups Brown Sauce*	*diced*
1 medium-sized onion, minced	*1 bay leaf*	*3 cups clear stock*
4 medium-sized carrots, diced	*12 peppercorns*	*¼ tsp. basil*
	2 cloves garlic	

Have your butcher bone the saddle completely. At middle of saddle, place veal kidneys that have been cut in long strips. Roll meat tightly and fasten securely with string. Salt and pepper generously, place in oiled roasting pan and brown evenly as fast as possible in 425°[F] oven . When brown, add onion, carrots, celery, bay leaf, peppercorns, garlic and basil. Return to 350°[F] oven until vegetables are brown. Care must be taken to baste very frequently. As soon as vegetables are lightly browned, add mixture of white wine, Brown Sauce, tomatoes and clear stock. Cover the roaster, finish braising veal in 325°[F] oven until well done. This should take from 2½ to 3 hours. Remove string. Strain gravy and serve with sliced roast.

STUFFED CABBAGE

1 whole white cabbage	*½ lb. mushrooms, cooked*	*½ cup Parmesan cheese*
5 cups risotto, cooked	*with risotto*	*Salt and pepper*
	¼ cup butter	

Blanch cabbage, then cool in cold water. Break off all large leaves and cut off heavy stems. Into each leaf of cabbage, place 1/3 cup risotto and mushrooms. Roll tightly. Place in buttered baking pan. Sprinkle with Parmesan cheese and salt and pepper. Bake in 350°[F] oven for 20 minutes. Arrange Stuffed Cabbage neatly around Roast Saddle of Veal.

HUNGARIAN VEAL GOULASH

SERVES 8

½ cup butter
3 lbs. onions, sliced
3 lbs. veal shoulder, cut in
    1½-in. pieces

4 tbs. paprika
1 bay leaf
2 cloves garlic, chopped fine,

2 qts. clear stock or water
2 medium-sized tomatoes
    peeled, chopped fine
Salt and pepper

Heat butter in a good-sized kettle. Add onions and brown very lightly. Add veal shoulder and mix in the paprika, bay leaf, garlic, clear stock and tomatoes; season to taste with salt and pepper. Cover the kettle and simmer on slow fire for 1 ½—2 hours. Remove bay leaf and serve with noodles.

EMINCÉ OF VEAL PIQUANTE

SERVES 4

1/8 lb. butter
1 lb. veal julienne
1 medium bell pepper, chopped fine
2 tbs. finely chopped celery

4 tbs. finely chopped green onion
1 tsp. English mustard
¼ tsp. basil

½ cup white wine
1 cup Brown Sauce
1 tbs. Worcestershire Sauce
Salt and pepper

Heat butter in heavy skillet. Add veal julienne, bell pepper, celery, green onion and sauté golden brown. Add English mustard and basil. Mix well. Add wine, Brown Sauce and Worcestershire Sauce. Bring to gentle boil. Salt and pepper to taste.

ROULADE OF VEAL DERBY

SERVES 6

1½ lbs. veal in 6 cutlets
1 tbs. English mustard
2 small dill pickles, quartered
6 pieces green onion, width of cutlet

6 pieces carrot, width of cutlet
Butter or olive oil
6 strips salt pork, width
    of cutlet

1 cup white wine
2 cups Brown Sauce
6 oz. noodles
1 tbs. chopped chives

Flatten cutlets with side of cleaver until very thin. Arrange on board preparatory to filling. Make paste of mustard and water. Brush each cutlet with paste. On each cutlet, arrange a quarter of dill pickle, section of green onion, piece of carrot and a strip of salt pork. Care must be taken not to have fillers wider than the cutlet. Next, roll cutlet very tightly around the fillers. Secure them with two toothpicks or with string. Dredge or roll lightly in flour. Season with salt and pepper. Fry golden brown in butter or olive oil. Transfer to heavy covered kettle. Add white wine to remaining butter or oil. Reduce by one-third and pour over roulades. Add Brown Sauce. Cover kettle and braise slowly until done. This will require about 1 hour. If gravy reduces too fast, add small amounts of hot water as needed. Serve on heated platter with noodles. Pour gravy over all and sprinkle with chives.

Roulade of Beef Derby is made as above, substituting 1½ lbs. of beef round. Cooking time will be slightly longer.

A Cook's Tour With Cutlets

Almost every country has a different and delicious way to prepare veal cutlets. Here are Hungarian, German, Austrian, American, Italian, French and even Swedish variations.

HUNGARIAN VEAL CUTLETS (VEAL PAPRIKA)
SERVES 4

1½ lbs. veal in 4 thin cutlets
¼ cup butter

1 tbs. paprika
1 tsp. finely chopped onion
1 cup pastry cream

½ cup Brown Gravy
Salt and pepper

Flatten cutlets as thin as possible with side of cleaver. Heat butter in a good-sized, heavy skillet. Add cutlets and sauté golden brown on both sides. Sprinkle with paprika; add onion and smother 1 minute. Add cream, Brown Gravy and season with salt and pepper to taste. Bring to gentle boil. Remove cutlets to heated platter. Reduce gravy by one-third. Strain through fine sieve. Serve with noodles of Spaetzels Polonaise.

RAHM SCHNITZEL
SERVES 4

1½ lbs. veal in 4 thin cutlets
½ cup butter

1 cup pastry cream

1 cup Brown Sauce
Salt and pepper

Flatten cutlets with side of cleaver as thin as possible. Salt, pepper and flour them. Heat butter in skillet. Add cutlets and fry golden brown on both sides. Add cream and Brown Sauce and bring to a boil. Remove cutlets. Reduce gravy by one-third. Season with salt and pepper to taste. Pour over cutlets on heated platter. Serve with noodles and gravy over all.

WIENER SCHNITZEL GARNI
SERVES 4

1½ lbs. veal in 4 thin cutlets
½ cup butter or oil
1 cup Brown Derby
*   Tomato Sauce*

1 lemon in 4 round slices
1 tsp. chopped parsley
1 tsp. paprika

1 tbs. capers
4 anchovy filets, rolled
[Salt and pepper]

Flatten cutlets as thin as possible, using flat side of cleaver. Season with salt and pepper. Bread them. Heat butter in heavy skillet and fry cutlets over slow fire until golden brown on both sides. Serve on heated platter which has been coated with Tomato Sauce. Garnish each cutlet with lemon slice, each coated half with parsley and half with paprika. In center, place capers. Arrange anchovy filets around capers. Serve with noodles or Spaghetti Derby.

BREADED VEAL À LA HOLSTEIN

SERVES 4 - 6

1½ lbs. veal in 4-6 cutlets
½ cup butter or oil
1 cup Brown Derby
      Tomato Sauce

4 - 6 eggs, fried singly
2 - 3 dill pickles, halved
            lengthwise, fan-shaped
4 - 6 slices beet
1 lemon in 4-6 round slices

1 tsp. paprika
3 tsp. chopped parsley
4 - 6 anchovy filets, rolled
1 tbs. capers

Flatten cutlets as thin as possible with flat side of cleaver. Season with salt and pepper to taste. Bread the cutlets. Heat butter or oil in heavy skillet. Add breaded cutlets and brown golden brown on both sides over slow fire. Serve cutlets on hot Tomato Sauce. On top of veal cutlet, place a fried egg. Garnish fried egg with fan of dill pickle, fan of beet, slice of lemon that has been dipped on one side in paprika and other half in chopped parsley. In center of lemon, place ring of anchovy filled with capers.

BREADED VEAL MORNAY

SERVES 4

1½ lbs. veal in 4 thin cutlets
¼ cup butter

1 cup Brown Derby
      Tomato Sauce

1 cup Sauce Mornay
½ cup grated Cheddar cheese

Flatten cutlets with side of cleaver as thin as possible. Season with salt and pepper and bread them. Heat butter in heavy skillet. Add cutlets and fry golden brown on both sides. Cover and cook over low heat until tender. Remove to heated platter that has first been covered with small amount of Tomato Sauce. Completely cover cutlets with hot Sauce Mornay. On top of cutlets, sprinkle cheese and a little paprika. Brown under broiler or open fire until brown.

STUFFED VEAL CUTLETS ST. GALLE

SERVES 2

2 oz. butter or oil
2 6-oz. or 4 4-oz. veal cutlets,
      well pounded

½ cup Brown Derby
      Avocado Mushroom
      Stuffing

2 tbs. Parmesan cheese
4 tbs. Sauce Bercy
Salt, pepper and flour

Heat butter in heavy skillet. Salt and pepper the cutlets; then dip in flour. Sauté about 4 minutes on each side. Remove from the fire and place on heavy platter or pan. Divide the stuffing on top of the cutlets. Sprinkle with Parmesan cheese and brown under broiler. Pour the hot Sauce Bercy around the cutlets and serve.

BROWN DERBY AVOCADO MUSHROOM STUFFING

2 oz. butter
½ cup finely chopped mushrooms
2 tbs. green onion, finely chopped
1 very ripe avocado, peeled

1 medium-sized tomato, peeled
  seeds removed, charged
  fine
2 tbs. flour
½ cup white wine

½ cup chicken stock or
  consommé
1 tsp. celery salt
1 pinch basil
2 egg yolks

Heat butter in skillet. Add mushrooms and green onion; sauté for about 4 minutes. Mash and add avocado, add tomato and flour, and mix well. Sauté about 3 minutes more. Add wine, chicken stock, celery salt, basil and stir well. Cook for about 10 minutes on slow fire. Add egg yolks. Let the egg yolk thicken and remove from the fire. Cool in flat pan.

This stuffing can also be used to stuff any fish.

SWEDISH VEAL CUTLETS

SERVES 4

20 oz. veal
3 oz. butter

12 medium crab legs
½ cup Sauce Béarnaise

1 cup thin Brown Derby
  Tomato Sauce

Remove skin and sinews from meat. Cut in 4 equal pieces; flatten out with heavy mallet as thin as possible; salt and pepper and flour well. Heat butter in heavy skillet; then place cutlets in the skillet. Brown over slow fire on both sides, about 5 minutes for each. Remove the cutlets to a serving platter. On each veal cutlet, place 3 crab legs. Brown the cutlets and the crab legs under gas broiler for 1 or 2 minutes and remove. Cover crab legs with Sauce Béarnaise. Pour Tomato Sauce around the cutlets. Serve with any vegetable or rice.

VEAL CUTLETS CACCIATORA

SERVES 4

1½ lbs. veal in 8 cutlets
¼ cup butter
4 tbs. green onion, finely chopped
1/3 cup sliced mushrooms
2 tbs. finely chopped celery

6 finely chopped pepperoncini
1 medium-sized tomato,
  chopped fine
¼ tsp. basil
½ bead garlic

½ cup burgundy
1 cup Brown Sauce
2 cups rice or spaghetti,
  cooked

Ask butcher to pound veal with flat side of cleaver and cut into 8 equal cutlets. Season with salt and pepper. Flour them. Heat butter in heavy skillet. Add cutlets and brown as fast as possible on both sides. Remove cutlets to heated platter. Add green onion, mushrooms, celery and sauté lightly brown. Add peperoncini, tomato, basil and garlic. Sauté 2 minutes longer. Add wine and reduce to one-half. Add Brown Sauce and simmer 5 minutes. Add veal cutlets to sauce and bring to boil. Serve with steamed rice or spaghetti.

SCALOPPINE OF VEAL MASCOTTE

SERVES 4

½ cup butter
1½ lbs. veal in 12 thin cutlets
¼ lb. mushrooms, sliced
4 artichoke bottoms, in 8 pieces each
2 cloves shallot, chopped fine

1 medium-sized tomato, diced
2 oz. whole butter
½ cup white wine
1 piece lemon peel

¼ tsp. basil
1 cup Brown Gravy
Salt and pepper
1 tbs. finely chopped chives
2 cups cooked rice

Heat butter in good-sized, heavy skillet. Add veal cutlets and sauté golden brown on both sides. Add mushrooms and artichoke bottoms. Continue sautéing until lightly brown. Add shallot and tomato and sauté 1 minute more. Add wine and reduce by one-third. Add lemon peel, basil and Brown Gravy. Simmer for 10 minutes. Season with salt and pepper to taste. Bring to gentle boil. Remove veal cutlets and reduce one-third. Sprinkle with chives and finish sauce by adding whole butter. Serve with rice.

SCALOPPINE OF VEAL SAUTÉ MARSALA

SERVES 6

1½ lbs. veal in 12 thin cutlets
½ cup butter
¼ lb. sliced mushrooms

2 beads shallot
½ cup white wine

1 cup Brown Gravy
1 tsp. garlic salt
3 cups steamed rice

Sauté veal cutlets in butter to a golden brown on both sides. Add mushrooms, shallot and wine. Allow to cook 1 minute longer; then add Brown Gravy and garlic salt. Bring to quick boil. Remove veal to heated casserole which has been half-filled with steamed rice. Reduce sauce in skillet by one-third. Pour over veal and serve at once. Spaghetti may be substituted for rice.

BOILING SWEETBREADS

2 lbs. sweetbreads
1 onion, quartered
1 carrot, quartered

2 branches celery, quartered
1 bay leaf

1 cloves
Juice of 1 lemon
Salt and pepper

Wash sweetbreads, then soak in cold water for 2 hours. To cook, place in heavy kettle. Add onion, carrot, celery, bay leaf, cloves, lemon juice and salt and pepper to taste. Cover with water and boil 30—40 minutes. Drain and cool sweetbreads; then remove all sinew and fat.

VEAL SWEETBREADS FINANCIÈRE

SERVES 4

1 lb. sweetbreads
¼ cup butter
¼ lb. mushrooms, halved

16 ripe olives, pitted
½ cup Madeira

1 cup Brown Sauce
4 thin sliced truffle (optional)
3 beads shallot, chopped fine

Split sweetbreads lengthwise and season with salt and pepper and dust with flour. Place in heavy skillet with heated butter. Add mushrooms. Sauté until brown on both sides. Add olives and shallot and sauté 1 minute longer. Add wine and reduce to half. Add Brown Sauce and allow to simmer gently for 8 minutes on slow fire. Remove sweetbreads to heated plate. On each piece of sweetbread, place slice of truffle. Cover with sauce and serve with rice or Parisienne potatoes.

Also: Emincé of Veal Indienne and Veal Sweetbreads Indienne ("Curries") and Spaghetti Cacciatora with Veal Cutlets, Spaghetti Derby House ("Luncheon and Supper Combinations").

BROILED CALF'S LIVER DERBY
SERVES 4

1 lb. liver in 8 pieces
Salt and pepper
4 thick slices eggplant

4 slices tomato
½ cup oil or butter

4 slices crisp bacon
4 large button mushrooms,
sautéed

Remove all sinew and skin from liver. Salt and pepper to taste. Bread eggplant and tomato slices. Dip liver, eggplant and tomato in oil or butter and cook under broiler until done. Garnish with bacon and mushrooms.

CALF'S LIVER SAUTÉ WITH MUSHROOMS BERCY
SERVES 4

1 lb. liver in 8 slices
¼ cup butter
¼ lb. mushrooms, sliced

½ cup white wine
½ tsp. finely chopped lemon peel
½ cup Brown Sauce
1 tsp. finely chopped parsley

Salt and pepper
2 cups steamed rice
(cooked 20 minutes)

Remove sinew and skin from liver. Season with salt and pepper and dust in flour. Place in skillet with heated butter; brown briskly on both sides; remove and arrange on heated plate. Add mushrooms to the remaining butter and sauté until lightly browned. Add wine, lemon peel (outside only), and Brown Sauce. Reduce by one-third. Add parsley and salt and pepper to taste. Finish sauce by adding a few pieces of whole butter and stirring briskly over hot fire. Cover liver with sauce. Mold rice into timbales and place around liver.

BREADED CALF'S LIVER PARMESAN
SERVES 4

1 lb. liver, cut in 8 thin slices

3 oz. butter or oil
[Flour, egg, fine crumbs]

½ cup grated Parmesan cheese

Salt and pepper the slices of liver, then bread evenly by dipping first in flour; next in beaten egg; and then in fine crumbs. Sauté the slices in hot butter or oil until brown. Remove from skillet. Arrange on platter. Sprinkle with Parmesan cheese. Brown under broiler and serve with baked or stewed tomatoes.

EMINCÉ OF CALF'S LIVER MADEIRA

SERVES 4

¼ cup butter	2 tbs. minced onion	2 tbs. flour
1 lb. liver julienne	Salt and pepper	½ cup Madeira

Heat butter in skillet. Add liver, onion and season with salt and pepper. Sauté until brown. Add flour and blend well. Add Madeira and Brown Gravy. Bring to boil and serve. Care must be taken not to boil too long or liver will become tough.

EMINCÉ OF CALF'S LIVER SWISS
SERVES 4

¼ cup butter	½ minced onion	2 tbs. white vinegar
1 lb. liver julienne	¼ lb. mushrooms	½ cup white wine
Salt and pepper	2 tbs. flour	1½ cup Brown Sauce

Heat butter in skillet. Add liver seasoned with salt and pepper; add onion and mushrooms. Brown. Add flour and mix again. Add vinegar, wine and Brown Sauce. Bring to gentle boil and serve immediately. Care must be taken not to boil this dish too long or liver will become tough.

EMINCÉ OF CALF'S LIVER STROGANOFF
SERVES 4

1 lb. liver julienne	1 tbs. flour	1 cup sour cream
¼ cup butter	½ cup sherry	1/3 cup Brown Sauce
¼ lb. mushrooms, sliced	1 tbs. horseradish	Salt and pepper
2 tbs. finely chopped onion		1 tbs. chives

Remove sinews and skin from liver. Heat butter in heavy skillet and add liver, mushrooms and onion. Brown lightly, stirring frequently on fast fire. When golden brown, add flour. Blend well. Add wine, horseradish, sour cream and Brown Sauce and season with salt and pepper to taste. Bring to brisk boil. Add chives and serve immediately. Do not overcook. Serve with noodles or rice.

See "Barbecue" for Barbecued Calf's Liver Steak with Onions.

LAMB

The ideal weight for a leg of lamb is from 5 to 8 lbs. The color should not be too dark, although lamb is naturally darker than the other meats. It should have a medium-thick covering of white fat.

ROAST RACK OF LAMB PARISIENNE

SERVES 6

3 lbs. rack of lamb, French trim
Salt and pepper
1 tbs. oil or shortening
1 medium-sized onion, sliced
1 bay leaf

10 peppercorns
1 tbs. cornstarch (optional)
12 medium-sized carrots,
    peeled

½ cup diced celery
¼ tsp. orégano
2 cloves garlic
2 cups clear stock
12 small new piotatoes

Place seasoned rack of lamb in oiled roasting pan. Brown quickly in 400°[F] oven, basting often. When lamb is brown, add onion, bay leaf, peppercorns, carrots, celery and orégano. Lower over to 350°[F]. Continue cooking until vegetables are dark brown. Add garlic and clear stock. Cover roasting pan and braise 40 minutes. Add small potatoes. Cover roasting pan and finish braising until lamb is well done. Then remove to hot cassereole. Strain gravy through fine sieve into small kettle. Reduce by one-third to thicken, or else add 1 tbs. cornstarch which has been mixed with a little water. Decorate with Garniture Parisienne.

GARNITURE PARISIENNE

SERVES 6

½ head cooked cauliflower
Carrots from roast
Potatoes from roast

2 cups cooked peas
12 tomato halves, baked with
    Parmesan cheese

12 boiled small white onions
1 cup corn, cut from cob,
    sautéed in water

Heat all vegetables very hot and arrange potatoes in neat border around lamb. Place peas inside ring. Make other vegetables into neat little bouquets surrounding meat. Serve very hot, with gravy served separately.

LEG OF LAMB BOULANGÈRE

SERVES 8 - 10

6 lbs. leg of lamb
6 potatoes, peeled, sliced
¼ lb,. Butter

2 medium-sized onions,
    sliced fine
Spice bag containing:
    1 bay leaf

12 black peppercorns
¼ tsp. orégano
2 cups water

Select a young leg of lamb. Trim French style—remove shank and hipbone. Salt and pepper and rub with garlic. Place in roasting pan and roast 1 hour at 350°[F]. Arrange potatoes around the leg of lamb. On top of potatoes, sprinkle sliced onions. Cover with pieces of butter. Add spice bag, 2 cups of water and cover roaster. Roast in 350°[F] over 1 hour and 45 minutes. Care must be taken to baste lamb every 20 minutcs. When done, remove lamb to platter. Place potatoes and onions around the meat and serve.

* * * *

The first dining establishment to print a menu and offer its patrons a variety of food was Boulangere's Restaurant, which opened in Paris in 1765. Before that time, the only public eating houses were taverns which served an "ordinary" or regular meal at a common table at a fixed hour and price.

As Boulanger's was an instant success, scores of similar places were soon opened, each trying to outdo the others with a larger choice of foods. The climax came when one of them began serving 197 different kinds of meat dishes.

* * * *

ROAST RACK OF LAMB WITH BRAISED STRING BEANS
SERVES 4

2 lbs. rack of lamb	1 bay leaf	½ cup diced celery
Salt	12 peppercorns	½ tsp. orégano
1 tbs. oil	12 medium-sized carrots,	3 cups clear stock
1 medium-sized onion	scraped and diced	1½ lbs. Braised Swing Beans
2 beads garlic		à la Swiss

Place seasoned rack of lamb in oiled roasting pan. Brown quickly in 400°[F] oven. Baste often. When lamb is well browned, add onion, garlic, bay leaf, peppercorns, carrots, celery and orégano. Change oven temperature to 350°[F]. Continue cooking until vegetables are very dark brown. Add clear stock. Cover roasting pan and allow to braise 70 minutes or until meat is tender. Remove to heated casserole. Strain gravy through sieve into small kettle. Thicken with cornstarch blended with small amount water or reduce by one-third to thicken; glaze lamb with gravy. Serve with Braised String Beans à la Swiss as garnish.

BRAISED BREAST OF LAMB JARDINIÈRE
SERVES 6

2½ lbs. lamb breast	4 branches celery, diced	1 clove garlic
Salt and pepper	1 bay leaf	2 tomatoes, peeled and diced
1 medium-sized onion, diced	½ tsp. orégano	1 qt. Brown Sauce
3 carrots, diced	1/3 tsp. basil	12 new potatoes, peeled

Remove most of the fat and skin from lamb breast; then salt and pepper. Brown lamb on both sides under open fire. Place lamb in braising kettle; add onion, carrots, celery, bay leaf, orégano, basil and garlic. Place in 375°[F] oven and brown vegetables lightly. Add tomatoes, Brown Sauce and correct seasoning. Cover braising kettle and braise in 350°[F] oven 1 hour and 45 minutes. Add new potatoes and braise again until lamb and potatoes are done. Should gravy evaporate too fast, add a little hot water as necessary.

Place breast of lamb and potatoes in good-sized hot casserole. Strain gravy and season to taste. Cover lamb with gravy; garnish with bouquets of cooked vegetables and serve.

LEG OF LAMB WITH CAPER SAUCE

SERVES 8 - 10

5 - 6 lb. leg of lamb	1 cup diced celery	½ cup butter
1 bay leaf	1 medium-sized leek	1 cup flour
2 whole onions, peeled	4 cloves	1 cup heavy cream
10 medium-sized carrots, scraped	Salt and pepper	½ cup capers

Skin and tie leg of lamb securely. For slicing convenience, it should be boned completely. Cover lamb with cold water and bring to brisk boil; then take out and wash leg of lamb thoroughly.

Place blanched leg of lamb back in kettle, barely covering with water. Add bay leaf, onions, carrots, celery, leek, cloves and salt and pepper to taste. Cover and simmer until lamb is well done (approximately 2½—3 hours). Remove cooked leg of lamb onto a pan and strain lamb stock.

Heat butter in separate kettle. Add flour and blend well. Simmer a minute or two. Add 2 qts. strained lamb stock to flour mixture. Mix well and bring to gentle boil. Care must be taken to dissolve any lumps that may appear. Add cream and boil slowly 20 minutes. Season with salt and pepper to taste. Strain through fine sieve. Add capers. Serve with sauce over boiled leg.

Shanks of lamb prepared in this manner are also excellent.

BREADED LAMB CHOPS HAWAII À LA MORNAY
SERVES 4

8 lamb chops, 4 oz. each	½ cup oil	2 cups Sauce Mornay
Salt and pepper	1 cup Brown Derby Tomato Sauce	½ cup grated Cheddar cheese
½ tsp. powdered ginger	8 pineapple rings	¼ tsp. paprika

Flatten lamb chops lightly. Salt and pepper and sprinkle with a little ginger. Bread chops. Heat oil in heavy skillet. Brown chops on both sides on slow fire (approximately 5 minutes for each side). Remove to heated plate which has a light covering of Tomato Sauce. On top of each chop, place 1 ring of pineapple. Cover pineapple and chops with Sauce Mornay. Sprinkle with cheese and a little paprika and brown under broiler. Serve at once.

STUFFED LAMB CHOPS NELSON
SERVES 6

12 French lamb chops	12 rings bell pepper	1½ cups Brown Derby
4 tbs. oil	1 cup grated Cheddar cheese	Tomato Sauce
3 cups Soubise for Stuffing	2 tsp. paprika	[Flour]

Salt, pepper and flour lamb chops. Fry on one side only until brown. Place chops in oiled pan, raw side down. Cover cooked side evenly with Soubise paste; garnish with ring of green pepper, Cheddar cheese and sprinkle with paprika. Bake in 350°[F] oven for 20 minutes. Serve with Tomato Sauce.

* * *

Ozzie Nelson claims that it just happens to be a coincidence that his favorite meat dish is Stuffed Lamb Chops Nelson.

* * *

IRISH LAMB STEW DERBY

SERVES 6

2 lbs. lean leg or shoulder of lamb
Spice bag consisting of:
  1 bay leaf
  10 peppercorns
  ¼ tsp. nutmeg
  1 sprig thyme
  1 clove garlic

1 medium-sized white cabbage
1 cup flour (optional)
18 small white onions, peeled
12 small carrots, scraped
12 in.-long pieces celery

Salt and pepper
12 small potatoes, peeled
6 sprigs parsley
12 small Fluffy Dumplings
1 cup milk (optional)
1½ cups cooked peas

Remove most of fat from meat and cut in 1-in. squares. Place in heavy kettle and blanch by covering with cold water and bringing to rolling boil. Remove from water and wash meat lightly. Prepare spice bag. Cover bottom of a medium-sized kettle with blanched lamb and on top of meat place some of the cabbage, a few onions, a few carrots and celery pieces. Repeat this procedure until all meat and vegetables are used. Cover meat and vegetables with water. Add salt and pepper and spice bag. Cover tightly and simmer 1 hour. This stew should be skimmed every 20 minutes. After 1 hour of gentle cooking, add potatoes and parsley. Cover tightly again and continue to simmer until meat is well done.

When meat is very tender, drop dumplings on top of boiling stew. Cover quickly and tightly and steam dumplings 10 minutes without removing cover. Remove dumplings to heated platter. If you wish, thicken gravy of stew with milk and flour. Serve stew in heated casserole crowned with Fluffy Dumplings. Sprinkle cooked peas over all.

For more lamb recipes, see "Specialties of the House", "Curries", and "Barbecues".

PORK

Pork should be grain-fed, fresh and have a medium covering of white fat. It requires thorough cooking. Loin is the best cut. Use the leg for roasts.

ROAST LOIN OF PORK WITH BAKED APPLES
SERVES 8

½ onion, diced
2 medium-sized carrots, diced
2 branches celery, diced

1 bay leaf
12 black peppercorns
4 - 5 lb. pork loin
Salt and pepper

1 cup water
3 cups Brown Sauce
8 baked apples

Place onion, carrots, celery, bay leaf and peppercorns in bottom of heavy roaster. On top of vegetables, lay pork loin that has been salted and peppered. Add water. Place in 375°[F] oven. As soon as loin is golden brown, lower over temperature to 350°[F]. Baste loin frequently and roast for 1 ½ hours. Remove and drain off excess fat. Add Brown Sauce and allow to simmer 12 minutes. Strain gravy through fine sieve. Season with salt and pepper. Serve loin with gravy and place baked apples evenly around the sliced pork.

BREADED PORK FILETS DERBY

SERVES 4

4 filets of pork
½ cup butter or oil

1 cup country gravy

8 corn or apple fritters

Split filets of pork book style lengthwise. Pound evenly and season with salt and pepper; then bread. Fry in butter or oil until done. Serve with country gravy and corn or apple fritters.

BROCHETTE OF PORK FILET DERBY
SERVES 4

1 lb. filet of pork
8 strips bacon, blanched
8 button mushrooms
Salt and pepper

12 artichokes, baby size
    cooked and halved
½ cup bread crumbs
1/8 lb. butter

2 cups rice
1 cup Brown Derby
    Tomato Sauce

Remove all skin from lean filet of pork and cut into 1/8-in.-thick, half-dollar-size pieces. Cut bacon into 1-in. pieces. Arrange in following manner on 4 skewers or brochette needles: mushroom, piece bacon, piece pork, piece artichoke, piece bacon, pork and so on until brochette needle is full. Close needle with another mushroom on end. Season with salt and pepper and sprinkle with bread crumbs. Place in buttered pan and broil under open fire until done. Serve with cooked rice timbale and Tomato Sauce

EMINCÉ OF PORK FILET AND MUSHROOMS
SERVES 6

1/8 lb. butter
1½ lbs. pork filet, sliced
¼ lb. mushrooms, sliced

½ medium-sized onions,
    chopped fine
1 tbs. flour

½ cup white wine
1 cup Brown Sauce
Salt and pepper

Heat butter in heavy skillet. Add sliced filet of pork, onion and mushrooms. Sauté until lightly browned. Add flour, blend well, and sauté again a minute longer. Mix in the wine and Brown Sauce, blend well and bring to quick boil; salt and pepper to taste and serve.

BRAISED PORK CHOPS FLAMAND
SERVES 4

8 lean pork chops (2 lbs.)
Salt and pepper
1/8 lb. butter

4 peeled apples, cored
    sliced thin
½ cup white wine

1 cup pastry cream
1 tsp. celery salt

Pound chops lightly. Season with salt and pepper. Place in heavy skillet with hot butter and brown lightly as quickly as possible. Do not attempt to cook the pork chops as they must be underdone. Place sliced apples in buttered, heated casserole. On top of apples, arrange browned pork chops. Add wine and place in 360°[F] oven. Bake until wine evaporates (approximately 30 minutes). Next, add cream and dash of celery salt and salt. Bake 20 minutes more in 325°[F] oven. Serve.

STUFFED PORK CHOPS CALIFORNIA
SERVES 4

8 pork chops	*1 tbs. chopped onion*	*¼ tsp. nutmeg*
1/8 lb. butter	*3 oz. raisins*	*½ cup chicken broth*
2 apples, peeled and sliced	*2 cups bread croutons*	*16 toothpicks*
	¼ tsp. celery salt	

Pork chops should be 2 in. thick. Split the meat side and fold open like a book. Pound both sides quite thin and season with salt and pepper. Prepare following dressing: heat butter in heavy skillet; add apples, onion and then brown lightly. Add raisins, croutons, celery salt and nutmeg; sauté 8 minutes on slow fire or in oven at 300°[F]. Add ½ cup chicken broth and blend well. Place dressing in even portions on pork chops. Fold edges and secure each chop with 2 toothpicks. Place in buttered pan and roast in 350°[F] oven for 30 minutes.

BREADED PORK CUTLET MORNAY
SERVES 6

2 lbs. boned pork loin	*1 cup Brown Derby Tomato Sauce*	*4 tbs. grated Cheddar cheese*
¼ cup oil	*1½ cups Sauce Mornay*	*1 tsp. paprika*

Have butcher flatten cutlets with side of cleaver as thin as possible. Season with salt and pepper and bread them. Heat oil in heavy skillet. Add cutlets and fry golden brown on both sides. Cover and cook over low heat until tender. Remove to heated platter that has first been covered with small amount hot Tomato Sauce. Completely cover cutlets with Sauce Mornay. On top of cutlets, sprinkle Cheddar cheese and dash of paprika. Brown under broiler or open flame.

Many more pork dishes can be made by substituting lean pork cutlets for veal in the veal cutlet and scaloppini recipes. Use minced pork filet instead of veal for the emincé dishes.

BRAISED SPARERIBS
SERVES 8

8 lbs. spareribs	*¼ tsp. basil*	*1 bay leaf*
Salt and pepper	*1 medium-sized onion, diced*	*1 cup white wine*
1/3 cup oil	*2 medium-sized carrots, diced*	*2 cups Brown Sauce*
¼ tsp. orégano	*1 branches celery, diced*	*3 cups clear stock*

Select 8 pounds of lean spareribs. Season with salt and pepper. Put in heated skillet with oil.

Brown on both sides under broiler. Place in roaster and add orégano, basil, onion, carrots, celery and bay leaf. Roast in 350°[F] oven until vegetables are lightly browned. Add wine; cover roasting pan and return to oven 4 minutes. Add Brown Sauce and clear stock. Cover roaster and braise until well done, approximately 1½ hours. Should the sauce evaporate too fast, add a little hot water as necessary. Remove spareribs and cut into desired shape and size. Strain gravy and serve with baked beans or Sauerkraut.

Also see sparerib recipes in "Barbecues".

BROILED CENTER-CUT HAM STEAK

Have butcher cut steaks the desired thickness (they should weigh 8-12 oz.). Trim off excess fat, dip in butter or oil, put under broiler and broil 8 minutes on each side. Serve with Apple Fritters, fried yams and one of the following sauces: Champagne, Bigarade, Cumberland, Chafing Dish Steak, Madeira, Port Wine, Poivrade, Sweet Chutney Steak or California Raisin.

BAKED HAM STEAK HAWAIIAN
SERVES 4

4 8-oz. center-cut ham steaks
4 slices pineapple, canned or fresh
1 tbs. orange peel julienne

2 tbs. toasted shaved almonds
½ cup port wine
2 tbs. honey
4 tbs. soy sauce

1 cup water
2 tbs. chutney
½ cup tomato purée

Brown the ham steaks under gas broiler or over charcoal. Place them in heavy skillet. Add pineapple, orange peel, almonds, honey, soy sauce, water, chutney, wine and purée. Cover the skillet and simmer until the ham steaks are done — approximately an additional 80 minutes. Should the liquid reduce too fast, add a little water or pineapple juice.

HAM HOCKS AND SAUERKRAUT OR BAKED BEANS
SERVES 2 - 3

1½ -2 lbs. ham hocks   *Sauerkraut or baked beans*

Wash hocks thoroughly, place in pot, cover with water and simmer slowly until well done (2 - 2½ hours). Remove skin, bones and excess fat. Serve with kraut or beans.

Ham hocks and grilled frankfurters are prepared similarly, except that the frankfurters are split, dipped in butter and broiled, meat side to flame, until brown.

Other ham dishes: Baked Ham Brown Derby ("Specialties of the House"); Deviled Ham ("Hors d'Oeuvres"); several in "Luncheon and Supper Combinations"; and Barbecued Ham California ("Barbecues").

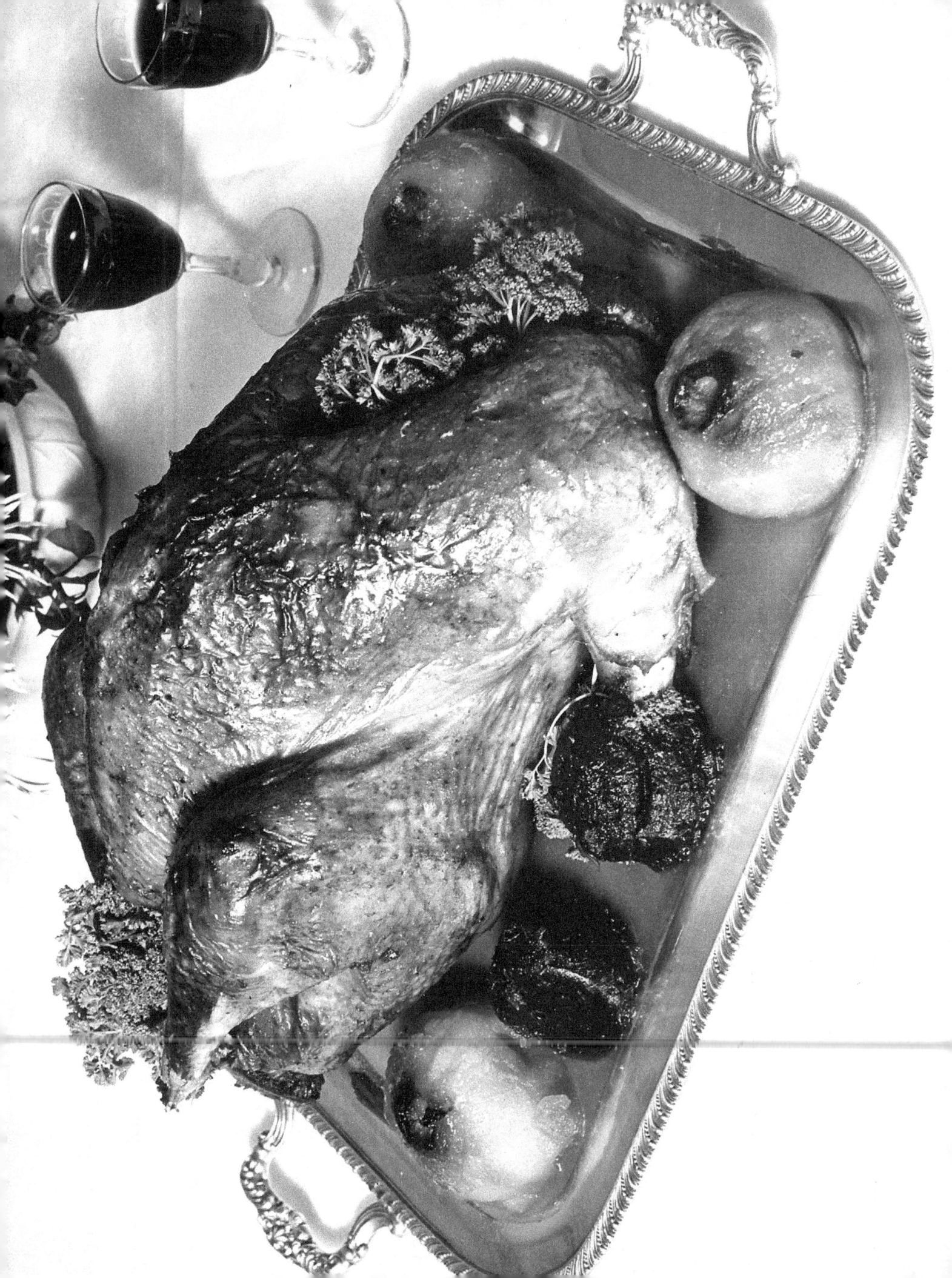

FOWL

FOWL

henever possible use fresh-killed poultry. If frozen, cook immediately after thawing out. A good bird shows a little yellow fat under the skin, has very few pinfeathers, and is nicely shaped—has a plump form and the breastbone does not stick out—but is well covered with meat.

Always wash and dry off the fowl thoroughly, inside and out, before frying or roasting. Since chicken and turkey are naturally dry, it is very important that they be basted frequently during roasting. Duck or geese do not require so much attention, since they help baste themselves with their own fat. However, with all fowl, the more basting, the richer and browner the color.

The professional method of telling when a fowl is cooked is to feel the joint of the drumstick. If the joint can be felt through the meat, the bird is usually done. In turning over a roasting bird, be careful not to run the fork through the breast or leg. Pierce the back or the neck.

With the larger fowl, such as turkey or geese, a good method is to brown, then cover well and steam by adding stock or water to drippings to provide moisture.

Wild game should be cleaned and plucked as soon as possible, then washed well and wrapped in wax paper until ready to use.

When a recipe calls for "1 breast of chicken", this means one-half or side of the white meat, not all of it.

CHICKEN IN THE POT

SERVES 4 - 6

5-lb. roaster or hen	6 black peppercorns	2 medium-sized bay leaves
6 pieces celery	1 gal water	4 sprigs parsley
1 leek	1 medium onion	Salt
	6 carrots, scrapped	

Place all ingredients with chicken in a large heavy kettle with close-fitting cover. Allow to cook slowly for 2 ½ —3 hours, until chicken is very tender but does not fall from bones. Allow to cool in stock. Here are the net results:

2½ qts, chicken broth	1 cup white meat or 2 pieces of	1 cup skin
2 cups dark meat	breast of chicken	6 oz. (¾ cup) bones

A variety of chicken dishes can be made with Chicken in the Pot as the foundation. The next 7 recipes are derived from this dish.

BAKED BREAST OF CHICKEN PRINCESS
SERVES 1

1 cup hot steamed rice	*½ cup hot Sauce Suprême*	*4 cooked asparagus tips*
½ breast of chicken, cooked		*1 tbs. Sauce Hollandaise*

Cover bottom of ovenware casserole with rice. Place boned breast of chicken on rice. Cover with hot Sauce Suprême. Bake in 350°[F] oven 3—5 minutes. Remove and arrange asparagus tips in neat line across center. Garnish with Sauce Hollandaise.

BREAST OF CHICKEN PETITE MARMITE
SERVES 2

1 breast of chicken, cut in 2 pieces	*Above ingredients are from Chicken in the Pot*	*1 cup cooked noodles*
6 carrots	*1 medium-sized tomato, chopped fine*	*6 Matzoth Balls*
1 medium-sized onion		*½ cup cooked peas*
1 qt. chicken broth		*½ cup cooked string beans*
		2 tsp. chives

Place chicken in a 1-qt. service casserole. Add carrots and onion, tomato, noodles, Matzoth Balls, peas and string beans. Cover with chicken broth, sprinkle with chives, bring to a boil and serve.

This can also be served separately as Chicken Broth or Soup, and Broiled Chicken and Vegetables.

DERBY CHICKEN POT PIE
SERVES 1

¾ cup hot Sauce Suprême	*2 small boiled onions*	*2 large mushrooms, cooked and sliced*
1 Matzoth Ball	*½ chicken breast or broiler, cooked*	*½ cup Brown Derby Pastry*
2 sliced cooked carrots	*1 tbs. cooked peas*	

In the bottom of a heavy earthenware individual oven casserole, place 3 tbs. of Sauce Suprême. Add Matzoth Ball, carrots, onions. On top of this, place breast of chicken which has been boned and halved. Arrange mushrooms and peas over chicken. Fill remaining space in the dish with balance of sauce. Then cover with pastry, crimping firmly at the edges. Using pastry brush, brush top lightly with egg yolk and milk. Bake in 400°[F] oven until crust is golden brown (approximately 20 minutes). Serve hot.

BREAST OF CHICKEN VIENNA
SERVES 1

½ chicken breast	*½ cup salad oil*	*2 strips crisp bacom*
½ cup Orly Batter	*½ cup Sauce Suprême*	*½ pickled peach*
	1 large thick sliced eggplant	

Flour cooked breast of chicken slightly. Dip in Orly Batter. Fry golden brown in oil. Arrange hot Sauce Suprême in the center of a very hot, deep service plate. In the sauce place slice of eggplant which has been breaded and fried golden brown. On top of eggplant, arrange chicken breast. Garnish breast with 2 strips of bacon. Serve with pickled peach or any other pickled fruit desired.

BREAST OF CHICKEN, FRICASSEE STYLE
SERVES 2

1 cup chicken broth	*6 mushrooms, sautéed well*	*1½ cups Sauce Suprême*
6 cooked small, white onions	*2 tbs. cooked peas*	*½ cup pastry cream*
6 very small cooked carrots	*1 breast of chicken, cooked,*	*Salt and pepper*
4 Matzoth Balls, cooked	*halved*	*1 egg yolk*

Heat onions, carrots, Matzoth Balls, mushrooms and chicken in little chicken broth. When hot, remove from broth into heated casserole. In a small heavy skillet, heat sauce, cream, and salt and pepper to taste. Simmer 4 minutes. Thicken with egg yolk that has been mixed with a little cream. Pour into casserole over vegetables and chicken. Sprinkle with fresh-cooked hot peas.

BREAST OF CHICKEN COTTAGE STYLE
SERVES 2

2 cups cooked egg noodles	*1 cup chicken broth*	*2 cups hot Sauce Suprême*
1 breast of chicken, cooked,	*6 large mushrooms, sautéed in*	*2 tsp. Sauce Hollandaise*
halved	*butter*	*2 tsp. whipped cream*

Using 2 small ovenware casseroles, place 1 cup egg noodles in each. Spread evenly and on top arrange ½ breast of chicken that has been heated in chicken broth. On top of chicken, arrange 3 large sautéed mushrooms. Cover all with hot Sauce Suprême. Blend together the Sauce Hollandaise and whipped cream. Cover chicken with this mixture. Place under broiler at 550°°[F] for 1—2 minutes. Care must be taken while browning to avoid burning.

CHICKEN À LA SOMBORN   SERVES 2

2 cups pastry cream	*1 breast of chicken, cooked, diced fine*	*3 egg yolks**
	Salt and pepper	

Bring cream to a gentle boil in a heavy skillet. Add chicken. Simmer for about 4 minutes on slow fire. Salt and pepper to taste. Thicken with egg yolks that have been mixed with a little cream. Serve on toast.

* * *

Chicken à la Somborn was created by Herbert K. Somborn, the founder of The Brown Derby Restaurants, which stand as a monument to his exacting taste and high standards in food and service.

* * *

*[Caution: Current health safety guidelines recommend caution when using raw eggs. Please observe. This recipe is included as presented in 1ˢᵗ edition.]

In addition to this recipe, and the other fine-cut chicken dishes which follow, see "Curries" for Fine-cut Chicken Curry Bengal and Calcutta.

FINE-CUT CHICKEN IN CREAM DERBY
SERVES 6

3 oz. butter
12 mushrooms
1/3 cup white wine
2 cups Sauce Suprême

1 cup pastry cream
4 lb. boiled hen, diced
3 cups steamed rice
        (cooked 20 minutes)

24 avocado balls
½ cup toasted shaved almonds
Salt and pepper

Heat butter in heavy skillet, add mushrooms and sauté till lightly browned. Add wine and cover; reduce by one-third. Add sauce and cream and blend well. Add diced chicken. Simmer 4 minutes on slow fire. Salt and pepper to taste. Thicken with egg yolks that have been mixed with a little cream. Spread cooked rice evenly in casserole. Cover rice with creamed chicken and garnish with avocado balls. Sprinkle with almonds.

Chicken broth may be used in place of Sauce Suprême, in which case, add 2 tbs. of flour while sautéing mushrooms.

CREAMED CHICKEN SUZETTE
SERVES 6

6 large russet potatoes, baked
4 oz. butter
12 mushrooms, diced, medium
2 cups Sauce Suprême

1 cup pastry cream
1 tsp. paprika
2½ cups cooked chicken,
        diced medium

Salt and pepper
2 egg yolks
1 cup Cheddar or American
        cheese, cut fine

Cut off tops of potatoes. Scoop out two-thirds of the potato. Place the shells in a pan. Heat butter in medium-sized heavy skillet. Add mushrooms and sauté until lightly browned., Add Sauce Suprême and cream. Blend well and bring to a boil. Add chicken and simmer 5 minutes. Season with salt and pepper to taste. Thicken with egg yolks that have been mixed with a little cream. Fill the potato shells with the creamed chicken, sprinkle with cheese and a little paprika. Bake under open flame until brown. Scooped-out portion of the potatoes may be pressed through a sieve, mixed with a little butter and cream, and served on the side.

If Sauce Suprême is not available, use 2 cups chicken broth and, while sautéing mushrooms, add 2 tbs. of flour.

FINE-CUT CHICKEN HASH À LA RITZ
SERVES 6

3 oz,. butter
10 mushrooms, diced
1/3 cup sherry
2 cups Cream Sauce Brown
        Derby

1 cup pastry cream
4-lb. boiled hen, diced
3 egg yolks
Salt and pepper

2 cups steamed rice
        (cooked 20 minutes)
2½ cups puréed peas
1/3 cup Parmesan cheese

Heat butter in heavy skillet. Add mushrooms and sauté until lightly browned. Add sherry, cover and reduce by one-third. Add Cream Sauce, cream and mix well. Add diced chicken, simmer on slow fire 5 minutes. Thicken with egg yolks that have been mixed with a little cream. Salt and pepper to taste. Place the cooked rice in casserole and speed evenly. Cover rice with the creamed chicken. Make a border around inside rim of casserole with purée of peas. Sprinkle with Parmesan cheese and brown under open flame.

PAN-FRIED CHICKEN HASH

SERVES 4

2 cups cooked chicken dark meat, diced very fine	1 egg, whipped well	1 tbs. onion (optional)
1 cup potatoes, diced very fine	1 tsp. A-1 or Worcestershire Sauce	Salt and pepper

In a medium-sized mixing bowl put chicken meat, potatoes, egg, sauce and onion. Salt and pepper to taste and mix well. Mold to desired portions and fry brown in heavy iron skillet.

SAUTÉED AND FRIED

CHICKEN SAUTÉ SEC

SERVES 2 - 4

6 tbs. salad oil	2 beads shallot, chopped fine (optional)	1 small piece lemon peel
2½-lb. broiler, unjointed, floured, salted and peppered	¼ tsp. basil	1 tsp. celery salt
4 oz. butter		1 cup dry white wine
		½ cup light brown stock

Heat oil in heavy skillet. Fry chicken until golden brown on both sides. Remove oil and add ¼ cup butter and the shallot, basil, lemon peel and celery salt. Sauté 1 minute. Add wine and cover skillet. Gently reduce wine to 2 tbs. Add brown stock and allow chicken to simmer slowly until cooked. Keep covered during cooking. Remove chicken to hot plate or casserole. Add remaining ¼ cup soft butter to gravy, mixing sharply so butter is absorbed by gravy. Strain ad pour over chicken.

CHICKEN SAUTÉ JERUSALEM

SERVES 2 - 4

3 oz., butter	1½ cups pastry cream	4 artichokes
2½-lb. broiler, unjointed	½ cup chicken broth	1 tbs. finely chopped chives
4 mushrooms, sliced	¼ tsp. celery salt	1 tsp. beurre manié
½ cup sherry		Salt and pepper

Heat butter in heavy skillet. Salt, pepper and flour chicken and fry golden brown on both sides. Add mushrooms and sauté 3 minutes more. Add wine, cover and reduce by one-third. Add pastry cream, chicken broth and celery salt. Cover and simmer 18 minutes. Now add artichokes. Should the sauce reduce too fast, add more cream or chicken broth. Allow to simmer until well done (approximately 15—20 minutes). Add chives. If a thicker sauce is desired, add beurre manié. Salt and pepper to taste.

SPRING CHICKEN SAUTÉ MARENGO
SERVES 2 - 4

4 tbs. olive oil	2 beads shallots, chopped	8 pitted green olives, sliced
2½-lb. broiler	fine (optional)	1 cup Brown Sauce
Salt and pepper	1/3 cup white wine	¼ tsp. basil
8 mushrooms, sliced	2 medium-sized tomatoes,	2 tbs. butter
	diced	

Heat olive oil in heavy skillet. Add chicken which has been unjointed into 6 pieces and rolled in flour with salt and pepper. Brown on both sides. Add mushrooms and sauté 3 minutes. Add shallot. Sauté ½ minute more. Add wine, cover and reduce one-third. Add tomatoes, green olives, Brown Sauce and basil. Cover skillet and simmer 18 minutes. Should gravy become too thick, add more Brown Sauce or a bit of chicken broth. Just before serving, work in whole butter. Serve with rice.

SPRING CHICKEN SAUTÉ EUGENE
SERVES 2 - 4

2½-lb. broiler	1/3 cup white wine	2 slices fried ham
3 oz. butter	1½ cups pastry cream	4 mushrooms, sautéed
½ cup diced mushrooms	½ cup Brown Gravy	in butter
2 beads shallot, chopped fine	1 English muffin, split	Salt and pepper

Unjoint chicken in 6 pieces; flour, salt and pepper. Heat butter in a heavy skillet. Add chicken and fry golden brown on both sides. Add mushrooms, sauté till lightly browned. Add shallot, sauté 1 minute more. Then add wine, cream and Brown Gravy. Cover skillet and simmer on slow fire until chicken is well done. Should gravy reduce too fast, keep adding a little more cream. Remove chicken, place half on top of each half of toasted muffin, which has been covered with 1 slice of ham garnished with mushrooms. Reduce gravy to desired thickness. Salt and pepper to taste. Cover chicken, ham and muffin with gravy.

CHICKEN SAUTÉ PRINCESS
SERVES 2 - 4

3 oz. butter	2 beads shallot, chopped fine	1 cup pastry cream
2½-lb. broiler	(optional)	¼ tsp. celery salt
8 mushrooms	½ cup Sauce Suprême	12 cooked asparagus
½ cup white wine	½ tsp. beurre manié	Salt and pepper

Heat butter in heavy skillet; add unjointed chicken which has been floured, salted and peppered and cook golden brown on both sides. Add mushrooms, sauté 3 minutes more. Add shallot, mix and sauté ½ minute more. Add wine, cover and reduce by one-third. Add Sauce Suprême, beurre manié, cream and celery salt. Cover skillet and simmer 18 minutes. If gravy should become too thick, add cream or chicken broth. When chicken is well done, salt and pepper gravy to taste. Arrange chicken on plate, cover with gravy and place bouquet of asparagus tips on side.

SPRING CHICKEN SAUTÉ CACCIATORA
SERVES 2 - 4

2½-lb. broiler
1/3 cup olive oil or butter
8 mushrooms, sliced
2 tbs. finely chopped green onion

2 tbs. green pepper julienne
¼ tsp. basil
1 bead garlic, chopped fine
1/3 cup white wine
1 medium-sized tomato, dice

4 peperoncini, cut in ¼-in.
pieces
1½ cups Brown Gravy
1 cup cooked rice or spaghetti

Unjoint chicken in 6 pieces; flour, salt and pepper. Heat olive oil in heavy skillet, add chicken and sauté golden brown on both sides. Add mushrooms and green onion and sauté about 3 minutes more. Add green peppers, basil, garlic and sauté 1 minute more. Add wine, tomato, peperoncini and Brown Gravy. Cover and smother on slow fire until chicken is well done. Should gravy reduce too fast, add more plain Brown Gravy. Serve with rice or spaghetti.

The next recipe is one of the greatest of French specialties—chicken made with wine and brandy. Tests of this Derby recipe made at home resulted in great enthusiasm for the dish as well as very avid conversation when it was served.

COQ AU VIN
SERVES 2 - 4

2½-lb. broiler
1/3 cup butter
8 button mushrooms
¼ tsp. basil
2 pieces lemon peel small
1 cup burgundy
1 cup chicken bouillon

2 beads shallot, chopped
(optional)
2 ponies brandy
12 small carrots, partially
cooked
4 small onions, sautéed
in butter

12 pieces of celery, 2-in. long
12 Parisienne or diced
potatoes sautéed
in butter
½ cup Brown Gravy
Salt and pepper

Unjoint chicken, skin, flour, and salt and pepper. Heat half the butter in skillet and add unjointed chicken and sauté until light brown on both sides. Add whole mushrooms, sauté till mushrooms are lightly browned Add shallot, basil, lemon peel and sauté about 1 minute more. Add wine, reduce by one-third. Add brandy. Light with a match. When brandy stops burning, add Brown Gravy and chicken bouillon, cover and simmer until well done. Place chicken in casserole with carrots, onions, celery and cooked potatoes. Return gravy to fire and reduce a little. Salt and pepper to taste. Finish by whipping into gravy remaining half of soft butter. Cover chicken and vegetables in casserole with the gravy and serve (or serve gravy separately).

SMOTHERED SPRING CHICKEN DERBY
SERVES 2 - 4

2½-lb. broiler
3 oz. butter
2 cups pastry cream

1 cup chicken broth
1 tbs. finely chopped green
onion

¼ tsp. celery salt
Salt and pepper
[Flour]

Unjoint chicken in 6 pieces; flour, salt and pepper. Heat butter in heavy skillet, add chicken and sauté golden brown on both sides,. Add cream, chicken broth, onion and celery salt. Cover and simmer 20 minutes or till well done. If gravy should reduce too fast, add more cream or chicken broth. Add salt and pepper to taste. Serve with noodles.

SPRING CHICKEN À LA MARYLAND
SERVES 2 - 4

½ cup oil
2½-lb. broiler
1 cup egg butter

1½ cups bread crumbs

1 cup country gravy
2 strips bacon
4 small Corn Fritters

Heat oil in heavy skillet. Add broiler that has been unjointed, salted and peppered, and well breaded. Sauté golden brown on both sides. Extra care should be taken to sauté the chicken very slowly so as not to burn bread crumbs. When chicken is browned on both sides, put into 300°[F] oven and finish until well done. Remove chicken from oil onto napkin to absorb any remaining oil. Serve with country gravy, bacon and Corn Fritters.

STUFFED ROAST CHICKEN DERBY
SERVES 4

5-lb. roasting chicken
Salt and pepper
1 qt. Brown Derby Dressing

1/3 cup oil, chicken fat or butter
1 cup chopped onion, carrot
and celery

1 cup white wine
2 cups Brown Gravy or
good stock

Chicken should be drawn and cleaned well and seasoned with salt and pepper outside as well as inside. Stuff bird with Brown Derby Dressing. Tie securely with string and place in roasting pan. Cover bird with chicken fat, oil or butter. Roast in 350°[F] oven until golden brown. Care should be taken to baste repeatedly. When bird is brown, add vegetables. Finish roasting bird in 325°[F] oven until well done. Remove bird to heated platter. Remove string. Place roasting pan over flame. Remove excess fat drippings; add white wine, reduce a little and add Brown Gravy. Simmer to right thickness. Season with salt and pepper to taste. Use some gravy to glaze bird. Serve the remainder on side.

ROAST CHICKEN GARNI BOUQUETIÈRE

SERVES 4

5-lb. roaster
1/3 cup salad oil, chicken fat
    or butter
1 cup Sauce Vegetables (carrots,
    celery, chopped onion,
    spices, pepper, bay leaf
4 large mushrooms

4 little bouquets cauliflower
12 cooked asparagus tips
3 cups Brown Gravy
8 new potatoes, cooked and
    and sautéed
1 cup cooked carrots
1 cup cooked peas

12 small, white onions,
    cooked and glazed
4 small baked tomatoes,
    sprinkled with
    Parmesan cheese
1 cup white wine

Use a bird that has been drawn and cleaned well. Tie securely with string,. Salt and pepper outside as well as inside. Cover with salad oil, chicken fat or butter and place in roasting pan. Roast in 350°[F] oven until brown (approximately 12 minutes). When bird is brown, add Sauce Vegetable. Finish roasting the bird on slow fire until done (approximately 50 minutes). Care must be taken to baste bird about every 8 minutes. Remove to large heated platter and remove string. Garnish with all vegetables in individual bouquets around the bird. Put the roasting pan with drippings and Sauce Vegetables on top of stove. Remove excess fat drippings, add wine, reduce by two-thirds and add Brown Gravy. Mix well and reduce gravy to desired thickness. Strain through sieve. Use some of the gravy to glaze roasted bird.

CHICKEN CREOLE WITH RICE

SERVES 4

2½-lb. chicken in 8 pieces
½ cup olive oil
2 medium-sized green peppers,
    sliced very thin
4 branches celery, sliced fine
1 medium-sized onion, minced

1 clove garlic, minced
2 cups hot stock or water
Salt and pepper
1 bay leaf
½ tsp. sweet basil

½ lb. mushrooms
½ cup dry white wine
1 No. 2 can solid-pack
    tomatoes or 6 peeled
    fresh tomatoes
1 cup raw rice

Sauté chicken in olive oil until golden brown. Add green peppers, celery, onion, garlic, bay leaf and basil. Simmer 3 minutes. Add mushrooms, wine, tomatoes, rice and hot stock. Simmer 30 minutes more. Cover and cook 20 minutes more. Should it become too dry, add more stock until rice is steamed tender. Season to taste.

CHICKEN LIVERS AU MADEIRA

SERVES 4

1½ lbs. chicken livers
2 oz. butter
¼ lb. mushrooms

½ medium-sized onion, chopped fine
1 cup Madeira
1 cup Brown Gravy
½ cup heavy cream

Salt and pepper
2 cups steamed rice (cooked
    20 minutes)

Clean livers well. Put into heavy skillet and cover with milk. Bring to a boil. Strain off milk and again wash livers well. Place on towel to dry. Heat butter and add livers, mushrooms, chopped onion and sauté until brown (approximately 5 minutes), stirring constantly. Add wine. Reduce by two-thirds. Add Brown Gravy and simmer 10 minutes. Add cream and salt and pepper to taste. Serve with cooked rice.

BROCHETTE OF CHICKEN LIVERS
SERVES 6

60 chicken livers
18 pieces bacon, lightly cooked
12 button mushrooms

1 cup bread crumbs
Salt and pepper

1½ cups Brown Derby
Tomato Sauce

Clean chicken livers well. Place in skillet, cover with milk and bring to a boil. Strain off milk and again wash livers well. Place on towel to dry. Cut bacon into 1-in. pieces. Arrange on 6 skewers or brochette needles: first a mushroom, then piece of chicken liver, piece of bacon, piece of chicken liver, piece of bacon, etc., until needle is nearly full. Close needle with another mushroom. Sprinkle brochettes with
bread crumbs. Salt and pepper to taste. Place in buttered pan and broil under open flame. Be sure to cook evenly on all sides. Remove from needle and serve with tomato sauce.

CHICKEN CROQUETTES DERBY STYLE
SERVES 4

1/3 cup butter
¼ medium-sized onion, minced
2 cups diced chicken
     (white and dark meat)

1 cup Cream Sauce Brown Derby
½ cup pastry cream
1/8 tsp. nutmeg

¼ tsp. celery salt
Salt and pepper
6 egg yolks
½ cup egg batter

Heat butter in heavy skillet. Add onion and sauté 2 minutes, taking care it does not brown. Mix together diced chicken, cream sauce, cream, nutmeg, celery salt, salt and pepper to taste; and add to onion. Cook 5—6 minutes over very slow fire, stirring frequently. Blend egg yolks with small portion of cream. Add to first mixture and stir constantly over very slow fire until thickened. Salt to taste. Pour into shallow pan and allow to cool sufficiently to handle. Sprinkle flour on board. Divide paste into even portions. Roll in flour to shape of ball. Press the ball into cone shape and dip in egg batter and roll in bread crumbs. Shape cone to perfection before storing in refrigerator to chill thoroughly. Fry in deep fat at 400°[F] until golden brown. Serve with Sauce Suprême or Cream sauce.

ROAST DUCK DERBY

SERVES 4 - 6

5 - 6 lb. duck, drawn	2 medium-sized carrots, cut in	Juice and peel of 1 orange
1 qt. Brown Derby Dressing	½-in. pieces	2 cups Brown Sauce
4 tbs. water	1 bay leaf	1 cup chicken broth or water
1 medium-sized onion, cut in	12 peppercorns	2 tbs. current jelly
½-in. pieces	1 sprig thyme	¼ tsp. ground ginger
2 pieces celery, cut in ½-in. pieces	1 cup port	1/8 lb. butter

Wash and dry duck well. Salt and pepper inside and out. Stuff with Brown Derby Dressing and tie securely. Place in roasting pan and baste with 4 tbs. water. Roast in 400°[F] oven until golden brown (approximately 15 minutes). Add onion, celery, carrots, bay leaf, peppercorns and thyme. Cover with lid and return to 350°[F] oven for 1 hour and 40 minutes, basting duck frequently. Then remove excess fat from drippings and add the wine, orange juice, Brown Sauce, chicken broth, current jelly and ground ginger to the drippings and return to oven. Braise for 20 minutes, basting frequently. Meanwhile, cut the outside of the orange peel in strips, preferably with a potato peeler, discarding the white pith. In a separate pot bring the orange peel to a boil with a little water and drain. When duck is done, remove to heated platter and remove string. Strain the drippings through a fine sieve, remove excess fat again and bring to a boil. Add whole butter slowly while finishing sauce by mixing sharply. Now add the orange julienne to the sauce and taste for salt and pepper. Glaze the duck with a little gravy and serve the remainder in gravy boat.

WILD DUCK DERBY

SERVES 4

2 wild ducks	1 bay leaf	1 cup burgundy
1 bunch celery	18 peppercorns	2 cups Brown Sauce
½ onion, chopped	1 sprig thyme	2 ponies brandy
2 medium-sized carrots	¼ tsp. basil	¼ lb. butter
	2 tbs. oil	

Ducks should be well-dressed, the pinfeathers removed. Salt and pepper inside as well as outside. Stuff with branches of celery. Place onion, carrots, bay leaf, peppercorns, thyme and basil in roasting pan and place ducks on top of vegetables. Cover each duck with 1 tbs. of oil; place in 420°[F] oven for 20 minutes (for medium-sized ducks). Baste frequently while in oven. Remove ducks to heated platter, drain off excess fat from drippings and add wine; then reduce by half. Add Brown Sauce and simmer for 5 minutes. Strain gravy through fine sieve into hot chafing dish, keeping sauce simmering. Serve ducks with sauce from chafing dish. At the table, remove breasts, placing skin side down on hot silver platter. Put platter on flaming Richeau (electric plate warmer or hot plate). Now place carcasses of ducks in heated duck press. Chafing dish, with simmering sauce, is placed under the faucet of the press and all essence of duck is pressed into chafing dish. Keep stirring evenly. Add brandy to sauce and burn. When brandy is burned add butter in small pieces to the sauce, mixing sharply, cover duck breasts with sauce and serve.

When a duck press is not available (about 99 percent of the time), place carcass in pot and crush with mallet or potato masher, straining juice through sieve into chafing dish.

SALMIS OF DUCKLING DERBY

SERVES 4 - 6

5 - 6 lb. duck, drawn	*12 ripe olives, pitted*	*½ cup chestnuts*
¼ lb. butter	*1 cup port*	*Salt and pepper*
1 medium-sized onion, chopped fine	*1½ cups Brown Sauce*	*6 thin slices truffle*
12 medium-sized mushrooms, sliced		*½ lb. wild rice*

Wash and dry duck well. Salt and pepper inside and out. Place in roasting pan and roast with a little oil or water for 1 hour in 350°[F] oven. Remove and allow to cool. Disjoint to 8 pieces, separating 2 drumsticks from second joints and cutting each breast in 2 pieces. Heat butter in a good-sized heavy skillet, add pieces of duck and sauté 4 minutes. Add onion, mushrooms and olives and sauté 2 minutes more. Add wine and reduce by half. Then add Brown Sauce, chestnuts, salt and pepper to taste and simmer until very tender. Arrange duck in casserole with thin slices of truffle on top. Glaze with the hot gravy and serve with wild rice which has been cooked 30 minutes.

ROAST STUFFED TURKEY

16-lb. turkey	*2 carrots, diced*	*1 cup flour*
2½ qts. Brown Derby Dressing	*1 onion, diced*	*1 qt. chicken stock*
2 cups oil or chicken fat	*1 stalk celery, diced*	*6 cups cranberry sauce*

Salt and pepper outside and inside of a drawn and well-cleaned turkey. Stuff with dressing and tie securely. Place in roasting pan and cover turkey with oil or chicken fat and roast in 350°[F] oven until brown. Care should be taken to baste repeatedly. Roasting should take 3½—4 hours. While turkey is in oven, cook giblets. About an hour before turkey is done, add to pan the carrots, onion and celery. Brown the vegetables with the turkey. When done, pour off drippings and let stand a few minutes to allow charred bits to sink to bottom. Skim fat from top and place one cup of drippings in medium-sized saucepan. Heat well, then add flour and brown lightly. Add chicken stock and remainder of drippings, with all fat skimmed off again, as well as vegetables. Blend well and simmer for 20 minutes. Strain through fine sieve and add the cooked giblets, which have been chopped very fine with a knife. Serve turkey with gravy and cranberry sauce.

SCALLOPED TURKEY DIABLE

SERVES 2

2 oz. butter	*1 tbs. very finely chopped*	*½ cup Cream Sauce*
6 oz. cooked flaked turkey	*green pepper*	*Brown Derby*
white meat	*2 tbs. Brown Derby*	*½ cup heavy cream*
4 mushrooms, quartered	*Diable Sauce*	*Salt and pepper*
1 tsp. English mustard		*2 oz. dry sherry*

Heat butter in skillet. Add turkey, mushrooms and green pepper. Sauté about 6 minutes. Add sherry. Reduce by two-thirds. Add mustard, Diable Sauce, Cream Sauce and cream. Then simmer for 10 minutes on slow fire. Salt and pepper to taste. Serve on toast.

***

AUTHOR: *Robert, this recipe for Roast Quail Napa Valley serves 12 people. How about cutting it down to family size?*

CHEF: *Any man who goes hunting and can't bring back 12 quail doesn't deserve to eat them this way.*

ROAST QUAIL NAPA VALLEY
SERVES 12

12 quail, dressed and stuffed with celery tops	1 bay leaf	1 cup Brown Gravy
	15 peppercorns	Juice of ½ lemon
12 slices bacon	¼ cup butter	1 cup fresh grapes
½ onion, chopped	1 cup burgundy	12 crouton setups
	2 tbs. grape jelly	

Salt and pepper quail to taste; roll slice of bacon around each and secure with toothpick. Place in roasting pan; add onion, bay leaf and peppercorns and cover quail with butter. Roast in 325°[F] oven for 15 minutes. Remove, place quail on heated plate and add burgundy to gravy; reduce by half. Add grape jelly, Brown Gravy, lemon juice and fresh grapes; simmer 8 minutes. Add whole butter in small pieces while mixing sharply. Meanwhile prepare crouton setups, which are sections of bread cut with trough or groove down center so that each will hold a quail, by browning crisply in butter or oil. Arrange quail on setups, glaze with the sauce and serve at once.

BROWN DERBY DRESSING, 1 qt.

½ celery heart	½ lb. white bread, diced and browned in oven	1/8 tsp. celery salt
1 medium-sized onion		1 tbs. chopped parsley
1 medium-sized apple	1/8 tsp. sage	1/8 tsp. nutmeg
1 small strip bacon	½ cup chicken fat	Salt and pepper

Chop celery, onion, bacon and apple fine. Smother in chicken fat for about 8 minutes. Add toasted bread, sage, celery salt, parsley, nutmeg and salt and pepper to taste. Mix well. Put in covered kettle and place in oven for 10 minutes. To make dressing [more] moist, add drippings from turkey or a little brown turkey gravy.

Chestnuts, oysters or raisins may be added to this basic dressing.

WILD RICE POULTRY DRESSING, 1 qt.

¼ cup butter	¼ lb. mushrooms, chopped fine	4 cups chicken broth
½ medium-sized onion, chopped fine	2 cups wild rice, washed	Salt and pepper

Heat butter in heavy kettle or pottery casserole. Add onion and mushrooms. Smother a few minutes without allowing to brown. Add wild rice and mix well. Pour in hot chicken broth, salt and pepper to taste; mix well. Cover and place in 350°[F] oven for 30 minutes.

SAUCES

The popularity of French cookery is based to a great extent on the French wizardry with sauces— the great glamour ingredient and the final touch which can make or break a dish. It takes practice to attain perfection in sauce making. Be patient, remember the mistakes to avoid the next time and heed these rules:

1. Never make too much of a sauce. Prepare only as much as is needed, in order to get the full flavor.

2. Never over salt or over spice.

3. Unless specified, a sauce should not be either too thick or too thin. Practice with the thickening agents, flour and egg yolks. Use stock, cream or milk to thin down.

4. Cook all sauces a little to attain the shiny stage.

The three basic sauces are Suprême, Brown and Cream. Many others are built up from one of these. The sauces which have attained the most favor at The Derbys are Hollandaise, Mornay, Bercy, Béarnaise, Bordelaise and, of course, the Meat Sauce for Spaghetti Derby and the De Luxe Sauce which accompanies the Hamburger Steak Derby.

BROWN SAUCE, 2 qts.

5 lbs. beef and veal bones, chopped in 1-in. square pieces
1 onion, chopped medium fine
2 beads garlic, chopped medium fine
2 carrots, chopped medium fine
Salt and pepper

3 pieces celery, chopped medium fine
½ leek, chopped fine
1 bay leaf
¼ tsp. basil
1 tsp. peppercorns
1 cup flour
2 cups burgundy

1 No. 1 can tomato purée
2 qts. stock or water
1 No. 1 can solid-pack tomatoes or 4 fresh tomatoes
2 sprigs parsley
1 tbs. paprika

Place bones in roasting pan; brown in 350°[F] oven, turning frequently to brown evenly. When brown, add onion, garlic, carrots, celery, leek, bay leaf, basil and peppercorns. Return to oven until onion and vegetables are lightly browned. Sprinkle with flour to thicken and mix well. Return to oven for 5 minutes. When flour is lightly browned, add wine, purée, stock, tomatoes, parsley and paprika. Mix well. Pour into large saucepan; season to taste. Simmer slowly for 2½ hours. Strain through fine sieve. Should gravy become too thick, add a little water from time to time.

Here is a simple, speedy version of Brown Sauce which can be added to the drippings from a roast or sautéed meat.

BROWN GRAVY, 1 pt.

2 heaping tbs. butter	*2 cups consommé or any meat*	*Pinch of monosodium*
3 heaping tbs. flour	*or chicken stock (except ham)*	*glutamate [optional]*
	3 tbs. tomato purée	*Salt and pepper*

Heat butter in heavy pot; add flour and stir well until flour is a light brown. Add hot stock, stir well again to dissolve all lumps; add tomato   purée, monosodium glutamate (to enhance flavor), salt and pepper to taste. Boil on slow fire for 12 minutes and strain through sieve. Add to 1 cup of drippings.

SAUCE SUPRÊME, 1 qt.

½ cup butter or salad oil	*1 qt. chicken stock*	*1 tbs. salt*
½ cup flour	*(heated)*	*Juice of ½ lemon*
1 tsp. peppercorns	*1 small carrot, cut*	*½ cup cream*
	1 branch celery	

Heat butter or oil. Add flour and mix until smooth. Add hot chicken stock, peppercorns, carrot, celery and salt. Mix well. Cook for 20 to 30 minutes. Strain through fine sieve. Add lemon juice, mix again and add cream. Simmer 5 minutes more.

Use with chicken, mushrooms, artichokes, sweetbreads and fish. With latter, use fish stock.

CREAM SAUCE BROWN DERBY, 1 pt.

2 tbs. butter	*2 cups milk (heated)*	*1 pinch salt*
2 heaping tbs. flour		*1 pinch nutmeg*

Heat butter and add flour. Mix well until smooth and all lumps have disappeared. Add milk, salt and nutmeg. Cook 15—20 minutes. Strain through fine sieve.

COUNTRY GRAVY, 1 pt.

2 pieces crisp bacon, finely chopped	*1 pt. Cream Sauce*	*1 tsp. finely chopped chives*
1 tbs. chopped onion	*Brown Derby*	

Brown bacon and onion in skillet. Add Cream Sauce. Mix well and sprinkle with chives.

SAUCE HOLLANDAISE, 1 qt.

1 tbs. whole white pepper, crushed	6 egg yolks*	1 lb. butter, melted
3 tbs. white wine vinegar	Juice of 2 lemons	Salt
	3 tbs. water	

Boil together pepper and vinegar for 1 minute; allow to cool. Blend together egg yolks, lemon juice and water in the top of a double boiler. Stir briskly as egg yolks begin to thicken. When mixture has reached the consistency of thick cream sauce, remove from heat and slowly add warm, melted butter. Add the butter only as long as eggs will absorb it. Continue to beat until a new stage of absorption is reached, until all the butter is used. Add salt to taste. Strain through a fine sieve.

Use immediately. Hollandaise is splendid blended with egg, fish, vegetable and chicken dishes.

*[Caution: Current health safety guidelines recommend caution when using raw eggs. This recipe is included as presented in 1st edition.]

Béarnaise Sauce is a more piquant version of Hollandaise and is used with fish, eggs, beef and veal.

SAUCE BÉARNAISE, 1 pt.

1 tbs. peppercorns, crushed	½ cup tarragon vinegar	2 tbs. fresh tarragon,
4 beads shallot, finely chopped	1/8 tsp. cayenne pepper	finely chopped
	2 cups Sauce Hollandaise	

Place peppercorns, shallots and vinegar in saucepan and reduce to 1 tsp. Remove from heat and allow to cool. Add Sauce Hollandaise and stir sharply. Strain through sieve. Add tarragon and cayenne and serve.

SAUCE BERCY, 1 pt.

1 cup white wine	1½ cups Brown Sauce	1/8 tsp. cayenne pepper
4 beads shallot, finely chopped	Juice of 1 lemon	1 tbs. parsley
Outside yellow peel of ½ lemon	¼ tsp. celery salt	¼ cup butter
	Salt and pepper	

Place wine, shallot and lemon peel in heavy, medium-sized skillet and reduce one-half. Add Brown Sauce, lemon juice, celery salt and cayenne pepper. Allow to simmer 10 minutes. Remove lemon peel. Add parsley, salt and pepper to taste. Whip in butter to complete sauce.

SAUCE MORNAY, 1 pt.

1 cup thick Cream Sauce	1 cup pastry cream	1/8 tsp. cayenne pepper
Brown Derby	1 cup American cheese	Salt and pepper

Place Cream Sauce and pastry cream in small saucepan. Mix well. Bring to a gentle boil. Add cheese and cayenne pepper. Allow to simmer until cheese is melted and the sauce has smooth appearance. Salt and pepper to taste.

* * *

Two bordelaise sauces are popular with Derby diners. The first is the traditional recipe, which has only a slight and optional accent on the garlic. The second is a California version, more high-powered in seasoning and spices. Both are for steaks and barbecued meats.

* * *

SAUCE BORDELAISE, 1½ pts.

1 cup burgundy	*1 clove garlic, finely chopped*	*1/8 tsp. cayenne pepper*
4 beads shallot, finely chopped	*(optional)*	*½ cup butter*
1 tbs. peppercorns, crushed	*1 pt. Brown Sauce*	*4 oz. marrow from bone*

Cook together in saucepan wine, shallot and peppercorns, reducing by one-third. Add Brown Sauce, garlic and cayenne pepper; again reduce by one-third. Strain through fine sieve. Bring to a boil again and add small pieces of butter, stirring sharply until all butter is whipped in. Just before serving add blanched marrow. (Marrow should be cooked in plain water for 2 minutes before adding to sauce.)

CALIFORNIA BORDELAISE SAUCE, 1 pt.

½ cup butter	*2 beads shallot*	*1 tbs. parsley, finely chopped*
4 cloves garlic, finely chopped	*¼ tsp. basil*	*1 tbs. chives, finely chopped*
1 cup burgundy	*1 cup thick Brown Sauce*	*Salt and Pepper*

In heavy medium-sized skillet, heat ¼ cup butter. Add garlic and shallot and brown lightly. Add burgundy. Reduce one-half. Add basil and Brown Sauce. Simmer for 12 minutes and strain. Add parsley and chives and season with salt and pepper to taste. Work in remaining ¼ cup butter, whipping constantly.

SPANISH OR CREOLE SAUCE, 2 qts.

1½ cups olive oil	*1 cup green pepper*	*2 cups chicken stock*
1 cup ham trimmings or	*½ cup flour*	*1 tbs. celery salt*
salt pork, chopped	*½ tsp. thyme*	*2 cups tomatoes, fresh or*
1 cup onion, sliced thin	*½ tsp. orégano*	*solid pack*
4 cloves garlic, chopped fine	*1 tsp. Gumbo Filé**	*1 cup tomato purée*
1 cup celery julienne	*1 cup white wine*	*1/8 tsp. Tabasco*
2 tbs. salt		*1 bay leaf*

Heat olive oil in heavy kettle. Add ham trimmings. Sauté until lightly browned. Add onion and garlic and continue cooking until lightly browned Add celery and green pepper and mix well. Sauté 5 minutes more. Add flour, thyme, orégano and Gumbo Filé and allow to smother 3 minutes. Add wine, stock, celery salt, tomatoes, tomato purée, Tabasco, salt and bay leaf. Cook 30 minutes on slow fire.

* * *

*Filé consists of the young and tender leaves of sassafras made into a fine powder. It was first prepared by the Choctaw Indians who lived in the woods around New Orleans. The leaves were gathered by the squaws and spread on stones to dry. When thoroughly dry, they were pounded and rubbed through a sieve. Twice a week the Indians would come to the famous French Market in New Orleans to sell their Filé. It has quite a distinctive flavor but must be used with discretion, as it thickens the sauce and make it "tacky".

* * *

PORT WINE SAUCE, 1 pt.

1 cup port wine	*Juice of ½ lemon*	*1 pinch cayenne pepper*
2 beads shallot, finely chopped	*Peel of ½ orange julienne*	*1 cup Brown Sauce*
1 pinch thyme	*(outside only)*	*(not too thick)*
2 oranges (juice)	*Salt*	*¼ cup butter*

Place wine, shallot and thyme in medium-sized skillet and reduce one-half. Add orange juice, lemon juice, orange peel, cayenne pepper and Brown Sauce. Allow to simmer 10 minutes. Remove orange peel. Add butter while stirring vigorously. Salt to taste and serve.

WHITE MUSHROOM SAUCE, 1 pt.

2 oz. butter	*1½ cups Sauce Suprême*	*¼ tsp. celery salt*
½ lb. mushrooms	*1 cup pastry cream*	*1/8 tsp. cayenne pepper*
½ cup white wine		*1/3 cup lemon juice*
(optional)		*Salt and pepper*

Heat butter in medium-sized skillet. Add mushrooms and sauté lightly. Add wine and reduce one-half. Add Sauce Suprême and pastry cream and mix well. Add celery salt, cayenne pepper and lemon juice and allow to simmer 10 minutes. Salt and pepper to taste.

BROWN MUSHROOM SAUCE, 1 pt.

¼ cup butter	*½ cup white wine*	*2 cups thick Brown Sauce*
½ lb. mushrooms, sliced thin	*¼ tsp. basil*	*Salt and pepper*
3 beads shallot, finely chopped		

Heat butter in medium-sized skillet. Add mushrooms and shallot; brown lightly. Add wine and basil and reduce one-half. Add Brown Sauce. Allow to simmer 10 minutes on slow fire. Add salt and pepper to taste.

MUSTARD SAUCE

4 tbs. Cream Sauce

1 tsp. English mustard

1 tsp. Brown Derby Diable or
    A-1 Sauce

Salt and pepper

Heat together and mix well.

SAUCE MADEIRA, 1 pt.

¼ cup butter

2 beads shallot, finely chopped

1 cup Madeira wine

Peel of 1/3 lemon (outside only)

2 cups Brown Sauce

Salt and pepper

Heat butter in medium-sized skillet. Add shallot; sauté until lightly browned. Add wine and reduce one-half. Add lemon peel, Brown Sauce, salt and pepper to taste. Allow to simmer 10 minutes. Remove lemon peel and serve.

Madeira Sauce is used over calves' liver, chicken livers, poultry, emincé of beef and veal.

SAUCE VIN BLANC, 1 pt.

1 cup white wine

2 beads shallot, finely chopped

1½ cup Sauce Suprême

1 cup pastry cream

Juice of ½ lemon

1 pinch cayenne pepper

1 pinch celery salt

Salt and pepper

3 egg yolks*

Place wine and shallot in a small saucepan. Reduce by one-third. Add Sauce Suprême and pastry cream and mix well. Add lemon juice, cayenne pepper and celery salt; simmer on slow fire 10 minutes. Season to taste. Add egg yolks that have been blended with a little cream. Mix quickly and remove from fire.

Vin Blanc Sauce is for fish, mushrooms, baby artichokes and palm hearts.

CHAMPAGNE SAUCE, 1pt.

1 cup champagne or dry white wine

2 cloves

1 tsp. whole peppercorns

½ bay leaf

2 cups Brown Sauce (not too thick)

1 tsp. sugar or jelly

Juice of 1 orange

Juice of 1 lemon

Salt

¼ cup butter

Place champagne, cloves, peppercorns and bay leaf in medium-sized skillet. Reduce by one-third. Add Brown Sauce, sugar, orange and lemon juice; simmer for 10 minutes. Add salt to taste and strain through fine sieve. Whip in whole butter.

*[Caution: Current health safety guidelines recommend caution when using raw eggs. This recipe is included as presented in 1st edition.]

CALIFORNIA RAISIN SAUCE, 1 qt.

2/3 cup raisins, washed	*Juice of ½ lemon*	*1 tbs. honey*
1 cup burgundy		*4 cups Brown Sauce*

Place raisins in kettle or saucepan. Cover with wine and boil 3 minutes. Add lemon juice, honey and Brown Sauce; simmer for 5 minutes more. Serve.

Champagne and California Raisin Sauces are used principally with baked ham and tongue.

* * *

According to a steady Derby patron, John Nesbitt, the Passing Parader of radio and motion pictures, capers are the unopened flower buds of the caper bush, a shrub of the genus Capparis, which is a member of the family Capparidaceae. After they are picked, they are salted and pickled in either tarragon or wine vinegar.

* * *

CAPER SAUCE, 1 pt.

1½ cups Sauce Suprême	*2 tbs. capers*	*1/8 tsp. cayenne pepper*
1 cup pastry cream		*Salt and pepper*

Place Sauce Suprême and pastry cream in small saucepan. Mix well and bring to gentle boil. Add capers and cayenne pepper and season to taste. Simmer for 10 minutes. Serve.

Used for beef and veal tongue, sweetbreads, kidneys and lamb.

CHAFING-DISH STEAK SAUCE
SERVES 1

This sauce is served at the table at all Brown Derbys when requested by patrons. It has become quite famous and is mixed in the following manner:

The water bed is taken off the chafing dish and the heat is applied directly to the dish until it is quite hot. Two pats of butter are melted and ½ teaspoon English mustard is added and the two ingredients mixed briskly. Then, while stirring constantly, 2 tablespoons of Brown Derby Diable Sauce are measured into the dish, followed by ½ teaspoon of Worcestershire Sauce, 1 teaspoon of catsup and salt and pepper to taste. The stirring is continued until all the ingredients are well-blended together. The sauce is served over the steak.

SWEET CHUTNEY STEAK SAUCE

1 pt. chili sauce	*½ cup butter*	*1 tbs. celery salt*
1 pt. Brown Sauce, thick	*2 tbs. Worcestershire Sauce*	*2 tbs. Brown Derby Diable or*
3 tbs. chutney, chopped	*3 tbs. English mustard*	*A-1 Sauce*

Mix all ingredients well and cook about 10 minutes.

SAUCE TYROLIENNE, 1 pt.

1 cup white wine
½ cup white vinegar
1 tsp. peppercorns

1 tsp. shallot, finely chopped
1 pinch basil
6 egg yolks

1 cup tomato purée
½ c. butter or olive oil
Salt and pepper

Place wine, vinegar, peppercorns, shallot and basil in heavy saucepan and reduce by one-third. Remove peppercorns; cool pan off slightly. Add egg yolks and mix well with a French whip. Place back on slow fire or in double boiler. As egg yolks thicken, add tomato purée slowly. Keep stirring vigorously until all purée is worked into egg yolks. Add butter very slowly while mixing. Season to taste and serve.

An interesting sauce for steaks, veal cutlets, chicken and some fish.

SAUCE BIGARADE, 1 qt.

1 cup port
1 orange, medium, juice and
  julienne outside peel

4 tbs. currant jelly
1 medium bay leaf
1/8 tsp. coriander

3 cups Brown Sauce or
  roast drippings
Salt

Heat port, orange peel and juice in a skillet; reduce by two-thirds. Add currant jelly, bay leaf, coriander, Brown Sauce or roast drippings. Reduce by one-fourth. Remove bay leaf; salt to taste.

If roast drippings are used, thicken sauce with 2 tsp. of cornstarch that has been mixed with a little of the port.

This is the sauce served with Baked Ham Brown Derby Style at the Derby on Saturday nights. It is also recommended for duck, quail and squab.

SAUCE POIVRADE, 1 pt.

1 tbs. crushed peppercorns
4 beads shallot, finely chopped
1 bay leaf

1 sprig thyme
1 cup burgundy
½ lemon peel (yellow only)
1 dash cayenne pepper

2 cups Brown Sauce
½ cup butter
Salt and pepper

Place peppercorns, shallot, bay leaf, thyme and wine in medium-sized skillet. Reduce by two-thirds. Add lemon peel, cayenne pepper and Brown Sauce and simmer 10 minutes. Strain through fine sieve. Work in butter, whipping constantly. Season to taste.

To serve with steaks, venison, duck and wild game, the English Bread Sauce which follows is also a wild-game sauce.

ENGLISH BREAD SAUCE, 1 pt.

3 cups pastry cream
½ onion, small

1 clove

1 cup white bread crumbs
Salt to taste

Place pastry cream in small, heavy skillet. Add onion into which clove has been stuck. Bring to gentle boil. Add crumbs and simmer about 8 minutes. Season to taste. Remove onion and clove before serving. If sauce becomes too heavy, add small amounts of cream.

COLD SAUCE CUMBERLAND, 1 pt.

2 lemons, peel only
2 oranges, peel only
1 cup port

4 tbs. currant jelly
2 tbs. wine vinegar

1 tsp. English mustard
1/8 tsp. cayenne pepper
½ cup white wine

Slice lemon and orange peel thin without removing pith and place in small skillet. Cover with water and boil 3 minutes. Remove water and place blanched lemon and orange peel in small mixing bowl. Add port, currant jelly, vinegar, English mustard, cayenne pepper and white wine and mix to smooth consistency. Serve.

Another wild-game sauce. May also be served with cold ham.

SAUCE DUXELLES, 1 pt.

1/8 lb. butter
¼ lb. mushrooms, chopped fine
3 tbs. Virginia ham, finely chopped

4 beads shallot, finely chopped
1 cup white wine
½ cup tomato purée

1 cup thick Brown Sauce
1 tbs. parsley, finely chopped
1 tbs. chives, finely chopped

Heat butter in medium-sized skillet. Add mushrooms and ham; brown lightly. Add shallot. Sauté 1 minute more. Add wine and reduce one-half. Add tomato purée and Brown Sauce and simmer on slow fire 10 minutes. Add parsley and chives. Serve.

Here is one of the most versatile of sauces. It goes well over fish, veal cutlets, chicken, sweetbreads and may be used as a spaghetti sauce.

EGG SAUCE, 1 pt.

1½ cups Brown Derby Cream Sauce
1 cup pastry cream

3 hard-cooked eggs, finely chopped
1/8 tsp. cayenne pepper
¼ tsp. celery salt

¼ tsp. nutmeg
Salt and pepper

Place Cream Sauce and pastry cream in small saucepan. Mix well and bring to a boil. Add eggs, cayenne pepper, celery salt and nutmeg. Simmer on slow fire 10 minutes. Salt and pepper to taste. Serve.

May be used over poached fish, finnan haddie and any timbale of fish.

SAUCE POULETTE, 1 pt.

2 oz. butter
¼ lb. mushrooms, sliced
2 beads shallot, finely chopped
1 cup white wine

1½ cups Sauce Suprême
1 cup pastry cream
1 pinch cayenne pepper

1 pinch celery salt
Juice of 1 lemon
2 tbs. chives, chopped fine
Salt and pepper

Heat butter in medium-sized skillet. Add mushrooms and brown lightly. Add shallot and sauté 1 minute more. Add wine and reduce one-half. Add Sauce Suprême and celery salt and mix well. Add lemon juice and simmer on slow fire 10 minutes. Add chives, season to taste and serve.
Use with crabs, oysters, filet of sole, sweetbreads and boiled chicken.

SAUCE FINES HERBES, 1 pt.

¼ cup butter
2 tbs., mushrooms, finely chopped

1 tsp. chervil, finely chopped
1/3 tsp. tarragon
1 cup white wine

2 cups Brown Sauce
1 tbs. parsley, finely chopped

Heat butter in medium-sized skillet. Add mushrooms and sauté until lightly browned. Add chervil, tarragon and wine and reduce two-thirds. Add Brown Sauce, chopped parsley and simmer on slow fire 8 minutes.
Served mainly with fish or sweetbreads.

SAUCE PROVENÇALE, 1 pt.

½ cup olive oil
4 beads shallot, finely chopped
2 cloves garlic, finely chopped
½ cup white wine

2 fresh tomatoes, peeled
    and diced
1 pinch basil
Salt and pepper

1 cup Brown Sauce
    (not too thick)
2 tbs. whole butter
1 tsp. parsley, finely chopped

Heat olive oil in medium-sized skillet. Add shallot and garlic. Brown lightly. Add wine and reduce one-half. Add tomatoes, basil, Brown Sauce and season to taste. Allow to simmer 10 minutes on slow fire. Work in butter, whipping constantly. Add parsley. Serve.
Adds flavor to chicken, sweetbreads, veal or pork.

SAUCE ROBERT, 1 pt.

½ cup white wine
3 beads shallot
2 peppercorns
1 cup Cream Sauce

1 cup Brown Sauce
2 tbs. English mustard
1 tsp. cayenne pepper

1 tbs. celery salt
3 tbs. Worcestershire Sauce
4 tbs. Sauce Hollandaise
Salt

Boil together wine, shallot and peppercorns; reduce by two-thirds. Add Cream Sauce and Brown Sauce; then mustard, cayenne pepper, celery salt and Worcestershire Sauce. Cook 15 minutes over low heat. Strain through fine sieve. Return to heat but do not boil. Whip in Sauce Hollandaise and salt to taste.
Used with chicken, fish and oysters.

* * *

Not satisfied with plain horseradish as a dressing for his roast beef, Rupert Hughes, the celebrated dean of authors, telephoned from his table at The Hollywood Derby to his cook at home for her version of Horseradish Sauce. The Derby took note and has been preparing it in this way ever since.

* * *

HORSERADISH SAUCE, 1 pt.

1½ cups Sauce Suprême (thick)   *¼ tsp. nutmeg*   *3 egg yolks*
1 cup pastry cream   *2 tbs. horseradish*   *Salt and pepper*

Place Sauce Suprême and pastry cream in medium-sized skillet and mix well. Bring to gentle boil. Add nutmeg and horseradish and simmer 8 minutes. Thicken with egg yolks that have been mixed with a little cream. Remove from fire. Season to taste.

WHITE BRANDY SAUCE, ¾ pt.

3 egg yolks   *2 tbs. sugar*   *4 oz. good brandy*
½ pt. pastry cream   *2 drops vanilla*

Mix all ingredients. Place in top of double boiler over boiling water. Beat with wire whip constantly until thickness of heavy cream is reached.
Used as a dressing for various desserts, pies, puddings and fruitcake.

CALIFORNIA ONION SAUCE, 1 pt.

¼ cup butter   *½ cup white wine*   *1 bay leaf*
2 onions, sliced very thin   *1 pinch nutmeg*   *Celery salt*
    2 cups Brown Sauce

Heat butter in saucepan. Add onions and brown lightly. Add wine; reduce by one-third. Add nutmeg, Brown Sauce, bay leaf and celery salt to taste. Simmer on slow fire 15 minutes. Should gravy get too thick; add a little water. After 15 minutes remove bay leaf and serve.
This is an all-purpose sauce for meats, being equally nice for hamburgers, pork chops and broiled meats.

SAUCE ZINGARA, 1 pt.

¼ cup butter   *2 oz. tongue julienne*   *2 cups Brown Sauce*
¼ lb. mushrooms julienne   *4 beads shallot, finely chopped*   *1 pinch cayenne pepper*
3 oz. Virginia ham julienne   *1 pinch cayenne pepper*   *1 truffle julienne*

Heat butter in medium-sized skillet. Add mushrooms, ham and tongue and sauté until lightly browned. Add shallot and sauté 1 minute more. Add wine; reduce one-half. Add Brown Sauce, cayenne pepper, truffle and simmer 10 minutes.
For what? For sweetbreads, chicken sauté and turkey.

GLACE DE VIANDE

An almost solid distillation of meat stock which is prepared and used in restaurants (it is the result of forty-eight hours of concentrated cooking) is now offered for household use as "beef concentrate" under several trade names. In liquid or crystal form, it can be combined with consommé, stock or water and thickened for a quick Brown Sauce. Bouillon cubes can also be used for this purpose. For each pint, take 2 level teaspoons of beef concentrate liquid, or 2 heaping teaspoons of crystals, or 2 bouillon cubes which have been dissolved well. Add a pint of consommé, beef stock, or water and thicken with 2 tablespoons of Beurre Manié or 1 teaspoon of cornstarch.

Also see Brown Derby Tomato Sauce, Derby Meat Sauce and Derby De Luxe Sauce ("Specialties of the House"); Curry Sauce ("Curries"); and sauce section of Barbecue chapter.

VEGES

VEGETABLES

Vegetables are usually cooked too long in the home. Try undercooking, using the least possible amount of water and the least possible time. And arrange the schedule so that they are served as soon as they are ready. If it is necessary to reheat vegetables, never put them back in water. Sauté in butter instead.

Brown Derby chefs prefer Russet potatoes for baking and frying and Burbank varieties for boiling and hash brown.

BRAISED LENTILS

SERVES 8

2 oz. butter
½ cup chopped onions
Salt and pepper

1 lb. lentils, washed and
    soaked overnight

1 ham bone or hock
1 bay leaf
1 qt. water

Heat butter in cooking pot. Add onions and braise lightly. Add lentils. Braise about 3 or 4 minutes. Stir well, then add ham bone or hock, bay leaf and the water. Add a small amount of salt and pepper. Bring to boil. Cover pot and simmer until lentils are done—approximately one hour. If too much liquid remains, drain.

Lentils may be served with ham hocks and grilled frankfurters or used as any other vegetable.

BAKED SQUASH DERBY

Carefully clean Banana Squash and cut into pieces 3 in. square. Steam until half done (approximately 10 minutes). Brush with melted butter, sprinkle with paprika and salt and bake in pan in moderate oven for 20 minutes. Serve with melted or whole butter.

GLAZED CARROTS

SERVES 4

Wash and scrape 1 pound baby carrots. Then steam or cook in as little water as possible. Dry them well. Place in buttered skillet and add 1 tbs. granulated sugar. Sauté until nice and brown, turning constantly with spoon in order to glaze them evenly.

CREAMED SPINACH

SERVES 4

2 oz. butter
1 cup chopped cooked spinach

½ cup Brown Derby Cream Sauce
2 tbs. table cream

1 pinch nutmeg
Salt and pepper

Heat butter in skillet until brown. Add spinach and stir well. Add hot Cream Sauce, cream and mix well over slow fire. Add nutmeg, salt and pepper to taste. Heat a little more. Serve.

SAUERKRAUT

SERVES 6

3 tbs. leaf lard
½ cup chopped onion
1 ham bone

1 No. 2 can sauerkraut, washed
lightly
1 bay leaf

Fill the No. 2 can with water
1 medium potato, grated
very fine

Heat lard in heavy cooking pot. Add onion. Simmer lightly for about 3 minutes. Add sauerkraut, ham bone, bay leaf, water. Cover pot and simmer for 1½ hours. Add raw grated potato. Cook an additional 20 minutes. Serve with ham hocks, frankfurters or spareribs.

FRESH CUCUMBERS IN SOUR CREAM

SERVES 4

6 medium-sized cucumbers
1 tbs. cooking salt

1½ cups sour cream

Salt and pepper
1 tbs. chives, finely chopped

Peel cucumbers, split lengthwise, scoop out seeds with a small spoon, slice as thin as possible. Place in chilled bowl, sprinkle with salt and blend well. Stand in refrigerator 1 hour. Place cucumbers between dry towels and press firmly until free of water. Return to chilled bowl, add sour cream along with salt and pepper to taste. Blend well and sprinkle with chives.

ZUCCHINI PORTUGUESE

SERVES 4

1 lb. zucchini
3 oz. butter or olive oil

2 medium-sized tomatoes,
peeled and diced

1 tbs. chopped green onions
1 pinch fresh garlic
Salt and pepper

Wash zucchini, drain and cut crosswise in thin slices. Heat butter or oil in skillet, then add the zucchini. Stir frequently till browned lightly. Add tomatoes, green onions and garlic. Sauté about 8 minutes more. Add salt and pepper to taste. Cover skillet and place on slow fire about 5 minutes. Serve in casserole dish. If desired, Parmesan cheese may be sprinkled on top of zucchini and browned under broiler, before serving.

ZUCCHINI FLORENTINE

SERVES 6

Wash and drain one pound zucchini and cut lengthwise into sticks the size of a thin French-fried potato. Salt and pepper, dip in flour and egg batter and toss in fine bread crumbs. Care should be taken to coat the zucchini evenly with crumbs. Fry in deep fat for about 4 minutes and serve on napkin.

CORN SAUTÉ O'BRIEN

SERVES 2

2 oz. butter	1 tbs. green pepper, finely chopped	1 tbs. pimiento, finely chopped
1 cup kernel corn, canned or off the cob		Salt and pepper

Heat butter in skillet. Add corn and green pepper. Sauté until lightly brown, stirring often in order to brown evenly. When color desired is obtained, add pimiento. Salt and pepper to taste. Sauté 1 minute more.

CORN FRITTERS   18 FRITTERS

3 eggs	1 cup kernel corn	2 tsp. baking powder
No. 1 can cream-style corn	3 tbs. butter, melted	¼ tsp. nutmeg
	2 cups flour	

Whip eggs well in a medium-sized mixing bowl. Add stewed corn, kernel corn and butter. Mix lightly. Add flour. Mix until smooth. Add baking powder and nutmeg and mix well. Mold fritters with tablespoon and drop into skillet in hot oil (300°F) about ¼ in. deep. Brown nicely on one side, turn and finish in medium hot oven.

Should batter be too thin after you have added 2 cups flour, add more until it is sufficiently heavy and does not run too freely.

APPLE FRITTERS   12 - 14 FRITTERS

3 whole eggs, well-beaten	1 tsp. orange and lemon peel, finely ground	½ cup milk
1 cup pastry flour		4 large apples (Roman Beauties
2 drops vanilla	½ tsp. salt	preferred) cut in ½ in.
2 tbs. sugar	2 tbs. melted butter	slices

Place beaten eggs in mixing bowl. Add flour. Mix well. Add vanilla, lemon and orange peel, sugar, salt and butter. Mix well again to dissolve all lumps. Add milk and mix to smooth consistency. Dip apple slices in flour, then in the batter and fry in deep oil or butter 3 to 4 minutes on each side until golden brown. Sprinkle with powdered sugar or cinnamon sugar and serve.

STUFFED TOMATO SOUBISE

SERVES 8

8 tomatoes	1 cup Soubise	1 tbs. butter
	4 tbs. Cheddar cheese, grated	

Scoop seeds from tomatoes lightly, salt and pepper and stuff with Soubise. On top of Soubise, sprinkle Cheddar cheese and a little paprika. Place in buttered pan and bake in 375°[F] oven for 20 minutes.

SOUBISE FOR STUFFING, 1 pt.

½ cup onions, cooked	2 eggs	¼ tsp. nutmeg
½ cup rice, cooked		Salt and pepper

Grind onions and rice through fine grinder. Place in mixing bowl. Add eggs, nutmeg, salt and pepper to taste and blend well. Keep in refrigerator until used.

BRAISED STRING BEANS À LA SWISS

SERVES 4

1 lb. string beans	1 small clove garlic finely	Pinch crushed black pepper
3 oz. butter	chopped	1 cup consommé or water
½ cup chopped onions	6 strips bacon finely chopped	

Clean string beans and julienne lengthwise. Heat butter in a medium-sized cooking pot. Add onions, bacon, garlic, pepper and sauté lightly for about 4 minutes. Add string beans and consommé or water. If water is used, add salt to taste. Cover pot and braise slowly about 20 minutes. Serve.

FRESH ASPARAGUS ST. GALLE

SERVES 4

2 lbs. asparagus	½ cup cream	8 strips crisp bacon, chopped
½ cup white wine	Salt and pepper	2 egg yolks*
½ lb. Swiss cheese, chopped		½ cup bread croutons
or grated		

Heat asparagus in salt water. Meanwhile, make sauce. Reduce wine by two-thirds in skillet; then add cheese and half of the cream, mixing thoroughly until they are blended. Salt and pepper to taste. Add bacon and egg yolks which have been mixed with balance of cream. Remove immediately from fire. Drain asparagus and place on heated plates. Pour sauce over; sprinkle with bread croutons and serve immediately.

Fresh Broccoli St. Galle is prepared in the same manner.

*[Caution: Current health safety guidelines recommend caution when using raw eggs. This recipe is included as presented in 1st edition.]

STUFFED MUSHROOMS DUXELLES

SERVES 2

8 button mushrooms (large)   1 tbs. butter   2/3 cup Sauce Duxelles
(very thick)

Place mushrooms upside down in buttered pan. Salt and pepper lightly. Stuff with very thick Sauce Duxelles and bake in moderate (350°F) oven for 10 minutes.

MUSHROOMS AND ARTICHOKES NICOISE

SERVES 4

½ cup butter   8 artichoke bottoms   2 cups pastry cream
1 lb. mushrooms   2 tbs. chives, finely chopped Salt
3 beads shallot, finely   1 tsp. chervil, finely   5 egg yolks*
    chopped (optional)   chopped (optional)   4 slices toast or English
½ cup sherry   1 tsp. English mustard   muffins

Heat butter in heavy skillet. Add mushrooms and sauté until tender. Add shallot and sauté ½ minute longer. Add sherry and reduce by two-thirds on brisk fire. Add artichokes, chives, chervil, mustard and 10 tbs. cream. Salt to taste and reduce by one-third over brisk fire. Stir constantly. Add egg yolks that have been mixed with 6 tbs. cream. Remove immediately from fire. Serve on toast or muffins.

*[Caution: Current health safety guidelines recommend caution when using raw eggs. This recipe is included as presented in 1st edition.]

FRENCH-FRIED DEVILED EGGPLANT

SERVES 4

1 large eggplant   2 eggs   1½ cups toasted bread
½ cup Mustard Sauce   2 tbs. water   crumbs
                            Fat for deep frying

If eggplant is not very fresh, peel it; otherwise leave unpeeled. Slice eggplant, spread with Mustard Sauce; then cut in finger-length strips as for French-fried potatoes. Beat eggs and water together. Dip eggplant fingers in bread crumbs, then in egg mixture, then back in bread crumbs. Chill 1 hour, then fry in deep, hot fat until golden brown. Drain on paper towel and serve at once.

FRENCH-FRIED TOMATOES

SERVES 4

2 tomatoes (medium size)   1 egg
2 tbs. milk   1 cup bread crumbs

Cut tomatoes in thick slices. Season to taste and bread as follows: Cover carefully with flour. Dip in mixture made of egg and milk beaten together. Cover with bread crumbs. Fry in deep fat at 380°[F] for approximately 1 minute or until golden brown. Do not overcook.

SWEET POTATO BALLS

SERVES 4

1 lb. sweet potatoes, cooked and peeled

6 small pieces pineapple
3 maraschino cherries, halved

1 cup maple syrup
6 large marshmallows, halved

Mold the sweet potatoes into balls about the size of a peach. Place in buttered baking pan. On each potato ball, place 1 small piece of pineapple. On top of pineapple place 2 halves of marshmallow. Garnish the marshmallow with ½ maraschino cherry. Add maple syrup. Bake in very moderate oven for 20 minutes.

SPECIAL DERBY BAKED POTATO

SERVES 1

1 large Idaho russet potato
1 tsp. chives, chopped
1 tbs. chopped crisp bacon
Paprika

Paprika
1/8 tsp. nutmeg

2 tbs. sour cream
1 slice American cheese, cut in strips

Scrub potato; dry thoroughly; rub well with salad oil. Roll in salt. Bake in 425°[F] oven for 45 minutes. Pierce with fork to permit steam to escape so potato will be mealy. When done, cut off top, scoop meat into heated bowl and mash thoroughly. Add chives, bacon, nutmeg and sour cream, blending well. Put mixture back into potato shell. Smooth over and arrange strips of American cheese in criss-cross fashion over top. Dust lightly with paprika. Return to oven (324°) 10 minutes or until cheese is melted and golden brown. Serve immediately.

COTTAGE-FRIED POTATOES

SERVES 2

2 good-sized russet potatoes

½ cup oil
Salt and pepper

2 tbs. melted butter

Peel raw potatoes, slice very thin crosswise. Heat one-third of the oil in small skillet. Arrange potatoes in rosette form about 4 layers deep. Salt and pepper to taste. Add the rest of the oil. Cover the pan; fry for 10 minutes on slow fire. Drain off oil and turn potatoes over. If properly fried, they will turn in one place. Pour oil back into pan and brown on the other side. Remove oil. Add butter, fry a little more and serve.

HASHED-IN-CREAM POTATOES

SERVES 2

1 cup steamed russet potatoes

1 cup table cream
Dash of nutmeg

Salt and pepper

Chop potatoes into small dices. Boil cream in pot. Add potatoes and stir will. Add nutmeg and salt and pepper to taste. Cook until well thickened (approximately 10 minutes).

AU GRATIN POTATOES

SERVES 2

1 cup steamed russet potatoes
1 cup table cream
Dash nutmeg

Salt and pepper
Dash paprika

2 tbs. grated Parmesan or
Cheddar cheese

Proceed exactly as with Hashed-in-Cream Potatoes; then place in casserole and sprinkle with cheese and paprika. Place under broiler until brown.

BROWN DERBY SCALLOPED POTATOES

SERVES 6

2 lb. Idaho russet potatoes
3 oz. butter
1 lb. crisp bacon, chopped fine

1 tbs. chives
Salt and pepper

2 cups milk
Dash nutmeg
½ cup Parmesan cheese

Peel potatoes and slice very thin crosswise. Arrange in buttered baking pan in even rows. Sprinkle with bacon and chives. Add salt and pepper to taste, milk and nutmeg. Sprinkle with cheese. Bake in moderate oven under broiler.

NEW POTATOES IN SOUR CREAM

SERVES 2

12 small potatoes, boiled

2 cups sour cream

2 tbs. chives

Place potatoes, slightly warm, in deep heated dish. Cover with sour cream. Sprinkle with chives and serve.

DUCHESSE POTATOES

2 cups mashed potatoes   *2 egg yolks**

Mix well and form into little patties or use a border on any planked dishes.

POTATO DUMPLINGS

2 large potatoes   *¼ tsp. nutmeg*   *Salt and pepper*
Whole egg, well beaten   *1 tbs. flour*   *12 bread croutons*

Slice potatoes in pieces 1-inch thick and steam until well done. (If no steamer is available, care should be taken to remove the water when potatoes are cooked and place back on slow fire for 5 to 8 minutes until well dried.) Strain through ricer or sieve into mixing bowl. Add egg, nutmeg, flour and salt and pepper to taste. Mix lightly but thoroughly. Mold the potato paste into 6 equal portions. In center of each, press 2 toasted bread croutons. Roll the potato mixture smoothly around the croutons so they are in middle and boil in salt water for 20 minutes. Serve immediately with Polonaise Garniture.

Also see "Barbecue" chapter for more vegetable recipes.

*[Caution: Current health safety guidelines recommend caution when using raw eggs. This recipe is included as presented in 1ˢᵗ edition.]

RICE,
ROLLS,
CHEESE, ETC.

What is there to say about this chapter except that the dishes are all very delicious—and fattening?

PLAIN RISOTTO

SERVES 4

½ cup butter or olive oil
¼ medium onion, finely chopped

1 medium-sized bay leaf
1 cup long-grain rice

4 cups chicken broth, hot
Salt to taste

Heat butter or olive oil in heavy skillet. Add onion, bay leaf and smother gently for 2 minutes. Do not allow onions to take color. Add rice; sauté a minute longer. Add hot chicken broth and salt. Blend well. Cover skillet. Place in 400°[F] oven for 20 minutes.

RISOTTO À LA ROSA

SERVES 4 - 5

2 tbs. minced onion
6 tbs. butter

1 cup raw rice
3 cups chicken broth, heated
2 large fresh tomatoes

Salt and pepper
½ cup Parmesan cheese

Sauté minced onion in butter for 2½ minutes. Add rice and heated broth. Cover. Bring to a good rolling boil. Add tomatoes. Place in heated casserole. Add salt and pepper. Sprinkle with cheese. Cover. Bake in 350°[F] oven 35 minutes.

TWENTY-MINUTE RISOTTO

SERVES 4

1/3 cup onion, finely chopped
½ cup butter
1 cup raw rice

3 cups chicken consommé
*   or stock*

1 tsp. salt
1/3 cup sweet butter
*   (optional)*

Sauté the onion in butter until tender but do not permit it to take color. Add washed and dried rice (preferably long-grain), blending well. Sauté 1 minute, then add hot chicken stock and salt. Bring to a quick boil. Cover securely. Place casserole in oven (400°F) for 20 minutes. When finished, if desired, stir in with fork few lumps sweet butter.

PIÉMONTAIS RISOTTO

SERVES 2

½ cup onion, finely chopped
½ cup butter
¼ tsp. saffron
1 cup rice, washed and dried

3 cups chicken stock or
*   consommé, hot*
1/3 cup sweet butter

½ cup Parmesan cheese,
*   grated*
1 tbs. shaved white truffles or
*   diced Virginia ham*

Sauté chopped onion in butter until tender but not colored. Add saffron and rice, blending well, so that rice is coated with butter. Add hot chicken stock; bring to rolling boiling. Cover securely and place in 400°[F] oven for 20 minutes. When finished, stir in few lumps sweet butter and cheese garnished with shaved white truffles or diced Virginia ham.

TURKISH RISOTTO

SERVES 4

¼ cup butter
1 tbs. onion, finely chopped

1 cup rice

½ cup Sultana raisins
3 cups chicken broth, very hot

Heat butter in a heavy kettle. Add onion and sauté lightly; do not brown. Add rice, mix well and sauté for 2 or 3 minutes without taking color. Add raisins and broth. Bring to a boil. Mix again. Cover kettle. Place in 400°[F] oven for 20 minutes. Serve.

CROISSANTS (CRESCENT ROLLS), 7 doz.

¼ cup sugar
1 tsp. salt
½ cup butter, soft

½ tsp. mace
2 whole eggs
2 egg yolks
1 pt. milk

6 cups flour, sifted
2 cakes (2 oz.) yeast
1 lb. sweet butter

PART 1. Cream together sugar, salt, butter and mace until light and fluffy. Add eggs and egg yolks, blending well. Add 1½ cups warm milk. Finally, add half the flour, blending well. Add the remaining ½ cup of milk in which yeast has been dissolved. Beat well. Add remaining flour, blending very well into smooth dough.

PART 2. Form dough into loaf shape, arrange on floured canvas. Place in refrigerator 1 hour. Remove dough from refrigerator. Roll on floured canvas until twice as long as wide and ¼ in. in thickness.

PART 3. Break butter into pieces size of walnut; divide evenly over two-thirds of surface of dough. Fold remaining one-third over to center and finally fold over last section to center. Butter is then evenly distributed over inner surface of dough. Roll again in rectangle to ½-in. thickness. Fold 3 ways, as before. Wrap in floured canvas and place in refrigerator for 1 hour. Repeat process of rolling in rectangle to ½-in. thickness. Fold 3-ply and return to refrigerator 4 to 24 hours before making into rectangle 12 x 4 in. Cut into small triangles and roll into crescents for baking.

Bake 25 minutes in a moderate oven (300° - 325°F).

CORN DODGERS

SERVES 4

4 cups corn meal	*3 tbs. bacon fat*	*1 tsp. salt*
2 cups boiling water		*1 tsp. baking powder*

Add boiling water mixed with bacon fat, salt and baking powder to the corn meal. Dip hands in cold water and form mixture into very thin finger-shaped cakes. Brown on a hot greased griddle. Place in a slow oven (300°F) until crisp. Serve hot.

SPAETZELS

SERVES 6

4 whole eggs	*1 tbs. melted butter*	*1 pinch nutmeg*
1 cup flour	*1 pinch salt*	*½ cup milk*

Break eggs into large mixing bowl and beat lightly. Add flour, butter, salt and nutmeg and mix well. Beat about 3 minutes. Add milk and mix well until a smooth consistency is obtained. Put 2 quarts of water and pinch of salt into a 4-qt. cooking pot and bring to boil. Place dough on a small wooden scraping board and cut into strips about 1-in. long, 1/5-in. wide and 1/8-in. thick. Put the strips carefully into the water so as to keep it boiling constantly. Boil 10 minutes on brisk fire. Drain off water. Spread Spaetzels to cool, arranged evenly.

Put a fair amount of butter in a skillet. When butter is hot, put in the cooled Spaetzels. Sauté until lightly browned. Remove from skillet and serve with Polonaise Garniture. Spaetzels may be served in place of any potatoes.

POLONAISE GARNITURE

SERVES 6

6 oz. butter
6 tbs. white bread crumbs

1½ hard-cooked eggs, very
finely chopped

1½ tbs. chopped parsley

Heat butter in skillet. Add bread crumbs and sauté until nice and brown. Remove from fire, add chopped hard-cooked egg, parsley and serve.

FLUFFY DUMPLINGS   12 dumplings

1½ cups pastry flour
½ tsp. salt

1½ tsp. baking powder
2 tbs. melted butter or oil
¾ cup milk

1 tbs. chopped parsley
1 pinch nutmeg

Sift the flour, salt and baking powder in mixing bowl. Mix in butter or oil. Add milk, parsley, nutmeg and mix well. Be sure to dissolve all lumps. To mold dumplings, oil hands slightly and shape dough the size of an egg. Immerse in boiling salted water for 10 minutes or in steamer for 8 minutes.

SOUR-CREAM RAISIN BISCUITS, 1 doz.

2 cups flour
½ tsp. soda
1 tsp. cream of tartar

1 tsp. baking powder
1 pinch salt
2 tbs. shortening

½ cup raisins (seedless)
½ cup sour cream
½ cup sweet milk

Sift dry ingredients together; rub in shortening until well mixed; fold in raisins, then sour cream and some of the milk, mixing with fork and adding more milk until mixture forms soft ball. Pat out on floured board and cut with biscuit cutter. Bake from 12 to 15 minutes at 450°[F].

BROWN DERBY CHEESE ROLL

Split French roll in two; dip in one-half cream and one-half milk; dip in grated Parmesan cheese; pace under broiler until golden brown. Serve immediately.

CHEESE SOUFFLÉ

SERVES 4

½ cup water
¼ cup butter
Salt to taste

1 dash nutmeg
1¼ cups Parmesan cheese,
grated

4 eggs, whole
6 egg whites, stiffly beaten
3 tbs. flour

Boil water, butter, salt and nutmeg in a heavy saucepan until butter is dissolved. Add flour while butter and water are boiling. Mix sharply with wooden spoon until mixture forms a ball. Add whole eggs one at a time. Mix vigorously and blend into a smooth paste before adding next egg. After all eggs have been blended smoothly, add cheese and mix again. All this should be done over slow fire. After cheese has mixed evenly, remove from fire and fold in egg whites. Place mixture in buttered and floured soufflé pan, saucepan or angel-food baking tin, set in water and place in 425°[F] oven for about 35 minutes. This soufflé will rise several times its original size. When it stops rising, serve immediately with Cheese Sauce.

CHEESE SAUCE

1 cup cream   3 tbs. Parmesan cheese, grated

Heat cream over hot water, add parmesan cheese, cook until melted, blend well and serve over soufflé.

* * *

A noted chef once complained that after a meal he had prepared, Sarah Bernhardt gave such a magnificent performance he should have shared in the applause. The Brown Derby chefs who frequently prepared this Cheese Soufflé for Gracie Allen on the afternoon of her broadcasts like to think that they have a tiny bit to do with the success of her light and airy nonsense.

* * *

AVOCADO CHEESE SOUFFLE

SERVES 2

½ cup water   4 whole eggs
¼ cup butter   1 large, very ripe avocado,   ¾ cup Parmesan cheese
¼ tsp. nutmeg   puréed   6 egg whites, beaten stiff
4 tbs. flour

Boil water, butter and nutmeg in a heavy saucepan until butter is dissolved. Add flour while butter and water are boiling. Mix sharply with wooden spoon until mixture forms a ball. Add whole eggs one at a time, beating vigorously and blending into a smooth paste before adding another. After all eggs have been blended smoothly, add Parmesan cheese, avocado purée and blend again. All this should be done over a medium fire. Should paste get too hot, remove from heat for a minute or so, stirring constantly. After cheese has melted, fold in egg whites. Place the mixture in a buttered and floured soufflé pan. Bake in 375°[F] oven. This soufflé should rise three or four times its original size. As soon as it reaches this stage, serve immediately with Cheese Sauce.

To make sauce, heat 1 cup cream over hot water, add 3 tbs. Parmesan cheese and cook until melted.

WELSH RABBIT

SERVES 4

3 cups Cheddar cheese, grated	1 tbs. English mustard	½ cup beer
1 tsp. cornstarch	1 tbs. Worcestershire Sauce	Salt to taste

Mix well-grated cheese and cornstarch in a heavy casserole. Add mustard, Worcestershire Sauce, beer and salt to taste. Mix well again. Place on fire and bring to a boil. Mix very briskly. When all cheese is melted and a smooth consistency is reached, serve in very hot casserole with toast or English muffins.

GOLDEN BUCK

This is Welsh Rabbit in individual servings with a poached egg on top.

CHEESE BLINTZES

SERVES 6

2 eggs	½ cup flour	½ tsp. ginger
1 cup milk	3 tsp. butter	1 tsp. vanilla
½ tsp. salt	1½ cups cottage cheese	2 tsp. sugar
Little orange and lemon peel finely grated	1 cup sour cream	1 cup currant or strawberry jelly

To prepare batter: Beat eggs. Add milk, salt and peel. Pour into the flour slowly, stirring vigorously to obtain a smooth, thin batter. Pour 2 tbs. of the batter into a 7-in. frying pan that has been very slightly buttered, spreading thin over the entire bottom of the pan. When cooked, the edges will shrink away from the side of the pan., Remove the pancake and invert on cloth or paper that has been sprinkled with powdered sugar. Allow to cool.

FILLING: Blend cottage cheese, one-half of sour cream, ginger, vanilla and sugar. Put 2 tbs. of filling in the center of each of the pancakes. Roll like a jelly roll and place in a shallow pan. When all of the cakes have been filled, place a dab of butter on top of each and put under broiler (or in oven at 350°[F]) until heated through. Serve, topped with balance of sour cream and jelly.

ORLY BATTER, 1 pt.

3 eggs	½ tsp. salt	1 cup flour
1/8 tsp. nutmeg	3 tbs. salad oil	2/3 cup milk

Beat eggs very well with nutmeg, salt and oil. Add flour and milk alternately, beating until smooth after each addition to eliminate lumps. Unused batter will keep for several days in covered jar in refrigerator.

BROWN DERBY MATZOTH PANCAKES
SERVES 6

6 egg yolks, lightly beaten	1 pinch baking soda	1 tsp. sugar
1½ cups milk or buttermilk	1 pinch salt	½ tsp. vanilla
2 cups matzoth flour	6 tbs. melted butter or	6 egg whites, stiffly beaten
1 pinch baking soda	chicken fat	
1 pinch salt		

Place egg yolks in mixing bowl. Add milk, matzoth flour, soda, salt, sugar, melted butter or chicken fat and vanilla. Mix well. Care should be taken to dissolve all lumps. Fold in the egg whites lightly. Fry in heavy skillet in hot butter, chicken fat or oil. Spoon batter into the hot grease, brown on one side, turn and put skillet into a medium-hot oven for about 8 to 10 minutes. Remove from skillet onto a towel in order to absorb the grease. Serve with stewed fruit or prunes, applesauce or maple syrup.

SPAGHETTI TETRAZZINI IN CASSEROLE
SERVES 2

3 oz. butter	2/3 cup pastry cream	2 cups spaghetti, cooked
4 mushrooms, julienne	1½ cups dark meat	8 minutes
4 slices truffle (optional)	2 egg yolks	½ cup Parmesan cheese
1/3 cup sherry	Salt and pepper	1 cooked chicken breast,
1 cup Cream Sauce		julienne

Heat butter in medium-sized heavy skillet. Add mushrooms and sauté until lightly browned. Add truffle. Add sherry and reduce by one-third. Add Cream Sauce, pastry cream and chicken. Blend well and allow to simmer 5 minutes. Thicken with egg yolks mixed with a little of the cream. Season to taste. Arrange well-drained spaghetti in heated and buttered casserole. Pour chicken in sauce over spaghetti. Sprinkle with Parmesan cheese. Brown under open flame. Serve at once.

SPAGHETTI CARUSO

SERVES 6

½ cup olive oil
1 lb. chicken livers, blanched
½ lb. sliced mushrooms
2 tbs. onions, finely chopped
¼ tsp. basil

1 cup Parmesan cheese
Salt and pepper
1 clove garlic, finely chopped
1 cup burgundy

2 medium-sized tomatoes,
    peeled and diced
1 cup Brown Sauce
1 lb. spaghetti
1½ cups tomato sauce

Heat olive oil in heavy skillet. Add chicken livers, mushrooms, onion, basil and salt and pepper to taste. Sauté till chicken livers are golden brown. Add garlic and sauté 1 minute more. Add wine, tomatoes and Brown Sauce and bring to a boil. Place on top of spaghetti that has been cooked 10 minutes and mixed with tomato sauce. Serve Parmesan cheese on side.

BROWN DERBY SPECIAL SANDWICHES

NUMBER 1   Use two big slices of large Russian rye bread. Butter one side and to one slice, add a layer of baked ham, fat removed, a layer of imported Swiss cheese, thin sliced, 2 tbs. of coleslaw, spread evenly.
Cover with second slice of bread, cut crosswise in 3 sections and serve with kosher dill pickle.

NUMBER 2   Instead of baked ham, use slices of tongue.

NUMBER 3   Fill with turkey and ham.

NUMBER 4   Use turkey, ham, and Swiss cheese.

MONTE CRISTO SANDWICH

Take three slices of white bread. Butter the first and cover with lean baked ham and chicken. Butter the middle slice on both sides, place on meat and cover with thinly sliced Swiss cheese. Butter the third slice and place, butter side down, over cheese. Trim crusts; cut sandwich in two; secure with toothpicks; dip in light egg batter; fry in butter on all sides until golden brown. Remove toothpicks and serve with currant jelly, strawberry jam, or cranberry sauce.

CURRIES

Curry, the national dish of India, has been gaining favor in the United States and some of the most popular items on the Brown Derby menus are the curried dishes in this chapter. They range from hors d'oeuvres and eggs to seafood, chicken, lamb and veal.

You will find three types of curries: à la Bengal—with fruit, such as dates, pineapple, coconut, et cetera; à la Calcutta—with tomatoes and cheese au gratin; and Madras or Indienne—plain.

For a successful curry always use the finest ingredients obtainable and, if possible, purchase curry powder packed in India. Curry powder is a combination of spices, such as turmeric, mustard, pepper, garlic powder, chili, coriander, fenugreek seed, Bengal gran and curry leaves. It is so widely used in Asia that it is known as "the salt of the Orient".

Curries should never be too strong in flavor. Even in India, they are served just the least bit nippy. If, on sampling, you wish to sharpen your curry, do not add more curry powder. Instead, add cayenne pepper or a pepper or Tabasco sauce. Some people season with more garlic. East Indians frequently add a small amount of lime or lemon juice to flavor their curries.

Serve with rice which has been cooked 20 minutes, as in Pilaff. That means the rice is in individual grains and has been well-boiled, drained, buttered and seasoned. The Brown Derby uses Vitamin B converted rice, which does not get soggy and which retains all nutritional value.

CONDIMENT TRAY

With curries, always serve Indian condiments. The best known is chutney, a combination of ripe fruits (mangoes, tamarinds, raisins, et cetera) with spices, herbs, peppers, vinegar and lemon juice in a sweet syrup. Other relishes are Popadums (corn cakes covered with Popadum leaves, which are fried in butter or oil); Bombay Duck, really a salmon-like fish, the Bummaloti, which is dried, smoked and salted; coconut, either shredded or sliced thin and toasted; chopped bell peppers; toasted peanuts or almonds; small sharp, sour, pickled peppers; chopped eggs; capers; and anchovies of Bombay Duck is not available.

CURRY SAUCE AND CURRIED LAMB, VEAL OR BEEF

1 large onion	*1 cup flour*	*1 bay leaf*
1 apple	*6 tbs. curry powder*	*1 tsp. whole black pepper*
3 outside pieces celery	*2 large ripe tomatoes, chopped*	*2 tbs. chopped chutney*
1 clove garlic	*2 tbs. coconut, shredded*	*Chicken bones or chopped*
2 carrots	*2 qts. chicken stock or*	*veal, lamb or beef*
¼ lb. butter or chicken fat	*consommé*	*bones*

Chop onion, apple, celery, garlic and carrots and simmer in butter or chicken fat for about 5 minutes. Add flour and simmer for another 3 or 4 minutes. Add curry powder, tomatoes and coconut. Add stock, bay leaf, pepper, chutney and bones. Cook for 45 minutes to 1 hour over very slow fire. Season with salt if necessary.

If used for chicken, shrimp or crab legs, add a little cream.

For Lamb, Veal, or Beef Curry, the bones are left out. Brown the meat lightly and cook together with sauce until meat is done, then remove meat, strain the sauce and serve over meat.

BROWN DERBY CALIFORNIA CHUTNEY, 1 gal.

A	B
1 cup wine vinegar	*1 cup raisins*
1 tsp. cominos	*2 apples, peeled and sliced*
1 tsp. coriander	*½ cup apricots, sliced*
10 cardamom seeds,	*1 tsp. horseradish*
crushed, finely chopped	*Peel of 2 oranges, julienne*
1 tbs. mustard seeds	*1 cup mango, sliced*
2 bay leaves	*2 cups sweet relish or*
2 tbs. powdered ginger or	*watermelon rind*
½ lb. candied ginger, sliced	*chips*
1 tsp. salt	*½ cup guava jam*
1 cup sugar	*1 cup dates, seeds removed*
2 cups honey	*2 Mexican long chili*
1 cup orange juice	*peppers, julienne*

Cook together all ingredients under heading "A" for 1 hour. Strain through fine sieve. Return to fire. Add ingredients under heading "B". Allow to simmer 1 hour. Serve with curry dishes or with cold meats.

SMALL PATTIES CHICKEN MADRAS
36 portions

1½ cups Curry Sauce	*4 tbs. chopped chutney*	*36 Hors d'Oeuvre Patty Shells*
½ cup pastry cream	*¾ cup finely diced chicken*	*3 tbs. minced parsley*

Heat Curry Sauce with cream and chutney in double boiler. When boiling, add chicken and heat thoroughly. Fill patty shells and serve at once, garnished with minced parsley.

Hors d'Oeuvre Patty Shells are made from 1-in. squares of Puff Paste molded into miniature shells which hold 1 tsp. and then baked. One pound of Puff Paste will make about 36 shells.

SMALL PATTIES LOBSTER INDIENNE
36 patties

1½ cups lobster	*½ cup pastry cream*	*36 Hors d'Oeuvre Patty*
1½ cups Curry Sauce	*4 tbs. chopped chutney*	*Shells*

Remove cooked lobster meat from shell and pack well in cup when measuring. Heat Curry Sauce. Add cream and chutney. Bring to a boil over direct heat. Add lobster which has been sautéed lightly in a little butter. Keep hot until ready to serve. Fill patty shells. Serve at once. Garnish with parsley and paprika lemon slices.

For Crab or Shrimp Patties Indienne follow above recipe, substituting same amount of crab meat or shrimp for lobster.

BAKED FILET OF SOLE CURRY CALCUTTA
SERVES 3

2 oz. butter (¼ cup), melted	*½ cup fish stock*	*2 tbs. chutney, finely chopped*
12 oz. filet of sole	*Salt*	*1 large tomato, peeled,*
½ cup white wine	*1½ cups rice, cooked*	*thinly sliced*
Juice ½ lemon	*1½ cups Curry Sauce*	*2 tbs. Parmesan cheese*

Pour melted butter into heavy skillet. Arrange filets of sole, which has been cleaned, boned and folded in half, in skillet. Add wine, lemon juice, fish stock and salt to taste. Cover and steam 8 minutes. Remove sole and arrange in heated casserole on rice. Return broth to heat and reduce by two-thirds. Add Curry Sauce and chutney. Bring to gentle boil and mix well. Pour over sole. On top of each filet lay 1 or 2 very thin slices of tomato. Sprinkle cheese on top and brown under broiler.

LOBSTER CURRY CALCUTTA
SERVES 2

2 oz. butter	*2 tbs. chutney*	*2 tbs. Parmesan cheese*
1 2-lb. cooked whole lobster,	*1 cup rice, steamed 20*	*1 lemon, sliced and sprinkled*
diced	*minutes*	*with paprika*
½ cup pastry cream	*1 large peeled tomato, thinly*	
1½ cups Curry Sauce	*sliced*	

Heat butter in heavy skillet; add lobster meat and brown lightly. Mix together pastry cream, Curry Sauce and chutney. Add to lobster. Boil 8 minutes.

Place cooked rice in center of heated casserole; pour lobster mixture over and around rice. On top of all, arrange neat line of tomato slices. Sprinkle with cheese. Place under broiler. Care must be used not to burn. Serve at once garnished with lemon-paprika slices.

If a particularly decorative touch is desired, the rice and the lobster curry may be blended, placed in empty lobster shell, sprinkled with cheese and put under broiler.

BAKED HALIBUT CURRY INDIENNE
SERVES 2

2 5-oz. filets of halibut	1 cup Curry Sauce	1 medium tomato,
2 cup Court Bouillon	1/3 cup pastry cream	thinly sliced
1½ cups cooked rice	1 tbs. chutney, chopped	2 tbs. shredded coconut

Poach halibut in Court Bouillon for 20 minutes on slow fire. Arrange steamed rice in buttered heavy casserole. Place halibut on rice and cover with Curry Sauce that has been heated with pastry cream and chutney. Arrange the tomato slices on top. Bake under open flame until tomato is well broiled. This should not take longer than 3 minutes. Sprinkle shredded coconut over top and return to flame for ½ minute. Serve at once, garnished with watercress.

For a simpler fish curry, try the scalloped halibut recipe below.

SCALLOPED FILET OF HALIBUT MADRAS
SERVES 4

4 5-oz. filets of halibut	2 cups Curry Sauce	3 tbs. chutney
3 cups Court Bouillon	1 cup pastry cream	3 cups cooked rice

Poach halibut gently in Court Bouillon* on slow fire. Flake poached halibut. Heat Curry Sauce, cream and chutney to boiling point in chafing dish. Add flaked halibut and simmer for 4 minutes. Serve at once with rice.

*Recipe in "Fish" chapter.

CURRIED LOBSTER À LA MADRAS
SERVES 2

2 oz. butter	1½ cups Curry Sauce	2 tbs. chutney, chopped
1 2-lb. lobster, cooked,	½ cup pastry cream	2 cups rice, steamed 20
meat diced		minutes

Heat butter in heavy skillet; add lobster; sauté until lightly browned., Add Curry Sauce with cream and lobster; cook 5 minutes on slow fire. Add chopped chutney. Serve in heated casserole with rice.

OYSTERS AND CRAB LEGS CURRY MADRAS

SERVES 3

2 oz. butter
9 large oysters (New York count)
12 crab legs, large (Dungeness if obtainable)
1½ cups Curry Sauce

½ cup pastry cream
2 tbs. chutney, chopped
2 cups Rice Pilaff cooked
20 minutes

Heat butter in heavy skillet. Add oysters and crab legs and sauté 3 minutes. Add Curry Sauce, cream and chutney. Allow to simmer 4 minutes more. Serve with Rice Pilaff.

FRESH SHRIMP CURRY À LA MADRAS

SERVES 4

4 oz. butter
1 lb. jumbo shrimp, split, cleaned
*   and cooked*

1½ cups Curry Sauce
½ cup pastry cream

2 tbs. chutney, chopped
2 cups rice, cooked 20
*   minutes*

Heat butter in heavy skillet. Add shrimp and sauté until lightly browned. Add Curry Sauce, pastry cream and chutney. Cook 6 minutes over slow heat. Serve with steamed rice.

OMELETTE AU SHRIMP INDIENNE

SERVES 1

3 eggs
1 oz. cream

1 pinch salt
1 oz. butter

½ cup Curried Shrimp
1 tbs. chutney

First prepare Plain Omelet (see "eggs" chapter) and Curried Shrimp. Place shrimp in center of omelet before folding sides to center. Turn over onto hot serving plate and serve chutney alongside. Garnish with watercress. Serve at once.

EGGS EN COCOTTE INDIENNE

SERVES 1

1 oz. butter

½ cup Curried Chicken,
*   finely chopped*

2 eggs
1 tbs. coconut, shredded

Butter 2 cocottes generously. Into each, place ¼ cup chicken. Then break an egg in each cup. Place cocottes in pan of boiling water and bake in moderate oven (350°F) for 8 minutes. Sprinkle coconut over top. Place cocottes immediately on heated serving plate with doily underneath and serve at once.

Eggs en Cocotte Bengal are made by substituting Curried Shrimp and ½ tomato, peeled and diced, for chicken and eliminating coconut.

ARTICHOKES WITH SHRIMP BENGAL
SERVES 2

½ lb. shrimp, cooked
6 artichoke bottoms
2 tbs. Parmesan cheese, grated

1 medium-sized tomato
thinly sliced
1 cup Curry Sauce

1 slice pineapple, chopped finely
1 tbs. chutney, chopped finely
2 cups rice, steamed 20 minutes

Peel shrimp, split in half lengthwise and clean. Put artichokes in buttered baking pan. Arrange shrimp on top to form mounds. Top with 1 thin slice of tomato and sprinkle with cheese. Bake 325°[F] oven for 10 minutes. Heat Derby Curry Sauce in double boiler. Add finely chopped pineapple and chutney. Bring to gentle boil. Arrange stuffed artichoke bottoms on heated plate. Pour Curry Sauce mixture around them and serve with rice.

SPRING CHICKEN CURRY À LA MADRAS
SERVES 4

2½-lb. broiler
3 oz. butter
1 cup Curry Sauce

½ cup pastry cream
1 tbs. chutney, finely chopped

Chicken broth, as necessary
1 cup rice, cooked 20
minutes

Unjoint chicken; roll in flour, salt and pepper. Heat butter in heavy skillet. Add chicken and sauté golden brown on both sides. Add Curry Sauce and pastry cream. Cover. Simmer 18 minutes. Add chutney. Cook gently until well done. If Curry Sauce reduces too fast, add chicken broth or cream. Serve with rice.

BREAST OF CHICKEN CURRY CALCUTTA
SERVES 2

1 tbs. butter
2 cups Rice Pilaff, hot
1 breast of chicken, cooked

2 cups Curry Sauce
2 tsp. chutney, chopped

2 medium-sized tomatoes,
thinly sliced
2 tbs. Parmesan cheese

Butter individual ovenware casseroles and in each place 1 cup hot rice. Over rice place half of breast of chicken which has been heated in chicken which has been heated in chicken broth. Cover with hot Curry Sauce to which chutney has been added. Cover with slices of tomato. Sprinkle over all with cheese. Dab lightly with melted butter. Brown under 550°[F] broiler flame for 1 to 2 minutes. Great care must be taken to avoid burning while browning. Serve at once.

FINE-CUT CHICKEN CURRY BENGAL

SERVES 4

2 cups Curry Sauce
1 cup pastry cream
1 slice pineapple, diced

1 medium-sized tomato,
        peeled and diced
1 breast of chicken, finely
        diced

1½ cups dark meat, finely
        diced
2 cups rice, cooked 20 minutes
1 tbs. chutney, finely cut

Heat Curry Sauce and pastry cream in heavy skillet. Add pineapple, tomato and chutney. Blend well and bring to a gentle boil. Add chicken and simmer on slow fire for 4 minutes. Serve with steamed rice.

FINE-CUT CHICKEN CURRY CALCUTTA

SERVES 6

4 lb. stewing chicken
3 cups Curry Sauce
1 cup pastry cream

2 tbs. chutney, chopped fine
2 cups cooked rice

3 tomatoes, peeled, thick slices
½ cup Parmesan cheese
4 oz. melted butter

Cook chicken till tender. Remove meat and dice. Mix Curry Sauce and pastry cream well in a heavy medium-sized skillet. Add chutney and bring to a boil. Add diced chicken and simmer 4 minutes on slow fire. Pour the chicken over rice. Cover the chicken with thick slices of peeled tomato. Sprinkle with Parmesan cheese. Pour melted butter over cheese and brown under open flame.

EMINCÉ OF VEAL INDIENNE

SERVES 4

¼ cup butter
1 lb. veal julienne

2 tbs. onion
Salt and pepper

1 cup Curry Sauce
½ cup pastry cream

Heat butter in heavy skillet. Add fine veal julienne, onion and season with salt and pepper to taste. Sauté until golden brown. Add Curry Sauce, pastry cream and bring to a slow, gentle boil.

CURRIED LAMB MADRAS

SERVES 6

2-lb. leg lamb cut in 1-inch squares
1/3 cup oil
1 medium-sized onion,
        finely chopped

2/3 cup flour
3 tbs. curry powder
2 cloves garlic, finely chopped
1 medium-sized apple, peeled,
        cored, chopped fine

½ cup celery, finely diced
1½ qts. lamb stock or water
1/3 cup coconut milk*
Salt and pepper

Toss lamb pieces in flour, salt and pepper. Heat oil in a good-sized heavy kettle and add pieces of lamb. Brown carefully until light brown. Add onion, flour, curry powder, apple, garlic and celery. Allow to smother 4 minutes, stirring often. Next add lamb stock or water which has been mixed with coconut milk. Season with salt and pepper to taste. Simmer gently 1½ hours or till well done. Serve with rice. Sprinkle each serving with shredded coconut.

*If coconut milk is not available, simmer ½ cup shredded dry coconut in 1 cup water for 20 minutes. Then strain and use liquid like fresh coconut milk.

VEAL SWEETBREADS INDIENNE
SERVES 4

1 lb. sweetbreads, soaked and boiled	¼ cup butter ½ cup pastry cream	2 cups rice, cooked 20 minutes 1 cup Curry Sauce

Split sweetbreads lengthwise and season with salt and pepper and dust with flour. Put in skillet with heated butter and brown lightly on both sides. Add Curry Sauce and pastry cream and simmer gently 8 minutes. Serve with rice and chutney.

MAYONNAISE BENGAL, 1 pt.

2 cups mayonnaise
1 tsp. curry powder
	1 tbs. finely chopped
	    Brown Derby Chutney
	3 slices pineapple, finely
	    chopped
		1 medium-sized tomato,
		    peeled, seeded, finely
		    chopped

Blend mayonnaise and curry powder in medium-sized mixing bowl, mixing thoroughly to dissolve all curry powder. Add chutney, pineapple and tomato and mix well again. Chill.

Try this dressing with cold fish, cracked crab, cold shrimp or lobster, cold chicken, cold cuts, or in making chicken salad or wherever a touch of piquancy should be added to plain mayonnaise.

EGGS

EGGS

The ideal procedure for cooking eggs is to use a special pan for omelets which is never used for anything else and another that is reserved exclusively for scrambling.

Always wait until the butter is quite hot and evenly distributed over the pan before adding the eggs. Butter shirred egg pans or cocottes well so that the eggs may be removed easily when eaten. If an egg poacher is not available, be sure the water is boiling briskly and has been salted before adding the egg. A little lemon juice in the water will draw the egg together.

Add a handful of salt to the boiling water when hard-cooking eggs. After 10 minutes, pour out the hot water and run cold water over them for 10 minutes more to make peeling easier.

PLAIN OMELET

SERVES 1

3 eggs
1 oz. cream

1 pinch salt
1 oz. butter

Beat eggs well. Add cream and salt. Since the skillet is all-important, use a clean 8-in black frying pan which is well broken in. If not, burn it out with oil brought to the smoking point for 5 to 10 minutes. Remove oil and clean pan with rag. *Never* wash this pan; always wipe out with cloth. Put butter in pan over a fairly fast heat. As soon as it is melted and quite hot, but not turning color, add egg mixture all at once. Keep shaking pan, tossing mixture over until omelet begins to take shape. Rest pan on stove for about ½ minute, then loosen omelet by hitting handle of pan sharply. Now fold each side one-third over toward the center and turn onto hot serving plate, smooth side up. If out of shape, shape by hand covered with clean cloth.

Minced Ham, Mushroom, or Chicken Omelets are made by sautéing the meat or mushrooms in the butter before adding egg mixture.

For Creamed Chicken or Spanish Omelet place 1 tbs. Cream Chicken or Spanish Sauce in the center of the omelet just before folding sides over and another alongside.

OMELETTE SAN SIMEON

SERVES 2

3 eggs
Salt
¼ cup butter

2 tbs. avocado, diced

2 tbs. chicken, white meat,
    finely diced
1 tbs. chopped chives

Beat eggs thoroughly in a small mixing bowl, adding salt to taste. Heat butter in heavy skillet. Add eggs, avocado, chicken and chives. Make a French omelet and roll onto a very hot service plate. Garnish with watercress. Serve at once.

OMELETTE HANGTOWN

SERVES 1

2 well-beaten eggs
1 tbs. butter
1 tbs. minced bell pepper

1 tsp. minced green onion
1 tsp. minced pimento

Salt and pepper
3 breaded oysters
2 slices bacon, crisp

Whip eggs with salt in mixing bowl. Heat butter in heavy skillet and sauté pepper, onion and pimento, stirring constantly for 1½ minutes. Add eggs. Blend well. Add salt and pepper to taste and finally add oysters which have been fried in butter. Make a flat omelet slightly browned on both sides. Place on hot service plate. Make a cross of crisp bacon. Garnish with watercress. Serve at once.

OMELET WITH CREAMED MUSHROOMS

SERVES 2

3 eggs
Salt

¼ cup butter

½ cup creamed mushrooms*
2 button mushrooms

Beat eggs thoroughly in small mixing bowl. Add salt to taste. Heat butter in heavy skillet and add eggs to make a French omelet. Fill with creamed mushrooms and roll on to hot service plate. Garnish top with 2 mushrooms which have been sautéed in butter, tip with a sprig of parsley. Serve at once.

*Creamed mushrooms are made by adding 1/3 cup Cream Sauce to 2 tbs. chopped mushrooms which have been sautéed in butter and bringing mixture to a boil.

SCRAMBLED EGGS LITTLE HAT

SERVES 2

3 eggs
Salt
3 tbs. pastry cream

1 oz. butter
3 tbs. diced ham
1 tsp. green pepper, chopped
1 tsp. pimento, finely chopped

½ cup fresh corn, sautéed in
    butter
4 pork sausages

Beat eggs well in small mixing bowl, with salt to taste and pastry cream. In a heavy, smooth skillet heat butter. Add ham, green pepper and pimento and sauté 1 minute. Add eggs, stirring very lightly while shaking pan until eggs reach soft stage. Heap eggs on a heated service plate, arranging in neat circle. Form a ring of corn around eggs. Place very hot sausages, nicely browned, in center, on top of eggs. Garnish with watercress. Serve at once.

OMELETTE LOS FELIZ

SERVES 2

3 eggs	*Salt*	*12 orange sections*
1 drop vanilla	*¼ cup butter*	*2 tsp. shredded coconut*
1 tsp. sugar		*1 tsp. powdered sugar*

Beat eggs well in a medium-sized mixing bowl. Add vanilla, sugar and salt to taste. Heat butter in heavy skillet. Add eggs and make a French omelet. Roll on to heated service plate. On top of omelet place orange sections. Sprinkle all over with coconut and powdered sugar. Place under broiler until lightly browned.

SCRAMBLED EGGS MISSION INN, RIVERSIDE

SERVES 2

3 eggs	*3 oz. butter*	*¼ tsp. basil*
3 tbs. pastry cream	*6 chicken livers, blanched in milk*	*3 tbs. burgundy*
Salt	*3 large mushrooms, sliced*	*½ cup Brown Sauce*
	1 tbs. green onions, minced	

Beat eggs in small mixing bowl with cream and salt to taste. Heat 2 oz. butter in a small heavy skillet, saving about 1 oz. Add livers to the butter, then the mushrooms and sauté until nicely browned. Add onions and basil and sauté 1 minute more. Add wine which has been mixed with Brown Sauce and reduce by one-third. In another heavy smooth skillet heat the remaining butter and add the well-beaten eggs. Stir lightly while shaking pan until eggs reach the soft stage. Place the cooked eggs on a heated service plate in a neat circle. Around the eggs arrange chicken livers and mushrooms with sauce. Garnish with watercress. Serve at once.

POACHED EGGS BENEDICT

SERVES 1

2 eggs	*2 slices ham (cut and fried)*	*2 very thin slices truffle*
1 English muffin	*½ cup Sauce Hollandaise*	*(optional)*

Poach eggs in salted water until soft stage is reached. Split and toast muffin which has been dipped in butter. Arrange toasted muffin on heated service plate. Put a slice of ham on each half. Arrange egg on top. Cover with Sauce Hollandaise. Garnish top with thinly sliced truffles. Serve at once.

POACHED EGGS VIENNA

SERVES 1

2 eggs
1 cup pastry cream

2 pieces toast

1 oz. butter
4 slices crisp bacon

Poach eggs in hot salted water to soft stage. Heat cream. Place toast on deep hot service dish. Place eggs on top. Cover eggs and toast with hot cream. Add a dab of butter for each egg. Garnish crisscross with crisp bacon curls. Serve at once.

FRESNO OMELET

SERVES 4

1 cup raisins
½ cup sherry
3 eggs, separated

1 tsp. salt
2 cups cream or evaporated
     milk

4 tbs. cake flour
6 tbs. butter
6 tbs. sugar

Soak raisins in wine until they are plump. Beat egg yolks with salt, 2 tbs. sugar, cream and flour until well blended and smooth. Add wine and raisins and mix well. Beat whites stiff and add remainder of sugar. Beat again ½ minute. Fold into mixture and blend well. Divide in half. Cook like an omelet in butter. Do not fold, but turn and cook until golden brown on both sides. Sprinkle with cinnamon and sugar. Pull apart with fork for serving, which must be done immediately.

NOTE: Current health safety guidelines recommend caution when using raw eggs. This recipe is included as presented in 1st edition.

SCRAMBLED EGGS MONTEREY

SERVES 2

3 eggs
3 tbs. pastry cream
Salt

1 tbs. melted butter
1 artichoke bottom,
     finely diced

2 strips bacon, cut very fine
1 tbs. chives, minced
2 mushrooms, finely diced

Beat eggs in small mixing bowl with cream and salt to taste. Heat butter in heavy, smooth skillet and add mushrooms and artichoke. Sauté 3 minutes on slow fire. Add bacon, chives and eggs. Stir eggs lightly while shaking pan until eggs reach the soft stage. Heap in a neat circle on heated service plate. Garnish with watercress. Serve at once.

POACHED EGGS BEVERLY DERBY

SERVES 1

2 medium-sized tomatoes	*1 oz. butter*	*2 eggs*
Salt and pepper	*½ cup creamed ham*	*2 tbs. Sauce Hollandaise*

Turn tomatoes upside down and scoop out bottom part. Sprinkle lightly with salt and pepper to taste. Place in buttered baking dish and bake until quite tender in 400°[F] oven. Place tomatoes on heated service plate. Fill with hot creamed ham. Poach eggs in salted water to soft stage. Place egg on top of each tomato. Cover with Sauce Hollandaise. Serve at once.

POACHED EGGS GOLDEN GATE

SERVES 1

2 eggs	*2 slices tomato*	*½ cup Sauce Mornay*
	2 slices ham	

Bread tomato slices and fry in butter. Arrange on hot serving plate. On top of each place a small slice of ham cut to fit tomato slices. Poach eggs in a little water to soft stage; then place gently on top of ham. Cover with Sauce Mornay.

SHIRRED EGGS À LA SUISSE

SERVES 1

1/8 cup butter	*2 strips crisp bacon, finely chopped*	*1 oz. pastry cream*
2 eggs	*3 tbs. Swiss cheese, grated*	*1 tsp. chives, minced*

Generously butter a shirred-egg service dish and break in eggs. Sprinkle bacon and cheese around egg yolks and add pastry cream gently so as not to break the yolk. Bake in 350°[F] oven 5 minutes. Sprinkle with minced chives. Serve at once.

SHIRRED EGGS CARUSO

SERVES 1

2 oz. butter	*¼ tsp. basil*	*½ medium-sized tomato, diced*
6 chicken livers, blanched in milk	*3 tbs. burgundy*	
2 mushrooms, sliced	*4 tbs. Brown Sauce*	*2 eggs*

Heat half of butter in small, heavy skillet. Add blanched livers, mushrooms and basil. Sauté until mushrooms are browned. Add wine mixed with Brown Sauce and tomato. Cook until reduced by one-third. Break eggs into buttered shirred-egg service dish. Place chicken livers and sauce around the eggs being careful not to cover the yolks. Bake in 350°[F] oven 5 minutes only. Garnish with minced parsley. Serve at once.

Shirred-egg dishes are low and shallow, being about 5 in. across and less than an inch deep. They hold two eggs. Cocotte dishes are 2 in. deep, 3 across and hold one egg.

EGGS EN COCOTTE BROWN DERBY
SERVES 1

1 tsp. shallot, chopped fine (optional)	2 mushrooms, finely chopped	2 slices truffles, chopped (optional)
1/8 cup butter (1 oz.)	½ tsp. parsley, minced	2 eggs
	1/8 tsp. nutmeg	
	Salt	

Sauté shallot in heavy skillet with butter. Add mushrooms, parsley, nutmeg and salt to taste. Add truffles. Heat for 1 minute only. Place in 2 cocottes that have been buttered generously. On top of sauce break egg. Place cocottes in pan of boiling water. Bake in 350°[F] oven 10 minutes. Remove cocottes at once from water; place on service plate. Serve at once.

EGGS EN COCOTTE À LA REINE
SERVES 1

1 oz butter	½ cup creamed chicken	6 asparagus tips
2 eggs	with mushrooms	2 tbs. Sauce Hollandaise

Butter 2 cocotte cups generously. On bottom of each place half the creamed-chicken mixture. Break an egg into each. Place 3 small asparagus tips on each, taking care not to break yolk. Place cocottes in pan of boiling water. Bake in 350°[F] oven 8 minutes. Remove cocottes from water immediately. Place on heated service plate and cover each egg with 1 tbs. Hollandaise Sauce. Garnish with large sprig watercress. Serve at once.

EGGS EN COCOTTE SMOKY MOUNTAIN
SERVES 1

1 oz. butter	½ creamed smoked	2 tbs. American cheese,
2 eggs	turkey	finely chopped

Butter 2 cocotte cups very generously. Place in each ¼ cup creamed turkey. Break an egg on top and sprinkle with cheese. Place cocottes in pan of boiling water. Bake in 350°[F] oven 10 minutes. Remove immediately from water and place cocotte cups on heated service plate. Garnish with a sprig of watercress. Serve at once.

EGGS EN COCOTTE BUCKINGHAM
SERVES 1

1/8 cup butter (1 oz.)	2 eggs	2 tbs. bread croutons, well
½ cup creamed ham	1 tbs. Parmesan cheese	browned

Butter 2 cocottes generously. Into each place ¼ cup creamed ham. Break egg on top of ham. Sprinkle with bread croutons and cheese. Place cocottes in pan of boiling water. Bake in 350°[F] oven 10 minutes. Remove cocottes from water and place on doily-covered serving plate. Garnish with parsley. Serve at once.

EGGS PRINCESS ALICE

SERVES 1

1 slice Pullman or sandwich bread, 1-in. thick	*1 egg*	*3 asparagus tips*
Melted butter	*1 slice bacon, cooked*	*2 tbs. Sauce Hollandaise*
	2 tbs. sliced mushrooms, sautéed	*½ tsp. chives*

Leave crust on bread; cut out center with round cutter, approximately 2½ inches wide. Soak bread in melted butter and place in hot skillet. Break egg, breaking yolk, into hole in bread. Place bacon and mushrooms on top of egg and sauté on slow fire for about 3 minutes. Turn over carefully, so as not to spill egg and sauté 3 minutes on other side. Turn back over and place on hot serving plate. Garnish top with asparagus tips, cover with Sauce Hollandaise and sprinkle with chives.

LUNCHEON AND SUPPER COMBINATIONS

For Sunday-night suppers, luncheons, casserole or one-dish meals and light dinners, The Brown Derby suggests some of the unusual entrees which are combinations of several foods, with sauces that blend them together, served in an interesting manner.

MELTED CHEESE WITH FRIED SHRIMP
SERVES 6

6 English muffins, split and
toasted

12 fried shrimp, breaded
3 cups Welsh Rabbit

Place half of muffin on heated plate. Alongside arrange 2 fried shrimp. Cover muffin with rabbit; cap with remaining half muffin. Cover with rabbit. Must be served on very hot plate as soon as possible.

MELTED CHEESE WITH CHIPPED BEEF
SERVES 6

6 English muffins, split and
toasted

3 cups Welsh Rabbit
1/5 lb. chipped beef

Place half a muffin on heated plate and cover with Welsh Rabbit. Put other half of muffin on top and cover again with rabbit. Sprinkle with small pieces of chipped beef which have been blanched in water.

DERBY PASTA RING

SERVES 4

8 oz spaghetti	*1 tsp. Worcestershire Sauce*	*¼ cup finely minced parsley*
¼ lb. grated cheese (equal	*1½ tsp. salt*	*½ tsp. paprika*
parts Parmesan and		*2 tbs. onion juice*
American		*2 eggs, separated and beaten*

Cook spaghetti in boiling salted water 15 minutes. Drain and force through a potato ricer. Add cheese, seasonings and beaten egg yolks. Fold in the stiffly beaten egg whites. Pour into a buttered and floured ring mold. Place in a pan of water. Bake in a 325°[F] oven 40 minutes. Turn out on hot plate. Fill center and cover ring with Creole Shrimp. Serve at once.

MELTED CHEESE WITH SMOKED TURKEY

SERVES 6

6 English muffins, split and	*1 cup smoked turkey julienne*
toasted	*3 cups Welsh Rabbit*

Place half muffin on very hot service plate. Along the sides place turkey. Cover muffin with hot rabbit. Top with remaining half of muffin and then with rabbit. Serve at once. Keeping the dishes very hot is the secret of a fine rabbit.

SPAGHETTI WITH SMALL SIRLOIN BALLS
AND MUSHROOMS

SERVES 4

1½ lbs. ground sirloin of beef	*1 cup chopped onion*	*3 cups cooked spaghetti*
½ cup butter	*¾ cup white wine*	*¾ cup Brown Derby*
1 cup mushrooms	*1½ cups Brown Gravy*	*Tomato Sauce*

Make very small balls of seasoned ground beef. Sauté in butter in heavy skillet.. Add mushrooms and onion. Add white wine, reduce by one-third and add Brown Gravy. Serve in a heated casserole over hot cooked spaghetti which has been tossed in hot Tomato Sauce.

SPAGHETTI CACCIATORA WITH VEAL CUTLETS

SERVES 4

2 lbs. veal in 8 cutlets
½ cup butter
4 tbs. green onion, finely chopped
½ cup mushrooms, sliced

2 tbs. celery, finely chopped
6 peperonicini, finely chopped
1 large tomato, finely chopped
¼ tsp. basil

½ clove garlic
½ cup burgundy
1 cup Brown Sauce
3 cups cooked spaghetti

Sauté floured and seasoned cutlets in butter, using brisk heat. Remove to heated platter. In same skillet place onion, mushrooms and celery and sauté lightly. Add peperoncini, tomato, basil and garlic. Sauté 2 minutes longer. Add wine and reduce one-half. Add Brown Sauce and simmer 5 minutes. Arrange cutlets in heated casserole which has been filled three-fourths with cooked hot spaghetti. Bring sauce to brisk boil and serve over all.

SPAGHETTI DERBY HOUSE

SERVES 6

1 lb. veal in small cutlets
4 oz. butter
1 lb. sweetbreads
12 button mushrooms

12 pork sausage, browned
1 clove garlic, finely chopped
¼ tsp. basil
½ cup white wine
1 cup Brown Sauce

1 lb. spaghetti
1 cup Brown Derby
Tomato Sauce
1 tbs. chives, finely chopped

Veal should be beaten thin, floured and seasoned with salt and pepper. Heat butter in medium -sized heavy skillet. Add veal and sweetbreads and brown on both sides. Add mushrooms and pork sausages that have been precooked a little. Sauté until mushrooms are brown. Add garlic, basil and wine. Reduce one-half. Add Brown Sauce. Simmer until veal cutlets are well done. You may remove pork sausages and sweetbreads before this, so as not to overcook them.

Cook spaghetti for 10 minutes and mix with Tomato Sauce. Place in deep casserole. Cover top of spaghetti alternately with veal cutlets, sweetbreads and pork sausages. Garnish with mushrooms, glaze with the sauce and sprinkle with chives.

STUFFED TOMATO WITH CHICKEN

SERVES 6

6 large tomatoes
3 cups chicken croquette paste

1 cup Cheddar or American
cheese, finely chopped
1 tsp. paprika

1 bell pepper, in 6 rings
1/8 lb. butter
2 cups White Mushroom Sauce

Cut off bottoms and scoop out one-third inside meat of tomatoes. Salt and pepper lightly. Fill tomatoes with chicken croquette paste. Sprinkle with cheese and paprika. Place ring of green pepper on top. Bake in buttered pan in 375°[F] oven for 25 minutes. Serve with White Mushroom Sauce.

STUFFED ARTICHOKE BOTTOMS WITH LAMB
PEBBLE BEACH

SERVES 4

1/8 lb. butter	½ cup burgundy	2 cups rice, cooked
1 lb. lamb filet, finely chopped	½ cup clear stock	2 medium-sized tomatoes,
½ medium-sized onion	Salt and pepper	peeled, sliced, breaded
¼ tsp. basil	8 artichokes, bottoms only	and fried
2 tbs. flour		1 cup American cheese, grated

Heat butter in medium-sized heavy skillet. Add lamb and brown evenly. Add onion and basil and sauté a few minutes longer. Add flour and blend well. Add wine, stock and salt and pepper to taste. Simmer on slow fire 5 minutes. Keep hot. Heat artichoke bottoms in salt water.

Arrange a neat bed of rice in center of plate. Place fried tomato slices on top. On top of each slice of tomato, place artichoke bottom filled with lamb and sauce. Sprinkle with American cheese. Melt cheese under broiler. Serve.

STUFFED ARTICHOKE BOTTOMS PRINCESS
SERVES 6

12 artichoke bottoms	24 asparagus tips	1 tsp. paprika
¼ cup butter	½ cup American cheese,	12 pimentos in inch-long
2 cups chicken croquette paste	sliced thin, 1-in	strips
in balls	square pieces	1½ cups Sauce Suprême

Arrange artichoke bottoms in buttered baking dish. Fill hollowed parts with paste balls. Press down lightly. Place 2 small asparagus tips on top of each and over them lay slice of cheese and sprinkle lightly with paprika. Bake in 325°[F] oven 12 minutes. Arrange on heated plate. Put strip of pimento on top of each stuffed artichoke bottom for garnish. Serve with hot Sauce Suprême.

STUFFED BELL PEPPERS
SERVES 4

4 large bell peppers	4 tbs. Cheddar cheese, finely	3 cups rice, cooked
2 cups chicken croquette paste	chopped	2 cups Mushroom Sauce
	½ cup butter, melted	

Slice off the bottoms and remove seeds from peppers. Stuff with chicken croquette paste. Press chopped cheese on top of paste. Arrange peppers in buttered casserole which is just large enough to hold them upright. Do not allow them to fall over. Pour melted butter over and bake in 375°[F] oven 25 minutes. Serve peppers in individual rice rings that have been filled with hot Mushroom Sauce.

MUSHROOMS AND CHICKEN CHEF'S DELIGHT
SERVES 4

¼ cup butter
½ lb. fresh mushroom, sliced
1 cup white wine
2 cups Sauce Mornay

½ cup pastry cream
8 slices chicken, white
*   or dark meat*
½ cup chicken broth
1 tsp. paprika

4 English muffins,
*   split and toasted*
1 cup American cheese,
*   finely chopped*

Heat butter in heavy skillet. Add mushrooms and sauté until tender. Add wine and reduce by two-thirds. Add Sauce Mornay and cream. Reduce by one-quarter. Keep warm over hot water (or in double boiler). Heat chicken in chicken broth. Arrange toasted muffins on heated plate. Cover with chicken and sauce. Sprinkle cheese on top, dust paprika lightly and brown under broiler. Serve at once.

FRESH MUSHROOMS SAUTÉ GEORGIAN
SERVES 2

3 oz. butter
½ lb. washed button mushrooms
1 tbs. raw Virginia ham julienne

1 tbs. roasted peanuts
½ cup white wine
Juice of ½ lemon

1/3 cup Brown Sauce
1 English muffin, split and
*   toasted*

Heat 2 oz. butter in skillet. Add mushrooms and sauté about 5 minutes, stirring to brown evenly. Add ham and sauté 10 minutes more. Add peanuts. Sauté 1 to 2 minutes more. Add white wine and lemon juice. Reduce by two-thirds. Add Brown Sauce. Simmer on slow fire for 5 minutes. Add remaining ounce solid butter. Mix well. Divide equally onto the English muffin halves. Serve.

FRESH MUSHROOMS BERCY AND
ASPARAGUS HOLLANDAISE ON HAM
SERVES 4

4 English muffins, halved
*   and toasted*

8 thin sliced Virginia ham,
*   fried or baked*
1 lb. Mushroom Buttons Bercy

1 lb. asparagus tips, cooked
½ cup Sauce Hollandaise

Place half of toasted muffin on heated plate. Arrange ham on top and mushrooms on top of ham. Pour Sauce Bercy over mushrooms. On other half muffin arrange asparagus in neat pile. Top with Sauce Hollandaise. Serve immediately.

FRESH ASPARAGUS MORNAY WITH HAM
SERVES 2

4 horseshoe cuts ham,
*   baked or fried*

1 lb. asparagus, cooked

1½ cups Sauce Mornay
1 tsp. paprika

Fry or heat ham. Heat asparagus in salt water. Heat Sauce Mornay in double boiler. Arrange two slices of ham on each plate. In center arrange half of asparagus and cover with sauce. Sprinkle with paprika and brown under broiler.

MUSHROOM, EGGPLANT, HAM, QUEEN SHEBA
SERVES 4

½ cup butter
1 lb. button mushrooms
½ cup white wine
2 tbs. brown mustard
1 tsp. black pepper
2 tbs. Worcestershire Sauce

2 tbs. chives, chopped
Juice ½ lemon
2 tbs. A-1 Sauce
1 cup Sauce Suprême
½ cup pastry cream

1 tsp. tarragon, finely chopped
½ cup Brown Gravy
Salt
4 eggplant slices, ½-inch thick
4 horseshoe-shaped ham
    slices (fried or baked)

Heat butter in heavy skillet. Add mushrooms and sauté until tender. Add wine and reduce by two-thirds. Add mustard, pepper, Worcestershire Sauce, chives, lemon juice, A-1 Sauce, Sauce Suprême, pastry cream, tarragon and Brown Gravy. Reduce by one-third. Add salt to taste. Keep warm over hot water. Bread eggplant slices. Fry in butter or oil until tender and golden brown. Then fry ham or heat baked ham. Arrange eggplant on heated plate. Top with ham, arrange mushrooms on ham and pour hot sauce over all. Serve at once.

FRESH ASPARAGUS ARDITH
SERVES 4

2 lbs. asparagus
¼ cup butter
8 oz. Virginia ham julienne

½ cup roasted peanuts
½ cup sweet white wine

2 cups pastry cream
5 egg yolks
8 small chicken croquettes

Cook asparagus in salted water. Heat butter in heavy skillet. Add ham and sauté until nearly crisp. Add roasted peanuts, wine and reduce by one-third. Add all of cream except 4 tbs. which is mixed with the egg yolks. Add egg mixture to thicken. Remove from heat. Fry chicken croquettes in deep fat. Arrange asparagus in center of plate, put 1 croquette on each side and cover all with ham and sauce. Serve immediately.

SLICED BREAST OF TURKEY DIVONNE PARISIENNE
SERVES 4

8 branches broccoli, cooked
1 cup American cheese, grated

8 large slices cooked turkey
    white meat

¼ tsp. paprika
3 cups Sauce Mornay

Drain cooked broccoli and arrange in bottom of casserole. Cover with slices of turkey and cover both completely with Sauce Mornay. Sprinkle with cheese and paprika and bake in moderate oven until brown (approximately 4 minutes).

FRESH ASPARAGUS CHEF'S DELIGHT
SERVES 4

½ cup butter
1 lb. mushrooms, sliced
1 cup white wine
½ cup pastry cream

2 cups Sauce Mornay
2 lb. asparagus, cooked
8 slices Virginia ham,
*   baked or fried*
1 tsp. paprika

1 cup Cheddar or American
*   cheese, finely chopped*
4 split English muffins
*   toasted**

Heat butter in heavy skillet. Add mushrooms and sauté until nearly done. Add white wine and reduce by two-thirds. Add cream and Sauce Mornay and blend well. Simmer 4 minutes. Remove from fire and keep hot. Heat asparagus in salted water. Toast muffins. Fry ham or heat baked ham. Arrange asparagus neatly on top of ham. Cover with sauce. Sprinkle cheese and paprika over top. Brown under broiler.

*If English muffins are not available, use toasted white bread.

JULIENNE OF TURKEY AND HAM HUSSARD
SERVES 6

3 oz. butter
1 cup Virginia ham julienne
1 cup mushrooms julienne
½ cup white wine
2 cups Cream Sauce

1 cup pastry cream
1 tsp. English mustard
2 cups turkey julienne, white
*   and dark meat*

2 medium-sized tomatoes,
*   peeled and sliced*
2 tbs. Sauce Hollandaise or
*   2 egg yolks*
1/8 tsp. cayenne pepper

Heat butter in heavy skillet. Add ham and mushrooms and brown lightly. Add white wine and reduce by two-thirds. Add Cream Sauce, cream and mustard. Blend well. Add turkey and simmer slowly for about 10 minutes. Add tomatoes and simmer again for 4 minutes. Thicken with Sauce Hollandaise or egg yolks. Sprinkle with cayenne pepper. Serve.

Chicken may be used in place of turkey.

BARBECUES

In Southern California, where outdoor living and outdoor eating have become almost a year-round custom, one of the most attractive modes of entertainment is the barbecue.

The national trend is toward cooking in the back yard, patio or garden for guests or family as a welcome change from more formal dinners or luncheons and many other parts of the country are adopting this pleasant way to eat during the warm season. For Americans everywhere are learning that there is a zest and flavor to a barbecue meal which come not only from the picnic atmosphere and the smell of charcoal and roasting, but from the hearty use of spices, herbs and condiments which give the food a Wild West aroma and the guest a sharp appetite.

Of course, an ideal barbecue has an electric revolving spit, but a barbecue pit need not be elaborate to get good results. Any combination of charcoal and iron grill will do. The important point is that the heat source be right. That means that the coals must be well burned out and glowing—one solid mass of fiery heat. Never use a burning fire.

The fire should burn from 1 to 1½ hours before any barbecuing is done over it. Light the charcoal or wood in ample time so that it will burn down to the coals stage. And keep a pail of water handy for fat drippings will ignite the coals and start a sputtering flame. In that case, douse quickly. If the coals are at the right stage, this will not kill the fire.

Barbecue small pieces very close to the fame—within two or three inches. If there is no rotator, larger pieces must be placed farther away, distance depending on size. Keep basting with the remainder of the marinade in which the meat or fish has been soaked. Use long-handled ladles and forks to work with. When done, large pieces should be kept in a warming oven until used. Small pieces should be prepared and timed to be eaten immediately. Steak, especially, should be barbecued so that they are finished when the guests are ready to start.

Beer is a traditional beverage to serve with barbecues. Good wines (cabernet, burgundy, etc cetera, with meat; sauterne with fish and chicken) also go well. An iced wine punch is another appropriate drink. However, a warning to the cook: Keep a clean head while barbecuing. It requires complete attention, good timing and a critical palate.

MEXICAN BARBECUE COLE SLAW
SERVES 8

1 head cabbage finely shredded
1 large onion, finely sliced
2 bell peppers, finely sliced

4 chorizo sausages,
finely sliced

1 cup Barbecue Mayonnaise
2 large pimentos, sliced

Place cabbage in mixing bowl. Sprinkle onion, sausage, peppers and pimento over slaw. Mix in 1 cup Barbecue Mayonnaise. (Old-fashioned French Dressing or Barbecue French Dressing may be used instead.) Serve at once.

BARBECUED CORN AND AVOCADO SALAD
SERVES 8

12 ears golden bantam corn
2 large avocados, peeled and diced

½ cup baked ham,
finely diced

1 tbs. chives
½ cup Barbecue Mayonnaise

Boil and cut corn from cob. Toss other ingredients well; add to corn and serve in salad bowl lined with lettuce leaves.

GARBANZO BEAN BARBECUE SALAD
SERVES 8

1 lb. garbanzos (chick-peas)
1 qt. beef stock
2 cloves garlic, finely chopped
½ cup green onion, finely chopped

½ cup crisp bacon, finely chopped
1 soaked Mexican chili pepper
or 1 tsp. chili powder

½ cup Barbecue French Dressing
Lettuce leaves
12 anchovy filets, finely
chopped (optional)

Boil garbanzos in beef stock or water until tender. Drain and allow to cool. Place in mixing bowl. Add garlic, onion, bacon, chili pepper or powder and mix with Barbecue French Dressing. Serve in bowl with pulled lettuce leaves. Sprinkle with chopped anchovies.,
    Canned chick-peas, already prepared, may be used instead of raw peas.
    Barbecue Lentil Salad is made in exactly the same way except that lentils are used instead of the garbanzos.

GARDEN VEGETABLES BARBECUE SALAD
SERVES 10 - 12

1 small head cauliflower
1 doz. small carrots, quartered
1 bunch celery cut in inch-
long pieces
12 zucchinis in inch-thick
slices

2 large onions, chopped
2 long Mexican chili pepper
julienne
6 small Mexican hot peppers
2 chili pods julienne
Salt

3 cloves garlic
20 crushed peppercorns
1 bay leaf
2 cups olive oil
2 cups wine vinegar
Water to cover vegetables

Place all vegetables in kettle. Add spices, oil, vinegar, salt and enough water barely to cover vegetables. Bring to boil, skim and boil 15 minutes. (Care should be taken not to cook the vegetables too well. They should still be crisp.) Let cool. Serve in salad bowl lined with lettuce leaves.

This salad is quite hot. To tone it down, omit the Mexican chili pepper.

SUCCULENT SALAD

Of course, a must for barbecue menus is a green salad. There is nothing so delicious as cold, crisp, crunchy head lettuce. Discard outer leaves and shred inner leaves with your hands. Never cut with knife. Place leaves in clean, dry towel on ice to chill for 2 hours. Just before serving, toss in wooden bowl with any of The Brown Derby salad dressings.

BARBECUE SALAD BOWL

Lettuce	*Chicory*	*French bread crust*
Romaine lettuce	*Quartered hard-cooked egg*	*Clove garlic*
Watercress	*Quartered tomatoes*	*Roquefort cheese dressing*

Fill mixing bowl with pulled lettuce, romaine lettuce in 1 in.-long pieces, pulled watercress and 1 in.-square pieces of chicory. Garnish with eggs and tomatoes. Cut off half-dollar-size pieces of crust from French bread. Rub each crust with clove of garlic on both sides. (These garlic crusts are called *chapeaux* by chefs.) Arrange them on top of salad. Serve with Roquefort cheese dressing.

BARBECUE LENTIL SALAD

SERVES 8

1 lb. lentils	*½ cup green onion finely chopped*	*½ cup Barbecue French*
1 qt. beef stock	*½ cup crisp bacon, chopped fine*	*Dressing*
2 cloves garlic finely chopped	*1 soaked Mexican chili pepper*	*Lettuce leaves*
	(or 1 tsp. chili powder)	

Boil lentils in stock until tender. Drain and allow to cool. Place in a mixing bowl. Add garlic, onion, bacon, chili pepper or powder. Mix with Barbecue French Dressing. Serve in a bowl garnished with pulled lettuce leaves.

BARBECUE FRENCH DRESSING, 1 pt.

2 cloves garlic, finely chopped	*1 medium-sized bell pepper*	*1 tsp. celery salt*
½ cup green onion, finely chopped	*julienne*	*1 pt. Brown Derby French*
1 tsp. barbecue spices	*3 eggs, well-beaten*	*Dressing*
	6 slices bacon, crisp,	
	finely chopped	

In a medium-sized bowl blend together garlic, green onion, spices, pepper, eggs and celery salt. While mixing sharply, add dressing very slowly. Finish by adding crisp, chopped bacon.

BARBECUE MAYONNAISE

SERVES 6 - 8

1 cup mayonnaise	1 tbs. finely chopped green onion	1/3 tsp. smoked salt
¼ tsp. coriander	½ tsp. chili powder	Juice 1 lemon
	¼ tsp. cominos	

Blend all ingredients well in mixing bowl. Use for salads, seafood and sandwiches.

* * *

The great secret of successful barbecuing is in the base or marinade used to pickle the meat or fish. Called upon to cater for many gala barbecue occasions, The Brown Derby years ago began to gather recipes for marinades. Some of these came from old-time chuck-wagon cooks, others from the famous Southern California and Mexico barbecue chefs who have followings comparable to movie stars. The Brown Derby chefs have tested these marinades and selected from them seven which cover every kind of barbecue.

* * *

BARBECUE MARINADE, 1 pt.

1 pt. oil	1 tbs. barbecue spices	1 sprig thyme
3 cloves garlic, finely chopped	15 peppercorns, crushed	4 green onions, finely chopped
Salt to taste	¼ tsp. basil	¼ tsp. celery salt

Mix ingredients in quart jar. Used to marinate shrimps, steaks, chops, liver, turkey steaks, chicken, quail or pheasant. Soak from 30 minutes to 1 hour, depending on size.

MARINADE FOR BARBECUED RAINBOW TROUT

SERVES 4

½ cup olive oil	1 tbs. salt	1 tsp. Worcestershire Sauce
½ cup white wine	1 tsp. celery salt	1 tsp. paprika
2 cloves garlic, finely chopped	1 tbs. barbecue spices	1 tbs. peppercorns, crushed

Mix all ingredients well. Also can be used for any other barbecued fish. For a different-flavored base, use the recipe which follows.

FISH BARBECUE MARINADE

1 cup oil
1 tbs. barbecue spices or
   chili powder
Juice of ½ lemon

1 tsp. smoked salt if chili
   powder is used
1 tbs. parsley, finely chopped

¼ tsp. orégano
¼ tsp. basil
Salt to taste
½ clove garlic

Place all ingredients in quart Mason jar and shake well to blend.

MARINADE FOR BARBECUED SHRIMP, 1 qt.

3 tbs. barbecue spices
3 cloves garlic, finely chopped
2 cups white wine

1 medium-sized onion, sliced
1 medium-sized bell pepper,
   sliced
1 tbs. whole black peppercorns

1 tbs. salt
1 cup water
1½ cups olive oil

Mix barbecue spices, garlic, wine, onion, pepper, peppercorns and salt well in large bowl. Add water and olive oil. Keep in refrigerator when not in use.

MARINADE FOR BARBECUED POULTRY
SERVES 12

1 cup oil
1 tsp. Derby Barbecue Spice
½ cup white wine

1 tbs. white vinegar
1 clove garlic, finely chopped

10 whole peppercorns
Salt to taste
¼ tsp. basil

Place all ingredients in a tightly sealed Mason jar and mix well. Soak pieces of poultry in this marinade for 20 minutes, then broil on charcoal.

WILD-GAME BARBECUE MARINADE

1 cup oil
½ cup red wine
¼ tsp. orégano
1 tsp. smoked salt

¼ tsp. basil
12 whole peppercorns, crushed
2 cloves garlic, finely chopped

½ onion, finely chopped
1 bay leaf
¼ tsp. coriander

Shake all ingredients together in a tightly sealed Mason jar, mixing well. Soak wild game in this marinade. The size and age of game govern time required for marinating, from 20 minutes to 1½ hours; the older and larger, the longer.

BARBECUED LAMB MARINADE

1 tbs. mint leaves, finely chopped
6 cloves
15 peppercorns, crushed

1 stick cinnamon
Salt
1 tbs. parsley, finely chopped

1 twig rosemary
1 cup salad oil
1 cup dry white wine

Mix together, blending well.

In addition to these marinades, here are two Mexican Salsas. These are hot, sour, nippy, chopped sauces for barbecued meat or fish. They may be used as condiments, on roasts, or as marinades before barbecuing. The first one is easy to prepare and not so sharp as the second.

HOT MEXICAN SALSA
SERVES 4 - 8

1 cup olive oil
1 medium-sized onion,
    finely chopped
2 tsp. chili powder or 4 dry
    Mexican chili pods
1 clove garlic, finely chopped
1 bell pepper, finely chopped
¼ tsp. cominos

¼ tsp. coriander
¼ tsp. orégano
½ cup white vinegar
½ cup string beans,
    finely sliced
2 drops Tabasco (more if hot
    sauce is desired)

4 medium-sized tomatoes,
    diced
2 tbs. pimento, finely chopped
1 cup corn cut from cob
1 cup clear stock
1 tbs. parsley, finely chopped
4 chorizo sausages, peeled and
    sliced

Heat oil in heavy deep kettle. Add onion, chili powder, garlic, pepper, cominos, coriander, orégano and chorizo sausages and brown lightly. Add vinegar, string beans, Tabasco, tomatoes, pimento, corn and clear stock. Simmer 15 minutes. Sprinkle with parsley. Serve hot or cold.

MEXICAN SALSA FOR BARBECUE
SERVES 4 - 8

4 strips bacon, finely chopped
½ cup olive oil
1 medium-sized onion,
    finely chopped
1 green pepper julienne

1 tsp. chili powder
1 clove garlic finely chopped
¼ tsp. orégano
¼ tsp. coriander
½ cup vinegar

15 ripe olives, pitted and sliced
1 avocado, peeled and diced
4 tomatoes, peeled and diced
1 cup clear stock or water

Sauté together bacon and olive oil in heavy deep kettle. Add onion, pepper, chili powder, garlic, orégano and coriander and brown lightly. Add vinegar, olives, avocado, tomatoes and clear stock. Simmer 20 minutes on slow fire. This sauce may be served either hot or cold.

BARBECUED SHRIMP

Peel raw shrimp, split lengthwise, and clean. Soak for 2 hours in Marinade for Barbecued Shrimp; remove and broil.

BARBECUED RAINBOW TROUT

SERVES 4

4 large rainbow trout

Marinade for Barbecued Rainbow Trout

Cover whole, cleaned trout with marinade for about 30 minutes. Remove and barbecue on brisk charcoal fire or under open gas flame. Serve with melted butter and lemon.

BARBECUED SALMON STEAKS

SERVES 2 - 3

1 lb. salmon, cut in 2 steaks

4 tbs. Brown Derby Fish Barbecue Marinade

1 cup cooked rice

Marinate the salmon steaks in the Fish Barbecue Marinade for about 30 minutes. Broil under gas broiler or on charcoal grill about 8 minutes on each side. Serve with rice and melted butter or Brown Derby Barbecued Fish Butter.

* * *

This is what Dinah Shore dashes into The Hollywood Derby to eat after she finishes a broadcast or a recording date.

* * *

BARBECUED JUMBO CRABS

SERVES 6

3 large crabs
1 cup oil

1 tsp. barbecue seasoning
½ tsp. chopped marjoram
½ tsp. paprika

1 tsp. celery salt
½ tsp. crushed peppercorns

Remove tops from crabs and wash well. Crack the legs open slightly. Mix oil and spice ingredients together. Dip crabs in the oil-spice mixture or brush with the mixture. Broil on fast charcoal fire about 4 minutes on each side. Crabs should be brushed frequently with the oil-spice mixture while broiling. Serve with barbecue mayonnaise and lemon.

Puget Sound Dungeness, Alaska or even soft-shell crabs may be used. If the latter, use more crabs.

BUTTER FOR BARBECUED FISH

SERVES 4 - 8

¼ lb. soft butter
½ tsp. chili powder or
barbecue spices

Juice of ½ lemon
1 tsp. parsley, finely chopped

¼ avocado, mashed through fine sieve
1 tsp. Worcestershire Sauce

Blend together butter, lemon juice, chili powder, parsley, avocado and Worcestershire Sauce. Serve over barbecued fish.

CALIFORNIA PARADISE BARBECUE SAUCE
SERVES 4

1 cup port
1 bay leaf
12 whole peppercorns
½ cup currant jelly

Juice of 2 oranges
1 cup Brown Sauce
¼ tsp. cayenne pepper
¼ tsp. ginger

6 tangerines, peeled and in
　sections
Salt and pepper
1/8 lb. (¼ cup) butter

Place wine, bay leaf and peppercorns in a heavy sauté pan and reduce one-half. Add currant jelly, orange juice, Brown Sauce, cayenne pepper and ginger and simmer 15 minutes. Strain through fine sieve. Bring to a boil again. Add tangerines, salt and pepper to taste. Finish sauce by adding butter slowly while stirring vigorously. This is a sweet sauce for duck, goose, squab or spareribs.

CALIFORNIA BARBECUE SAUCE (COLD)
SERVES 4

1 cup chili sauce
1 cup catsup
2 tbs. green onions, finely chopped
1 tbs. chili powder
1 tbs. olive oil
1 tbs. parsley, finely chopped

½ tsp. basil, finely chopped
1 tbs. Worcestershire Sauce
1 tsp. English mustard
1 tbs. green pepper,
　finely chopped
¼ avocado, diced small

1 tbs. green olives,
　finely chopped
1 clove garlic, finely chopped
1 tsp. smoked salt
Salt and pepper to taste

Shake all ingredients in a tightly sealed jar. Allow to stand 20 minutes before serving. Used as condiment with cold meats and cheeses.

RUSSIAN BARBECUE SAUCE, 1½ pts.

½ cup fat pork, diced
½ onion, finely chopped
¼ lb. mushrooms, sliced

½ clove garlic, finely chopped
¼ tsp. orégano
1/3 cup white wine
1 tbs. horseradish

1 cup tomato purée
Salt and pepper
1 cup sour cream

Heat pork in heavy sauté pan. Add onion and mushrooms. Brown lightly and add garlic, orégano and white wine and reduce one-half. Add horseradish, tomato purée and salt and pepper to taste. Simmer 7 minutes. Add sour cream and reheat. Serve with poultry, pork and fish.

CALIFORNIA OLIVE SAUCE, 1 pt.

3 beads shallot, minced (optional)
1 tbs. peppercorns
1 cup burgundy

2 cups Brown Sauce
Juice of ½ lemon
Salt

4 tbs. black olives, pitted and
　finely chopped

Heat shallot in small saucepan with peppercorns and wine. Allow to reduce by two-thirds. Remove peppercorns and add Brown Sauce, olives, lemon juice and salt to taste. Simmer 10 minutes.

This is delightful with barbecued poultry.

Here are two barbecue sauces. The first is Mexican in character and the second, more complicated to prepare, is a chutney type sauce.

BROWN DERBY BARBECUE SAUCE 1 qt. approximately

3 cups catsup
3 chili peppers, soaked,
    finely chopped
1 tsp. English mustard

1 tsp. black pepper, freshly ground
3 oz. barbecued spices
1 tbs. Worcestershire Sauce
1 clove garlic, whole

1 medium-sized onion, halved
¼ cup lemon juice
1 bay leaf
1 cup vegetable oil

Mix all ingredients. Use large jar with tight cover. When ready to serve, remove garlic, onion and bay leaf. Shake well before using.

DERBY BARBECUE SAUCE DE LUXE
SERVES 8 - 12

1 cup burgundy
1 bay leaf
1 tbs. peppercorns
½ cup wine vinegar
1 qt. Brown Sauce

1 tsp. orégano
2 tbs. paprika
1 tbs. chili powder
2 tbs. brown mustard
2 cloves garlic, chopped

1 tsp. coriander
1 tsp. basil
1 cup chili sauce
1 cup catsup
1 cup sweet relish

Place wine, bay leaf, peppercorns and vinegar in heavy kettle. Reduce by two-thirds. Add Brown Sauce, orégano, paprika, chili powder, mustard, garlic, coriander, basil, chili sauce, catsup and sweet relish. Cook gently 40 minutes. Strain through fine sieve.

Uses: Barbecued meats, fish, shrimp and chicken.

FRIJOLES BLANCO CON CHORIZO
(WHITE BEANS WITH SPANISH SAUSAGE)
SERVES 6

2 cups white beans
1 onion, minced
1 clove garlic, minced
¼ cup oil (preferably olive oil)

¼ cup chopped parsley
3 tbs. tomato sauce
6 cups warm water

3 chorizos Españoles or other
    highly seasoned
    sausages
Salt and pepper

Wash beans. Let soak overnight. Drain. Fry onion and garlic in oil until soft. Add parsley, tomato sauce, water, beans, whole chorizos. Cook, covered, until beans are tender (about 2 hours). Taste before adding salt and pepper because chorizos sometimes supply sufficient seasoning.

MARINATED ONION RINGS AND SLICED TOMATOES

Slice onions as thin as possible and lay them in 2-in.-deep pan. Sprinkle with a little sugar. Cover with Brown Derby Old-fashioned French Dressing. Add a little more wine vinegar. Marinate for about an hour. Arrange sliced ripe tomatoes on lettuce leaves on a chilled flat plate. Cover tomatoes with marinated onion rings. Sprinkle with chives. Serve. Mighty tasty for buffets, salads—and beer parties.

BARBECUED ONION SLICES

SERVES 4

2 large onions, sliced
2 tbs. oil

¼ tsp. orégano
Celery salt to taste

½ tsp. paprika
1 tsp. wine vinegar

Cut onions in ½-in.-thick slices. Soak in oil, orégano, celery salt, paprika and vinegar. Barbecue on slow charcoal fire. Good with barbecued steaks and salads.

BARBECUED EGGPLANT

SERVES 4

2 eggplants
3 tbs. oil
½ clove garlic, finely chopped

½ tsp. paprika
4 crushed peppercorns

¼ tsp. orégano
Salt

Peel eggplants and slice into ½-in.-thick pieces. Place slices in marinade made of oil, garlic, paprika, peppercorns, orégano and salt to taste. Marinate 7 minutes. Broil on slow charcoal fire.

Barbecue Zucchini is prepared similarly, except the zucchini is not peeled.

Both go well with barbecued meat, fowl or fish.

CORN ON THE COB BARBECUE

SERVES 4

8 ears corn with husks

Use very fresh corn in the husk. Cut off part of the stem and part of the top. Place ears on medium charcoal fire, turning frequently. Broil from 15 to 20 minutes. Pull off husks and serve with plenty of melted, seasoned butter.

PICKLED MUSHROOMS FOR BARBECUE

SERVES 8 - 10

12 whole peppercorns
½ cup salad oil
1 cup wine vinegar

1 cup water
2 cloves garlic, chopped
1 tsp. chili powder
¼ tsp. basil

Salt
1 bay leaf
2 lbs. mushrooms, washed

Mix together peppercorns, oil, vinegar, water, garlic, chili powder, basil, salt to taste, and bay leaf. Pour over mushrooms. Boil on slow fire 30 minutes. Allow to cool in broth. Drain before servings. If they are to be kept in refrigerator, store mushrooms, covered with broth, in glass jar.

An excellent hors d'oeuvre at a barbecue or cold buffet.

BARBECUED SQUAB

SERVES 4

4 1-lb. squabs
1 cup Barbecue Marinade
¼ lb. butter

6 beads shallots, finely chopped
    (optional)
1 tsp. chives, finely chopped

1 tsp. chervil, finely chopped
1 tsp. Worcestershire Sauce

Split squabs down the back and open. Clean. Remove breastbone. Dip squabs in any of the Barbecue Marinades except for fish. Soak 40 minutes. Place in hand broiler and broil over brisk charcoal broiler or fast gas flame until tender and brown. This should take about 30 minutes. While broiling it is necessary to turn frequently to avoid charring, also to baste every 4 minutes with the marinade.

Heat butter in heavy skillet. Add shallot and brown lightly. Then add chives, chervil and Worcestershire Sauce. Cook 1 minute. Pour sauce over the broiled squabs.

BARBECUED CHICKEN

Use 4-pound chicken, washed and cleaned. Soak in Poultry Marinade for 2 hours. Put on spit of rotating roaster and turn for 2½ hours. Use the drippings to make a sauce by thickening with flour or cornstarch and adding tomato purée or catsup.

BARBECUED TURKEY À LA LOS ANGELES

SERVES 12

This recipe is for the home that has a mechanical barbecue or one of the new electrical spits, since the turkey must be turned continuously for 3 hours.

1 16-lb. turkey
2 bunches celery
1/3 cup barbecue spices
2 cups white wine

2 cups olive oil
2 cloves garlic
1 tbs. basil, crushed
2 tbs. wine vinegar
2 cups water

1 lb. pork belly, thinly sliced
    sliced
Salt and pepper
1 qt. Barbecue Sauce

Salt and pepper outside as well as inside of drawn and cleaned turkey. Stuff with celery branches. This is done so bird will not collapse or dry out. Place in roasting pan. Mix barbecue spices, white wine, olive oil, garlic, basil, wine vinegar and water in medium-sized mixing bowl, blending well. Pour this over turkey and marinate 3 hours, turning and basting bird frequently. Then cover the breast as well as the back of the bird with thin slices of pork belly, securing them with skewer needles. Salt and pepper to taste. Tie turkey securely with string and place on barbecue skewer. Turkey should be turned over medium-hot charcoal fire for from 3 to 4 hours, basting every 15 minutes with marinade. When well done, serve with Barbecue Sauce.

BARBECUED CALF'S LIVER STEAK
WITH ONION SLICES

SERVES 4

2 lbs. calf's liver in 4 slices
1/3 cup oil
12 peppercorns, crushed

Salt
¼ tsp. orégano

2 tbs. onion, finely chopped
2 large onions cut in
    ¼-in. slices

Remove all sinews and skin from liver. Dip in mixture of oil, pepper, salt, orégano and onion. Broil on hot charcoal fire or under gas broiler. Dip the sliced onion in the same mixture and broil along with liver. Serve onions on the side.

MEXICAN BARBECUED LAMB

SERVES 8 - 10

1 8-lb. leg of lamb   Barbecued Lamb Marinade

Leg of lamb should be French trimmed and skinned, then placed in a deep pan and covered with Barbecued Lamb Marinade. Marinate for 3 hours, turning lamb frequently, as marinade will not cover. Begin cooking on a fast charcoal fire and sear evenly. Finish on a slow fire until done, basting repeatedly with marinade while barbecuing.

LAMB KABOB

SERVES 4

2 lbs. leg of lamb, skin and fat
    removed, in strips ½ inch
    thick and 1 inch wide
¼ tsp. orégano

Salt
8 whole peppercorns, crushed
1 clove garlic
2 tomatoes, quartered

8 small onions, peeled
4 strips bacon in inch-long
    pieces
1 eggplant, cut like lamb

Blanch pieces of lamb in cold water with a little salt. Bring to brisk boil and remove. Wash well. Rub lamb with oregano, salt, pepper and garlic. Arrange meat and vegetables on brochette needles in following order: Piece of lamb, tomato, onion, bacon, eggplant; repeat until brochette is full. Barbecue on medium charcoal fire.

BARBECUED LAMB KABOB

SERVES 6

2 lbs. leg of lamb or boned
    breast of lamb
2 cups sour red wine (or burgundy
    with 2 tbs. vinegar added)
3 cloves garlic
2 bay leaves

½ tsp. orégano, ground
½ tsp. basil, ground
1 tsp. celery salt
3 medium-sized onions, cut in
    1-in. pieces

½ cup olive oil
15 whole black peppercorns
1 tsp. paprika
12 slices bacon
3 tomatoes
24 button mushrooms

Cut meat into 1-in. long and ½-in.-thick pieces. Place in crock. Add wine, garlic, bay leaves, orégano, basil, celery salt, onions, olive oil, peppercorns and paprika. Keep in cool place 6 hours. Blanch bacon lightly and cut into square pieces. Cut tomatoes into 6 pieces, seed and remove part of inside. Arrange on 6 brochette needles in following manner: A mushroom, then a piece each of tomato, pickled onion, bacon, mushroom again; repeat until brochette is full. Put on brisk charcoal fire or under gas broiler. Should be basted with pickling marinade 2 or 3 times while cooking.

BARBECUED LEG OF LAMB
SERVES 8 - 10

1 5- or 6-lb. leg of lamb	*1½ cups burgundy*	*6 sprigs parsley*
6 small cloves garlic	*¼ tsp. basil*	*½ onion cut in small pieces*
1 lb. sow belly in thin slices	*¼ tsp. orégano*	*1 tbs. barbecue spices*
1 cup olive oil		*½ clove garlic, finely chopped*

Skin leg of lamb. Salt and pepper lightly. Insert garlic cloves evenly around lamb. Roll thin slice of sow belly around leg and tie securely with thin wire. Place leg in deep pan. Place olive oil, wine, basil, orégano, parsley, onion, barbecue spices and chopped garlic in mixing bowl and mix well. Pour this barbecue marinade over lamb. Marinate 3 hours. Leg should be turned frequently. Then brown the leg of lamb on brisk charcoal fire as fast as possible. When brown, remove from brisk heat and finish cooking on slow fire. While lamb is barbecuing, it should be basted frequently with the marinade. Cooking time: 1½—2 hours. Serve with Brown Derby Barbecue Sauce.

BARBECUED BREAST OF LAMB
SERVES 8

8 lbs. breast of lamb	*2 cups Barbecued Lamb Marinade*	*2 cups Brown Derby Barbecue Sauce*

Soak lamb in marinade 30 minutes. Barbecue on medium charcoal fire (approximately 2 hours). While barbecuing, baste the meat with the remaining marinade. When done, serve with Brown Derby Barbecue Sauce.

BARBECUED BEEF MEXICAN STYLE
SERVES 6

3 sour oranges	*1 twig thyme*	*Salt*
2 cloves garlic	*1 cup salad oil*	*6 lbs. beef, New York sirloin,*
2 bay leaves	*12 whole peppercorns,*	*boned and trimmed*
1 twig rosemary	*crushed*	

Chop the oranges very fine, also using the peel. Add garlic, bay leaves, rosemary, thyme, salad oil, peppercorns and salt to taste. Mix well. This is the marinade. Place beef in shallow pan. Cover with marinade and marinate 1 hour. Barbecue on fast fire. Baste repeatedly with marinade.

BARBECUED HAMBURGER STEAKS
SERVES 8

2 raw eggs
½ cup celery, finely chopped
½ cup onion, finely chopped

1 tsp. chili powder
1 tbs. Worcestershire Sauce
1 tsp. English mustard
Salt and pepper

1 peeled tomato, finely
   chopped
4 lbs. ground round steak

Mix eggs, celery, onion, chili powder, Worcestershire Sauce, mustard, salt and pepper and tomato. Add meat and blend well. Mold into desired size and shape. Barbecue on a well-oiled grill.

BARBECUED HAM CALIFORNIA
SERVES 12 - 15

1 12 - 14 lb. tenderized ham

To save time and insure thorough cooking, parboil ham in water for about 1 hour. Cool slightly, trim excess fat, and stick with cloves about 1 inch apart. Barbecue 20 minutes to the pound on slow fire, basting with Ham Barbecue Mixture every 10 minutes.

HAM BARBECUE MIXTURE

1 cup honey
Juice of 4 oranges

½ cup orange peel, cut very fine
¼ cup mild vinegar

1 tsp. hickory smoke salt
3 cups water

Mix well and use for basting.

BARBECUED SPARERIBS - On Grill or Spit
SERVES 10

8 lbs. spareribs

2 cups Barbecue Marinade

2 cups Brown Derby
   Barbecue Sauce

Spareribs should soak in the marinade 30 minutes and then be barbecued on medium charcoal fire from 40 to 50 minutes. Keep basting with the remaining marinade. When done, serve with Barbecue Sauce.

However, if grill or spit is not available, below is a recipe which can be made in any kitchen.

BARBECUED SPARERIBS
In the Oven - With Sauce

SERVES 4 - 10

8 lbs. spareribs
1 cup catsup
1 cup claret or burgundy
¼ cup vinegar
½ cup water

2 tbs. brown sugar
¼ tsp. cayenne pepper or
      Tabasco Sauce
1 tsp. English mustard

1 tsp. chili powder (optional)
1 onion, grated
2 tbs. Worcestershire Sauce
½ tsp. smoked salt
1 tsp. celery seed

Cook ribs for 7 minutes in 400°[F] oven. Combine all ingredients except celery seed and pour over ribs. Reduce to 350°[F] and bake for 45 minutes, basting occasionally. Then sprinkle with more smoked salt and the celery seed. Bake 15 minutes longer or until well done. Serves 4 as a main dish.

As an appetizer or with drinks, place cooked ribs on a rack in an open pan and heat slowly in oven or over grill until hot and fairly dry. Cut ribs apart and serve with plenty of paper napkins. Enough for 8 to 10.

BARBECUE BUTTER FOR FRENCH BREAD
(TOASTED)

SERVES 10

1 lb. soft butter
2 cloves garlic, finely chopped

1 tbs. Worcestershire Sauce
1 tbs. chives, finely chopped

1 tbs. parsley, finely chopped
1 tsp. celery salt

Place butter in mixing bowl. Add garlic, Worcestershire Sauce, chives, parsley, celery salt and mix well. Mold into desired shape. Keep in refrigerator. Delightful on French bread, especially when spread on before toasting.

GARLIC BUTTER

¼ lb. butter   ½ tsp. garlic powder

Let butter soften at room temperature. Add garlic powder, blend and melt.
Excellent on French bread. Cut the long loaf in half lengthwise; then into 3-in. pieces. Toast and apply garlic butter with basting brush.

DES
SERTS

DESSERTS

It would be impossible to communicate the know-how and skill of an experienced pastry chef in a dozen books the size of this one. However, a home baker with the inclination to improve her oven products can profit by observing the difference in procedure from the usual methods in the recipes which follow.

Fine pastry making is craftsmanship which is almost an art. Experience brings a knowledge of materials and how to blend them so that they will " hold to each other". A glance at the color and consistency of a "mix" and the way it works will tell a skilled baker if it is right or not. This sense of textures and blends can come only with practice and observation.

A good baker works at a steady pace, with assurance and without hesitancy, doing the right thing the first time. Once the desired result is achieved, that becomes standard operational practice and is followed without deviation or experiments from then on.

In The Brown Derby bakeshops the pastry chefs never taste as they work. They weigh ingredients, adhere to proven recipes, keep ovens at proper temperatures and know the finished product will taste right.

In commercial baking, uniform color is essential. This is achieved with good heat controls and even heat throughout the oven. In the cake recipes very little baking powder is used. Instead, pure and expensive ingredients are mixed with plenty of free air to make the cakes light and delicious.

VIENNA MIX, 2 10-in. cakes

1 1/5 cups pastry flour	5 tbs. cornstarch	1 1/5 cups melted butter
1 1/5 cups hard (winter wheat) flour	7 whole eggs	Grated peel 1 small lemon
	10 to 12 egg yolks	1 tsp. vanilla
	1 2/5 cups sugar	

Sift the flours and cornstarch together 5 times. Beat together eggs, egg yolks and sugar in top half of double boiler. Place over hot water, heat and continue beating constantly until mixture will hold points on the whip. Carefully fold in the dry ingredients. Finally fold in melted butter, lemon rind and vanilla. Bake in any type of pan or mold desired, in 350°[F] oven, baking time depending on size and depth of mold.

Vienna Mix is the basis for cakes of all kinds—Vanilla, Mocha, Banana Shortcake, Icebox Cake et cetera.

ICEBOX CAKE

SERVES 10 - 12

Vienna Mix   *Lady fingers*   *Chocolate chips or fresh*
Butter Cream   *Bavarian Cream*   *strawberries*
                      Whipped cream

Pour the Vienna Mix into a 10-in. ring, 1¼-in. high, and bake about 24 minutes or until done. Cool and remove from ring with spatula. Cut into 3 equal layers, but use only the bottom 2, as thin cake layers are required. Carefully trim about ½-in. off the outer edge of the 2 layers and spread Butter Cream between. Lay back inside the baking ring and stand lady fingers upright around the cake in the space left by trimming. Fill spaces in between with Bavarian Cream to which chocolate chips or fresh strawberries may be added. Allow to cool until firm. Cover with thin layer of whipped cream. The cake trimmings, diced, may be sprinkled over the top. Place in refrigerator until firm.

BUTTER CREAM

4 or 5 egg whites   *7 oz. sugar*   *½ lb. unsalted butter*
                            ½ tsp. vanilla

Put egg, sugar and vanilla in double boiler. Stir slowly until hot. Put in mixer; beat to a meringue consistency. While still slightly warm, break in well-kneaded butter until the butter and meringue "catch" together.

The result is a smooth, light cake filling which does not require that cakes be kept in refrigerator unless the weather is extremely hot, as the pure ingredients will stand up for a week without going sour.

BUTTER CREAM ICINGS

The above Butter Cream filling may be used as a soft icing on any kind of cake with the addition of various flavorings.

CHOCOLATE BUTTER CREAM ICING

Follow Butter Cream recipe and when finished add 3 oz. of melted chocolate (½ sweet and ½ bitter), pouring over cream and stirring rapidly.

Mocha Icing is made by adding 1 tbs. of mocha flavoring to the Butter Cream and blending well. Pistachio and almond flavorings may be used in the same way, with blanched, peeled and chopped pistachios, almonds or hazelnuts sprinkled over the icing.

Any kind of liqueur may be used to flavor the Butter Cream, with curaçao, kirschwasser, rum and crème de cocoa adding distinctive character to a cake icing.

COCONUT BUTTER ICING

½ cup sweet butter   1/3 cup thick cream   ½ tsp. vanilla
3 cups powdered sugar   1 cup grated fresh coconut

Cream butter and sugar together until smooth. Add cream and vanilla and beat thoroughly. Add half of coconut and mix thoroughly. (If necessary a little more cream may be added to make icing easy to spread.) Spread between layers and on top and sides of cake. Sprinkle remaining half cup of coconut on top and sides of cake.

ITALIAN MERINGUE

Butter Cream, after the egg whites, sugar and vanilla are beaten but before the butter is added, is known as Italian Meringue and makes a most successful cake icing. Using whipped cream for a filling and the Italian Meringue all around and on top, shredded, long-thread coconut may be sprinkled evenly around sides and all over top.

STRAWBERRY SHORTCAKE
SERVES 20

Take 1 layer of Vienna Mix cake. Slit in 2 pieces. Cover bottom half with thin layer of whipped cream, then put layer of whole, fresh, ripe strawberries. Put whipped cream on top of berries, filling the spaces between the berries to make layer solid. Place other half of cake on top of berries, pressing down slightly to make the cake even. Cover all the cake with whipped cream about ½-in. thick. Divide cake into 20 pieces and put large, perfect berry on each piece. Cover the berry with a film of strawberry Jello to keep fresh appearance, using a small paper tube filled with cool Jello just before it starts to set. All fruit used as cake decoration will look better if coated with Jello.

To make Banana Shortcake, use same procedure. Use bananas instead of strawberries. Divide again into 20 pieces, placing slices of banana on top. Cover banana with Jello to keep from turning dark.

To make Fresh Fig or Pineapple Shortcake, use same procedure.

RIO RITA CAKE

1 pt. milk   1 tbs. sugar   8 oz. flour
6 oz. butter   Pinch of salt   8 eggs

Place milk, butter, sugar and salt in pan on fire. When boiling fast, add flour. Boil to paste consistency, stirring rapidly while cooking. Milk and butter have to absorb the flour and change the mixture from thin to creamy smooth. Remove from fire and cool. When cool, stir in whole eggs. Spread mixture in 4 greased round tins 10-in. in diameter or in 4 10-in. circles on a large cookie sheet. Bake 10 minutes in 450°[F] oven. Gradually reduce temperature to 300°[F]. Bake to a crisp golden brown from 20 to 25 minutes.

FILING: Spread Bavarian Cream between layers and sprinkle shaved chocolate on filling.

* * *

Here are the Chiffon Cakes, mentioned in "The Story of The Brown Derbys", which were first introduced at The Original Derby more than [eighty] years ago.

* * *

BASIC CHIFFON CAKE

SERVES 16 - 20

2¼ cups sifted Softasilk
    Cake Flour
1½ cups sugar
3 tsp. baking powder
1 tsp. salt

½ cup Wesson or Mazola Oil
½ tsp. cream of tartar
5 medium-sized egg
    yolks, unbeaten

¾ cup cold water
2 tsp. vanilla
Grated rind 1 lemon
    (optional)
7 or 8 egg whites

Sift flour onto paper, then measure. Sift together into mixing bowl the flour, sugar, baking powder and salt. Make a well in center of ingredients and add, one at a time, oil, egg yolks, water, vanilla and lemon. Beat with wooden spoon until smooth.

Place egg whites and cream of tartar in large mixing bowl and whip until whites form very stiff peaks. Do not under beat, as this must be much stiffer than for angel food or meringue.

Pour egg-yolk mixture gradually over whipped egg whites, gently folding batter into whites with rubber scraper or heavy spoon until mixture is just blended. *Do not stir.* Pour into ungreased pan immediately. Bake in a 10-in. tube, 4-in deep, for 55 minutes at 325°[F] and then for 10 to 15 minutes at 350°[F]. If a 9 x 13 x 2-in. oblong pan is used, bake in 325°[F] oven for 45 to 50 minutes. Cake is done when top springs back when lightly touched.

Remove pan and immediately turn upside down, placing tube part over neck of funnel or bottle to cool. If loaf pans are used, turn upside down and rest edges on 2 other pans. Allow cake to hang, free of table, until cold. Loosen from sides of tube with spatula, turn pan over and hit edge sharply on table to loosen.

ORANGE CHIFFON CAKE

Use grated rind of 2 oranges (about 3 tbs.) instead of lemon rind.

CHOCOLATE CHIFFON CAKE

¾ cup boiling water
½ cup cocoa
1¾ cups sifted Softasilk
    Cake Flour
1¾ cups sugar

3 tsp. baking powder
1 tsp. salt
½ cup Wesson or Mazola
    Oil
7 unbeaten egg yolks

1 tsp. vanilla
¼ tsp. red food coloring
    (optional)
7 or 8 egg whites
½ tsp. cream of tartar

Stir water and cocoa together until smooth. Allow to cool. Sift together in the mixing bowl flour, sugar, baking powder and salt. Make a well in center and add, in following order, cooking oil, egg yolks, cooled cocoa mixture, vanilla and food coloring, if desired. Beat with spoon until smooth.

In another mixing bowl, whip the egg whites and cream of tartar until very stiff peaks will form.

Pour egg-yolk mixture gradually over whipped egg whites, gently folding with rubber scraper until just blended. Pour into ungreased pan immediately, then bake and cool as for Basic Chiffon Cake.

WALNUT CHIFFON CAKE

Proceed as for Basic Chiffon Cake until egg-yolk and egg-white mixtures have been blended. Then sprinkle over top of batter 1 cup of very finely chopped walnuts. Gently fold in with a few strokes and continue Basic Chiffon recipe.

CANADIAN CHOCOLATE CAKE

1 cup butter	*1½ cups brown sugar*	*1 tsp. soda*
2 oz. unsweetened	*½ cup white sugar*	*½ tsp. salt*
chocolate	*3 eggs*	*2/3 cup sour cream*
2/3 cup boiling water	*2 cups general-purpose flour*	*1 tsp. vanilla*

Let butter stand until it is at room temperature. Place chocolate in boiling water, stir until melted and stand until cool. Cream butter and sugar well together. Add eggs one by one, beating well after each addition. Sift flour, soda and salt. Fold melted chocolate and sour cream gently into creamed sugar, eggs and butter. While doing this, keep adding sifted ingredients slowly. Add vanilla. Mix in electric mixture set at slow speed for 3 minutes. Place mixture in 3 greased and floured cake pans. Bake at 350°[F] for 25 minutes. Test with toothpick until it comes out clean.

FUDGE FROSTING

2 oz. unsweetened	*1½ cups sugar*	*2 tbs. butter*
chocolate	*½ cup cream*	*1 tsp. vanilla*

Melt chocolate, cream and sugar over slow fire; boil until a few drops will form fairly firm balls in cold water. Add butter and vanilla. Let stand a few minutes; then beat until cool enough to spread. If too thick, use a little cream.

*** *

A recent addition to the list of Brown Derby-created cakes is one which causes much comment and brings many compliments.

*** *

BROWN DERBY GRAPEFRUIT CAKE

1½ cups sifted cake flour
¾ cup sugar
1½ tsp. baking powder

½ tsp. salt
¼ cup water
¼ cup vegetable oil
3 eggs, separated

3 tbs. grapefruit juice
½ tsp. grated lemon rind
¼ tsp. cream of tartar

Sift together flour, sugar, baking powder and salt into mixing bowl. Make a well in center of dry ingredients. Add water, oil, egg yolks, grapefruit juice and lemon rind. Beat until very smooth. Beat egg whites and cream of tartar separately until whites are stiff but not dry. Gradually pour egg yolk mixture over whites, folding gently with a rubber spatula until just blended. *Do not stir* mixture. Pour into an ungreased pan. Bake at 350°[F] for 25 to 30 minutes, or until cake springs back when lightly touched with finger. Invert pan on cake rack until cool. Run spatula around edge of cake. Carefully remove from pan. With a serrated knife, gently cut layer in half.

GRAPEFRUIT CREAM CHEESE FROSTING

2 6-oz. pkgs. cream cheese
2 tsp. lemon juice
1 tsp. grated lemon rind

¾ cup powdered sugar,
    sifted
6 to 8 drops yellow food
    coloring

1 1-lb. can grapefruit
    sections, well-
    drained

Let cream cheese soften at room temperature. Beat cheese until fluffy. Add lemon juice and rind. Gradually blend in sugar. Beat until well-blended. Add coloring. Crush several grapefruit sections to measure 2 teaspoons. Blend into frosting. Spread frosting on bottom half of cake. Top with several grapefruit sections. Cover with second layer. Frost top and sides, garnish with remaining grapefruit sections.

APPLESAUCE CAKE

½ cup butter
1 cup white sugar
1 egg, well beaten
1¾ cups cake flour
½ cup seedless raisins
½ cup currants

½ cup chopped walnuts
1 tsp. baking soda
½ tsp. cloves
½ tsp. nutmeg
¼ tsp. allspice

1 tsp. cinnamon
¼ tsp. salt
½ tsp. baking powder
1¼ cups thick, hot,
    unsweetened apple-
    sauce

Cream butter and sugar. Add well-beaten egg (beat white and yolk separately). Use ½ cup of the flour to dredge raisins, currants and walnuts. Sift remaining flour with other dry ingredients. Add dry ingredients and hot applesauce alternately to creamed mixture. Add raisins, currants and nuts last. Mix well. Bake in 2 8-in. cake pans for 30 minutes in 350°[F] oven. Put together with vanilla icing, spreading paper thin.

VANILLA ICING

1/8 lb. butter
½ tsp. vanilla

¾ lb. powdered sugar

2 tbs. cream
(approximately)

Cream butter well. Add vanilla. Add a little powdered sugar and beat until creamy. Add sugar and cream alternately and beat until creamy and fluffy, to consistency to spread.

BROWN DERBY FRUITCAKE
makes 4 2½-LB. cakes or 1 10-lb. cake

1 lb. flour
1 tsp. double-action
*   baking powder or*
*   2 tsp. cream of tartar*
½ tsp. each of cloves, mace,
*   and cinnamon*
1 lb. butter
1 lb. brown sugar
10 eggs, well-beaten
½ lb. glazed cherries

½ lb. glazed pineapple
1 lb. seeded raisins
1 lb. re-cleaned currants
½ lb. citron, diced
½ lb. orange peel
½ lb. lemon peel
½ lb. dates, pitted and
*   sliced*
1 tsp. salt

½ lb. fruitcake mix (pkg. of
*   fruits prepared for*
*   fruitcake)*
1 lemon rind, grated
1 pt. brandy
½ lb. nutmeats (pecans
*   preferred)*
1 cup honey, strained
1 cup dark molasses
½ cup cider

Sift flour; measure. Add baking powder and spices. Sift 3 times. Cream butter and sugar gradually; then add well-beaten eggs. Add fruits and peels which have been moistened with the brandy, nuts, honey, molasses and cider. Add flour mixture gradually. Place in four 2½-lb. size cake tins, greased throughout and lined with paper. Bake in 300°[F] oven 3 hours.

* * *

In Frankfort hot dogs are called Wiener (Vienna) wurst and in Vienna they are known as frankfurters. In somewhat the same perverse fashion the four-layer custard-filled pastry delight that Americans know as Napoleons are called Cream Slices in Europe.

Making the Puff Paste for a Napoleon is a task verging on a career. The ingredients are simple—flour, water, salt, cream of tartar and butter, but the procedure is another story. The dough is rolled out 6 different times, folded 5 times, and stored in the refrigerator 6 times for from 15 minutes to overnight.

Why? Because if handled too much, the delicate Puff Paste will become tough and rubbery. By working it briefly, cooling it between times, and letting the dough rest, a flaky, tender pastry is achieved.

* * *

NAPOLEONS
SERVES 10

PUFF PASTE

12 oz. flour
12 tsp. ice water

½ tsp. salt

½ tsp. cream of tartar
12 oz. butter

Knead into the flour the water, salt and cream of tartar. Continue kneading until dough is stiff. Cover with wet cloth and store in refrigerator for 15 minutes. Remove and roll out to 10 x 6 in. Place half of butter in center one-third, then fold one end on-third over, place remainder of butter on this and fold last one third over. Roll this out to 12 x 6 in., then fold again into 3 layers of equal size and store in refrigerator for 20 minutes. Remove, roll and fold again, this time into 4 folds. Store in refrigerator for 20 minutes more, then repeat, folding into 3 folds. Return to refrigerator for another 30 minutes, then repeat the rolling and fold into 4 folds. Store in refrigerator overnight, covering with wet cloth. The following morning roll dough into a thin sheet 16 x 12 in. Place on large baking sheet and puncture with fork. Store in the refrigerator for 20 minutes, remove, and bake for 10 minutes in 400°[F] oven. Then reduce heat to 300°[F] and bake until crisp and golden brown (approximately 20 minutes). Remove from oven and cool.

FILLING

¼ cup milk	½ dry vanilla bean or	½ cup hard (winter-wheat)
1 cup sugar	1 tsp. vanilla extract	flour
½ tsp. salt	6 egg yolks	1 pt. whipping cream

Mix milk, ½ cup sugar, vanilla and salt in top part of double-boiler and place over water. Cook to boiling point. While waiting for this, whip together the eggs and remaining sugar until white and creamy; add flour slowly. Pour one-half the boiling milk over the egg mixture and stir until smooth. Pour this immediately into the remaining milk, which is still in double-boiler, stirring until it comes to a boil. Remove from pot, pour on buttered stainless steel pan or baking tin to cool. Sprinkle top lightly with granulated sugar. When cold, fold in cream, which has been whipped. Be sure mixture is well-cooled or whipped cream will fall.

Take the 16 x 12-in. sheet of Puff Paste, cut in lengthwise into 4 pieces, each 16 x 3. Spread filling over 3 of the strips and place one on top of the other. Cover with fourth strip, which is spread with hot Apricot Glaze. Over glaze, spread lukewarm, thin fondant icing; then decorate with chocolate icing. Cut crosswise into 10 slices.

APRICOT GLAZE

Mix together 1 qt. of stewed or canned apricots which have been pulped and strained and 2 lbs. of granulated sugar. Boil for 15 minutes. Apricot Glaze is used in bakeshops throughout the world as a covering for French and Danish pastry, cookies and buns, keeping them fresh and appetizing.

FROZEN ÉCLAIRS OR CREAM PUFFS, 36 shells

1 pt. milk	Small pinch salt	½ lb. all-purpose flour
6 oz. butter	½ oz. sugar	6 - 7 whole eggs

Bring milk, butter, salt and sugar to fast boil. Allow to subside and then come up again. While boiling fast, sift in flour, stirring rapidly to avoid burning. Continue until mixture is smooth. Remove from fire, put into pan and cool. Put mixture into mixer at slow speed. Add 6 to 7 whole eggs, depending on size. Mix only until eggs are completely mixed; then put into batter bag. Drop onto greased and floured cookie sheet in éclair shape, cream-puff shape, or any other batter shape for filling. Bake at 300°[F] for approximately 25 to 30 minutes. Cool and split only enough to fill with custard, ice cream or whipped cream. Bananas or strawberries may be used.

This is the same base as the Rio Rita Cake except that fewer eggs are used.

DANISH PASTRY, REFRIGERATOR COFFEECAKE BASIC DOUGH

8 oz. sugar	Grated peel of 4 lemons	3 lbs. 12-oz. all-purpose
1 oz. salt	4 whole eggs	flour
4 oz. soft butter	12 eggs yolks	3 oz. yeast (3 cakes)
1 tsp. mace	1 qt. milk	2 lbs. sweet butter, well
		chilled

PART 1. Cream together sugar, salt, soft butter, mace and lemon peel until light and fluffy. Beat eggs and egg yolks and add, blending well. Add 3 cups warm milk. Add half the flour, blending well. Add the remaining cup of milk in which yeast has been dissolved. Beat well and add remaining flour. Blend into smooth dough.

PART 2. Form dough into loaf shape. Arrange on floured canvas. Place in refrigerator 1 hour. Remove dough from refrigerator. Roll on floured canvas until twice as long as wide and ¼-inch thick.

PART 3. Break 2 lbs. sweet butter into pieces size of walnut. Divide evenly over two-thirds surface of dough. Fold remaining one-third over to center of filled section and finally fold over last section. Butter is then evenly distributed over inner surface of dough. Roll again in rectangle to ½-in. thickness. Fold 3 ways, as before. Wrap in floured canvas and place in refrigerator. After 1 hour refrigeration, repeat process of rolling into rectangle to ½-in. thickness. Fold 3-ply and return to refrigerator for from 4 to 24 hours before making into vast assortment of coffeecakes and pastries.

In addition to the usual coffeecake shapes, this dough can be used for Crumb Cakes, Twists, Hazelnut Rings, Bear Claws, apricot and Plum Cakes. Almost any fresh-fruit topping except strawberries or raspberries may be used.

After the dough is raised, shape as desired and brush lightly with Egg Wash (whole eggs beaten together). For filling, use fruits such as crushed pineapple mixed with a small amount of the Napoleon Filling to hold it. Sprinkle with sliced blanched almonds and top with Apricot Glaze and a little white icing. Baking time is from 25 to 30 minutes in a 325°[F] oven.

COOKIES—BASIC DOUGH, 6 lbs.

1 lb. sugar	2 tbs. vanilla	3 lbs. flour
6 whole eggs	Rind of 1 lemon	1 tsp. salt
	2 lbs. butter	

Cream sugar, eggs, vanilla and lemon rind. Knead moisture out of butter, then work it into the creamed mixture. Rub in flour and salt. Give this mixture a quick kneading—about 10 seconds. Put in icebox pan and place in refrigerator overnight.

Roll out amount desired to ¼-in. thickness. Cut cookies from dough with cookie cutter of any design. Top with sliced almonds. Bake 20 minutes in 350°[F] oven until golden brown.

By adding almonds, filberts or diced fruit to basic dough, many different varieties of cookies may be made.

DANDIES, 4 lbs.

1 lb. powdered sugar	1 tbs. vanilla	1¾ lbs. flour, half soft and
1½ lbs. butter	1 pinch salt	half prepared cake
		½ pt. cream

Cream sugar and butter until light (mix in electric mixer). Add vanilla and salt. While mixer is still in motion, add flour and cream alternately. After all flour and cream has been added, run mixer at highest speed for a few seconds. *Speed* is very *essential* in this operation. Fill pastry bag with mix. Butter and flour cookie sheet in sufficient amount to make the size cookie desired. Bake 20 to 25 minutes in 300°[F] to 350°[F] oven.

The cream used in this recipe makes these cookies very tender. These are the melt-in-the-mouth cookies served with ice cream at The Brown Derbys.

ROUGH-AND-READY COOKIES, 4 lbs.

3 cups egg whites	18 oz. flour	Granulated walnuts
2 ½ lbs. sugar	1 oz. Cinnamon	Powdered sugar

Beat egg whites with electric mixer until very stiff. Add sugar slowly, taking about half a minute for this operation. Add flour and cinnamon. Using No. 5 plain tube in pastry bag, drop dough on paper-lined cookie sheet. Cover cookies with granulated walnuts, then powdered sugar. Bake in oven 250°[F] to 300°[F] for 15 minutes.

KISSES, 3½ lbs.

1 pt. egg whites	2¾ lbs. sugar
1 tsp. salt	2 tbs. vanilla

Beat egg whites with salt, using electric mixer, until very stiff. Add sugar slowly, taking about half a minute for this operation. Add vanilla. Drop on paper-lined cookie sheet with plain or No. 5 star pastry tube. Bake slowly in 200°[F] oven 20 minutes.

This mix may also be used for Meringue Glacé shells.

WALNUT KISSES, 4 lbs.

1 pt. egg whites	2¾ lbs. sugar	1 oz. cinnamon
1 tsp. salt	½ lb. walnuts	2 tbs. vanilla

Beat egg whites with salt, using electric mixer, until very stiff. Add sugar slowly, taking about half a minute for this operation. Remove from mixer; fold in walnuts, cinnamon and vanilla. When thoroughly mixed, put in pastry bag with plain tube and drop on paper-lined cookie sheet. Any shape desired may be made—round, in half-dollar size, lady-finger lengths, et cetera. Bake slowly in 200° [F] oven for 20 minutes.

TURKISH COOKIES, 3 lbs.

½ lb. powdered sugar
1 lb. butter
1½ eggs

½ tsp. salt
1 ½ lbs. flour

¼ lb. coarsely chopped
    almonds
½ oz. cinnamon

Cream sugar with butter until light. Slowly add eggs, salt and flour. Add almonds and cinnamon. Knead into a paste. Roll out in square 1½-in. thick. Place in refrigerator overnight. Slice in strips about 1½-in. wide. You now have long, square rolls which are then sliced into cookies about ¼-in. thick, placed on cookie tins, and baked in 350°[F] oven 25 minutes.

MACAROONS, 2 lbs.

1 lb. almond paste
1 lb. granulated sugar

6 large egg whites

½ tsp. bitter-almond
    flavoring

Mix almond paste, sugar and 2 egg whites until smooth. Add the remaining egg whites and flavoring. Place No. 6 tube (medium) in pastry bag. Use paper-covered baking sheet. Drop the mixture with pastry tube to make macaroon ¾-in. in diameter. Bake in a 350°[F] oven 10 to 12 minutes. When cold, wet the under side of the paper and remove the macaroons.

SOUR CREAM COOKIES, 8 doz.

4 cups flour
1 cup white sugar

1 tsp. baking soda
½ tsp. salt
1 cup butter

4 egg yolks
1 cup thick sour cream

Sift flour, sugar, baking soda and salt together. Add butter, mixing in as for pastry. Beat egg yolks very light, add to the sour cream and mix into the dry ingredients. Shape in rolls and chill in refrigerator for several hours. Slice thin and bake in hot oven until lightly browned.

These cookies will keep crisp and fresh indefinitely. Serve in pairs, with jam between, as Jam Jems.

* * *

Brown Derby fruit pies have their own particular style. The bottom crust is pinked at the edges, as for a custard pie. Then, when the top crust is added, it is cut out in the exact size to cover the fruit. After the pie has been covered, a little sugar and flour are sprinkled over top, then a few dots of melted butter. Bake in preheated oven 15 minutes at 450°[F] and then 35 minutes at 350°[F]. Cool free from drafts.

* * *

BROWN DERBY PASTRY
FOR COVERED FRUIT PIES, 1 8-in. piecrust

2 cups all-purpose flour
1 tsp. salt

2/3 cup pure-blend
    shortening

4 - 6 tbs. water

Sift flour and salt into mixing bowl. Divide shortening into 2 portions. Cut half of it into the flour until it is extremely fine. Cut the second half of the shortening into the mixture until the lumps of shortening are the size of a giant pea. Place the mixture in the refrigerator and chill thoroughly. Remove from refrigerator and blend in with fork just enough water (4 to 6 tbs.) to hold dough together. Care must be taken not to have the dough too wet. Roll this out on canvas-covered board with covered rolling pin.

BROWN DERBY PEACH PIE, 8 in.

¾ cup sugar	*Brown Derby*	*2 tbs. melted butter*
1 tbs. flour	*Fruit Pie Pastry*	*2 cups peaches, sliced*

Mix sugar and flour together well. Line an 8-in. pan with Brown Derby Pastry. Brush bottom and sides with melted butter. Add peaches, flour and sugar which have been mixed together well and dot with melted butter. Cover with pastry top.

BROWN DERBY CHERRY PIE, 8 in.

2½ cups frozen cherries (25	*Few drops red coloring*	*Brown Derby Fruit Pie*
percent sugar added)	*2 level tbs. Cornstarch*	*Pastry*
¼ cup sugar		*2 level tbs. melted butter*

Drain juice from partially sweetened cherries. Heat juice in heavy saucepan. Add sugar and coloring. Bring to boiling point over slow heat, stirring to avoid sticking. Moisten cornstarch with cold water or cherry juice to consistency of thick cream. Add to boiling mixture and cook until it becomes transparent (approximately 5 minutes). Pour over cherries and mix well. Allow to cool. Line an 8-in. pie pan with pastry. Brush bottom and sides with melted butter. Pour in cherry mixture and cover with pastry.

BROWN DERBY BERRY PIE, 8 in.

2/3 cup sugar	*Brown Derby Fruit Pie Pastry*	*2 cups berries, fresh or*
2 tbs. flour	*2 tbs. melted butter*	*frozen*

Mix sugar and flour together well. Line an 8-in. pan with Brown Derby Fruit Pie Pastry. Brush bottom and sides with melted butter. Add berries, then pour flour and sugar mixture over berries. Dot with melted butter and cover with pastry top.

* * *

Some time ago The Brown Derby set out to make the Perfect Apple Pie. No restrictions were put on budget or type of pastry or filling. There was no time limit on the search. More than a thousand recipes were considered.

Two years, 1,900 pies and $10,000 later, there emerged a new apple pie and a new crust which The Derby was proud to serve. Their pride has been justified; pie lovers, an extremely critical group, keep drooling their praises and keep coming back for more.

At The Derby bakeshops, trained crews make up the pies in small numbers—to retain the homemade flavor. Jonathan and Winesap apples, from Washington's largest orchard, are used. Then the pies are wrapped in special plastic covers and quick-frozen. Still unbaked, they are stored in deep-freeze boxes at all Brown Derby restaurants and baked as needed. Almost always the last piece has been devoured within an hour after they leave the oven. They are also sold at The Brown Derby Shops for home baking.

* * *

THE YEAR BOB COBB SPENT $10,000.00 TO DEVELOP THE PERFECT APPLE PIE.

FOR 10 GRAND IT BETTER BE GOOD!

BROWN DERBY $10,000 APPLE PIE, 1 8-in. pie

2 cups Brown Derby Pastry for Fruit Pies

2 cups apples, thinly sliced
¾ cup Apple Pie Seasoning: Equal amounts white and brown sugar, 1 level tbs. flour, 1/8 tsp. cinnamon, 1/16 tsp. nutmeg, few grains of salt

2 tbs. melted butter
2 tbs. water (if apples are dry)

Mix apples and seasoning together. Line an 8-in. pan with the pastry, fluting at edges as for custard pie. Brush bottom and sides with melted butter. Add apple mixture and dot with melted butter. If apples are dry, add enough water to moisten. Cover with pastry top and decorate as with other fruit pies, but bake in preheated oven longer—20 minutes at 450°[F], then 40 minutes (or until apples are tender) at 350°[F]. Cool free from draft.

VIRGINIA CHEESE PIE

SERVES 7 - 8

CRUST:

18 graham crackers   *¼ lb. melted butter*   *1 tbs. sugar*

Crumble crackers and mix well with butter and sugar. Pat into deep pie tin, molding to shape of tin. Bake in slow over for 20 minutes. Let cool until dried out.

FILLING:

5 pkgs. cream cheese	*4 eggs*	*¾ cup sugar*	*1 tbs. Vanilla*

Cream the cheese in mixer and add eggs, 1 at a time. Add sugar and vanilla and mix thoroughly. Put into cool graham cracker crust and bake at 200°[F] or 250°[F] for 1 hour.

TOPPING:

1 carton (about ½ pt.) sour cream

Add enough sugar to sweeten cream. Spread on top of pie about ¼-in. thick, sprinkle with graham cracker crumbs; put back into oven and bake for 10 minutes.

SHELL PASTRY DOUGH For Open-Faced Pies
2 10-in. shells

3/8 cup (¼ cup and 2 tbs.) sugar	*¼ tsp. lemon rind, grated*	*2/3 cup butter*
1 egg	*Small pinch salt*	*2¼ cups flour*
	½ tsp. vanilla (bean or extract)	*½ tsp. baking powder*

Mix sugar, egg, lemon rind, salt and vanilla in electric mixer until a creamy consistency is reached. Knead butter until smooth, then add to egg mixture. Add flour and baking powder, with mixer at slow speed, until a paste is formed. Switch to high speed for a few turns, to make sure everything is well-mixed. Roll out thin on lightly floured board and bake in 400°[F] oven for 10 to 12 minutes.

In addition to pie shells, this basic dough may be used for all kinds of cookies. By varying the amounts of baking powder, different degrees of crispness can be obtained, the less baking powder the crisper.

BLACK BOTTOM PIE, 1 10-in. Pie
SERVES 8

2 tsp. unflavored gelatin	*1 pinch salt*	*3 oz. sweet chocolate*
½ cup milk	*1 tsp. vanilla*	*1 pt. cream, whipped*
1 oz. sugar	*1 egg yolk*	*1 prebaked pie shell*

Soak gelatin in small amount of cold water for 15 minutes. Bring milk to boiling point. Beat together sugar, salt, half of vanilla and egg yolks until light, thick and creamy. Add ½ of the boiling milk over egg mixture. Blend well, then add to remaining hot milk. Return to heat, stirring constantly, for a few seconds. Remove from fire before boiling point is reached. Press soaked gelatin free of any excess water and dissolve in hot mixture. Strain through a very fine sieve. Add 2 ounces of the chocolate, which has been shaved; beat until smooth. Cool until it reaches cream-like consistency. Fold in half of whipped cream and remaining half of vanilla. Fill prebaked pie shell. Place in refrigerator for 30 minutes. Top with remaining whipped cream 1-inch thick. Remaining chocolate is now shaved into curled spears and stuck in top. Dust with grated chocolate.

LEMON SOUFFLÉ PIE, 1 10-in. pie
SERVES 8

½ pt. egg yolks
¾ cup granulated sugar

½ cup lemon juice
½ cup egg whites
1 tbs. lemon rind

1 10-in. partially prebaked
    pastry shell

Place egg yolks, ½ cup sugar and lemon juice in top of double-boiler, beating until very thick and at boiling point. Remove from heat and continue beating, using folding motion until cool. Then beat egg whites until firm, add remainder of sugar and the lemon rind and continue to beat until it reaches a wax-like meringue. Fold meringue into egg-yolk mixture. Pour into pastry shell, piling filling in so that pie will have a high-domed center. Bake 25 minutes in 350°[F] oven. It is important that these pies be cooled free from drafts. Top bakes golden brown and no topping is required; inside center is sunshine yellow.

DERBY PUMPKIN PIE, 1 10-in pie

1 tbs. flour
1 pinch salt
1 tsp. spice mixture
    (ginger, cinnamon,
    nutmeg, allspice)

4 eggs
1/3 cup molasses
5 oz. brown sugar
1½ pts. pumpkin purée

1½ pts. pastry cream
4 oz. melted butter
1 10-in. pastry shell

Sift together flour, salt and spices. Mix together eggs, molasses, sugar and pumpkin in electric mixer. Add flour and spices, beating well until smooth. Fold in cream and melted butter. Put mixture into pastry shell and bake at 350°[F] for 1 hour. Cool in a place free from drafts.

SOUR CREAM RAISIN PIE
SERVES 8

4 oz. raisins, bleached or
    dark according to
    preference
5 oz. brown sugar

1 egg
1½ pts. sour cream
1 tbs. vinegar

1 tsp. vanilla
1 tsp. salt
½ tsp. cinnamon
1 prebaked pie shell

Soak raisins overnight in cold water. Mix brown sugar, egg, sour cream, vinegar, vanilla, salt and cinnamon [together]. Last, add the thoroughly drained raisins. Fill into prebaked pie shell. Bake at 300°[F] for 35 to 40 minutes.

BAVARIAN CREAM, 1 10-in. pie

½ cup milk
4 tbs. granulated sugar
1 egg yolk

¼ tsp. salt
½ tbs. vanilla

1 tbs. gelatin
1 qt. whipping cream

Rinse saucepan with cold water. Place in it milk and two-thirds of sugar; bring to boil. Beat together egg yolk and remaining sugar. Pour hot milk mixture over yolk. Add salt and vanilla. Return to heat, stirring constantly. Remove before it reaches boiling point. Add gelatin which has been soaked in a small amount of cold water. Strain mixture through fine sieve and cool. Just before it begins to set, fold in stiffly beaten whipped cream.

STRAWBERRY BAVARIAN CREAM PIE
SERVES 8 - 10

1 qt. strawberries	*1 10-in. pastry shell, prebaked*	*Bavarian Cream from above recipe*

Strawberries should be washed and carefully picked. Arrange them in baked pastry shell, then pile on Bavarian Cream. Allow to settle all through berries; then place in refrigerator to become firm. Decorate top with a few choice berries.

OTHER BAVARIAN CREAM PIES

The same Bavarian Cream filling and the same method may be used in making pies with bananas, pineapple, pears, apricots, crushed macaroons, fresh whole raspberries, Kadota figs, peaches, coconut, chopped roasted hazelnuts and dates.

Bavarian Cream, with one of the above flavorings, also makes a delicious pudding.

BROWN DERBY CHOCOLATE PUDDING

This is the same as the filling used for Black Bottom Pie before the whipped cream is added. The pie-filling recipe is followed up to the point where the whipped cream is folded in; then pour the mixture into molds, cups or deep dishes. Chill. Serve with cream or whipped-cream topping.

CARAMEL CUSTARD
SERVES 8

Put ½ pound sugar in heavy pan on medium flame and melt, stirring constantly till smooth and light brown. Pour into custard cups about ½-in. deep. Cool. Grease the sides of the cups with butter and fill with the following custard:

1 qt. milk	*8 oz. sugar*	*½ vanilla bean or 1 tbs.*
8 whole eggs	*1 pinch salt*	*vanilla extract*

Bring milk to boiling point. Mix eggs, sugar, vanilla and salt. Pour half the milk over this egg mixture; then pour back into rest of milk. Stir for a few seconds but *do not boil,* as boiling will separate the mixture. Fill the cups and bake 15 to 20 minutes in pan half-filled with water. Baking time depends on thickness of custard cups used. Custard is done when a knife thrust into center comes out clean.

CUSTARD AND JELLO

SERVES 6 - 8

1 qt. milk	8 egg yolks	1 pinch salt
1 cup sugar	2½ heaping tbs. flour	1 tsp. vanilla

Boil milk and ½ cup sugar, stirring until it is a creamy, smooth mixture. Cream egg yolks with rest of the sugar. Stir in flour, salt and vanilla. Add to milk mixture and heat but do not allow to come to a boil. Fill Jello glasses half full of custard. Let cool; then fill up glasses with any kind of Jello desired. Set in refrigerator until Jello is firm. Decorate with whipped cream. Serve.

BROWN DERBY RICE PUDDING

SERVES 6

1 qt. milk	1 pinch each finely grated	3 oz. muscat raisins,
½ tsp. salt	orange and lemon	washed
½ tsp. vanilla	peel (optional)	3 tbs. sugar
½ stick cinnamon	4 tbs. long grain white	2 egg yolks
	rice, washed	1 pt. coffee cream

Bring milk to boil in a heavy pot. Add salt, vanilla, cinnamon, orange and lemon peel, rice and raisins. Boil very slowly over low flame for 20 minutes, or until tender, stirring frequently. Meanwhile, beat sugar and egg yolks together in a bowl until they are very light yellow and quite thick. Slowly, while stirring, add cream to sugar-egg mixture. Mix thoroughly, add to rice and bring to boiling point. Remove from fire and cool, stirring occasionally. Fill individual molds, being careful to distribute an even mixture to each. Sprinkle each mold lightly with powdered cinnamon. Place under broiler flame for few seconds to give delicate brown color. For this recipe, do not use converted rice.

BREAD-AND-BUTTER PUDDING

SERVES 8

1 qt. milk	1 tbs. vanilla	½ loaf very thinly sliced
4 whole eggs	1 pinch salt	bread, toasted
½ cup sugar		4 oz. melted butter

Bring milk to boiling point. Mix eggs, sugar, vanilla and salt thoroughly. Pour boiling milk over egg mixture, stirring while pouring. Put back on fire for few seconds but do not boil. Toast bread very dry. Cut in equal shapes to fit the serving dishes, place in the dishes. Half fill each dish with custard mixture. Allow bread to soak up mixture. Gradually fill dishes until all mixture is used. Divide butter in the dishes on top of mixture. Bake about 15 minutes in pan half filled with water till golden brown. Leftover coffeecake may be substituted for the bread.

GLAMOUR DEPARTMENT

FRESH STRAWBERRIES ROMANOFF

SERVES 4

1 basket choice strawberries
2 ponies brandy

2 ponies kirschwasser
2 ponies curaçao

1 cup whipped cream
1 pt. vanilla ice cream

This dessert is most effective when assembled at the table before the guests. The berries should be marinated in the liqueurs under refrigeration for 1 hour. At the table, arrange 3 bowls, one containing whipped cream, one ice cream and one strawberries set in a bed of ice. Combine ingredients for each guest, or ice cream and whipped cream may be blended together, the berries arranged in service dishes and the cream mixture piled on decoratively. Everything should be kept as cold as possible.

CHERRIES FLAMBÉ

SERVES 8

1 No. 2 can black pitted
*   cherries*
1 cup currant jelly

Juice of 1 orange
2 small pieces lemon peel
1 bay leaf
1 cup burgundy

2 oz. imported brandy
2 oz. cointreau
A chafing dish

Strain the juice off the cherries. Put cherries into chafing dish. Add half the juice, currant jelly, orange juice, lemon peel, bay leaf and wine. Simmer about 15 to 20 minutes. While mixture is boiling briskly, add brandy and cointreau. Ignite and mix with long-handled silver spoon, ladling liquid above the chafing dish so that it mixes with the air and the alcohol burns. As soon as flame dies out, serve over ice cream.

PEACH MELBA À LA DERBY

SERVES 1

1 scoop ice cream
½ peach, in syrup

1 tbs. raspberry syrup
1 tbs. shaved walnuts

1 heaping tbs. whipped
*   cream*

Place ice cream in chilled champagne glass. Cover with peach. Cover peach with raspberry syrup. Garnish with whipped cream. Sprinkle with walnuts. Serve.

MERINGUE ICE CREAM

SERVES 1

2 small meringue shells
1 scoop ice cream
2 tbs. whipped cream

2 tbs. strawberries, crushed
*   with berry*
*   granulated sugar*

Place ice cream between meringue shells. Cover with strawberries. Garnish with whipped cream. Serve.

COUPE DERBY

SERVES 1

1 scoop ice cream
12 melon balls, soaked in
    sweet white wine

½ pony curaçao

1 tsp. almonds, toasted and
    shaved

Put ice cream in champagne glass. Garnish with wine-soaked melon balls. Cover with curaçao. Sprinkle with shaved almonds. Serve.

BAKED ALASKA

SERVES 6

4 egg whites, beaten
8 oz. powdered sugar
2 drops vanilla

2 thin slices pound cake
4 scoops vanilla ice cream
12 lady fingers

12 large strawberries,
    marinated in kirsch
    and curaçao

Prepare meringue by beating egg whites stiff, then beat in slowly the powdered sugar and vanilla. Place the slices of pound cake in the center of a silver platter or a heavy china platter. On the cake, place 4 scoops of ice cream in line. Between the scoops, place the lady fingers around and on top of the ice cream. Add the remainder of the marinade very slowly so that the lady fingers and pound cake will absorb it. Cover with meringue, using pastry bag or spatula, ½-in. thick all over. Garnish with the 4 remaining strawberries. Sprinkle with powdered sugar. Bake in 450°[F] oven for approximately 8 to 10 minutes or until brown.

SABAYON

¼ cup sugar
8 egg yolks
1/8 tsp. orange peel, grated fine

¼ tsp. lemon peel, finely
    grated

1 cup Madeira
1 tbs. brandy

Put sugar, yolks, orange and lemon peel in top half of double-boiler and mix well. Add ½ cup wine. Mix thoroughly with French whip. Cook over water on medium heat, stirring vigorously, until mixture thickens. As mixture thickens, add remainder of wine. When cooked to consistency of Sauce Hollandaise, add brandy and mix well again. Serve. Be careful to use copper or glass pot—do not attempt to make it in aluminum.

May be served alone, with fruit, with a tea biscuit or over sponge cake soaked in rum.

GERMAN APPLE PANCAKE

SERVES 4

2 whole eggs
2/3 cup flour
4 tbs. melted butter

1/3 tsp. grated orange and
    lemon peel
4 tsp. sugar
1 pinch salt

2/3 tsp. vanilla
1/3 cup milk
2 tbs. whole butter

Beat eggs lightly in mixing bowl. Add flour, 2 tablespoons melted butter, grated peel, sugar, salt and vanilla. Mix well. Beat for about 3 minutes; then add milk. Mix well again until batter is smooth. Take a perfectly clean, well-broken-in 16-in. black frying pan and place in oven at 425°[F] for about 5 minutes. Take out pan and, using small amount (1 tablespoon) of melted butter, put a paper-thin coating of butter all over, rolling around and covering sides to rim. Use very little butter. Pour in 1 cup of pancake mixture and, by turning the pan, coat the entire inside surface. Place back into very hot oven and bake 10 to 12 minutes. If properly made, the pancake will rise two-thirds. After it is puffed high, remove and slide onto a large platter. Place in center with cooked apples prepared as follows:

APPLES FOR PANCAKE

4 medium-sized apples,	*2 oz. Butter*	*1 tsp. cinnamon*
peeled, cored, cut into		*3 tbs. sugar*
quarters and sliced extra fine		

Heat butter in skillet. Add apples, cinnamon and sugar. Stir slowly over slow fire until apples are done.

Before serving, add remaining 1 tablespoon melted butter and sprinkle a little more sugar and cinnamon over the pancake. Dot with whole butter in small pieces; then roll and cut into desired pieces. Serve.

BROWN DERBY FRENCH PANCAKES
SERVES 4

3 whole eggs	*1 tsp. Vanilla*	*2 tbs. sugar*
1 cup flour	*1/3 tsp. grated orange rind*	*1 pinch salt*
4 tbs. melted butter	*½ tsp. lemon rind*	*1 cup milk*

Break eggs into mixing bowl. Add flour, butter, vanilla, orange and lemon peel, sugar, salt and mix well. Beat for 2 or 3 minutes. Add milk. Mix well. Strain through fine sieve. Fry in small black frying pan about 7 inches in diameter—one pancake filling the pan. The pan should be oiled lightly. Care should be taken to cook on slow fire and to brown evenly on both sides.

FRENCH PANCAKES WITH JELLY
SERVES 1

Take 3 French pancakes and spread 1 tbs. any flavored jelly on each pancake. Roll them up. Lay them side by side on the platter. Sprinkle with powdered, confectioners' or extra-fine granulated sugar. Put under broiler to brown lightly. Serve.

The same pancakes, made slightly thinner, may be used for Crêpes Suzette.

CRÊPES SUZETTE DERBY

SERVES 1

2 oz. sweet butter
2 lumps sugar
1 orange, in halves

Rind of 1 lemon
1 pony cointreau
1 pony curaçao
1 oz. brandy

3 Derby French Pancakes,
*   made as thin as*
*   possible*

The preparation and serving of Crêpes Suzette is a deft ceremony at The Brown Derbys. First, the chafing dish is well-serviced, has plenty of fuel, and is spotlessly clean. As it is warmed, 2 pats of butter are melted. Then 1 lump of sugar is rubbed against the rind of an orange and the other against the rind of a lemon until they acquire the color of the fruit. The sugar is then added to the melted butter along with the juice of the orange squeezed out with the aid of a fork. The mixture is stirred gently until the sugar is dissolved and the liquid is blended and cooking. Then the cointreau and curaçao are poured in while the sauce cooks down to two-thirds and becomes syrupy. This takes approximately 15 minutes.

Next the pancakes are brought from the kitchen and each is gently folded twice (into quarter-circles) with fork and spoon. They are placed in the boiling sauce, the chafing dish is covered and they cook for 3 or 4 minutes longer. Then the cover is removed and the brandy is poured over all and lighted. While the fire is blazing, the sauce is gently stirred with a long-handled spoon. Now the pancakes are transferred to a hot serving plate and the still-flaming sauce is spooned out over them. Crêpes Suzette Derby are eaten with a fork.

Sally's
World Famous Candies

World Famed
Brown Derbys

Hollywood

The Vine Street Derby is the same great restaurant it was when...
MARGARET TRUMAN GOT THE SHOCK OF HER LIFE IN BOOTH 19.

It happened in 1951. At the Brown Derby, that zany, lovable restaurant at Hollywood and Vine.

Margaret Truman was in town for appearances on Jimmy Durante's TV show. In company with some NBC executives, Miss Truman arrived at the Hollywood Brown Derby for lunch.

The waiter came to the booth and said, "May I take your order." Miss Truman looked up and gasped! The waiter was her father, Harry S. Truman, President of The United States!

Miss Truman was so shocked that she forgot what she had decided to order.

Then everyone – including Miss Truman – broke-up laughing. It wasn't her father. It was only Apostoles Pooleon, a Brown Derby waiter who was a perfect double for the "Man from Missouri."

(Pooleon appeared in several movies and TV shows as Truman.)

The Brown Derby was one of the world's great restaurants when Margaret Truman was served and startled by "her father". It still is. The food is still prepared to a fare-thee-well. The service is still considerate. And the prices are still reasonable.

So dine with us soon, won't you.

HOW TO READ A MENU

The names of various dishes listed on menus of fine restaurants, their contents or manner of preparation need not remain a mystery if you will remember the definitions given here.

ALEXANDRIA. With artichokes, tomatoes and chicken livers.

BOULANGÈRE. With potatoes and onions.

BOURGEOISE. With vegetables which have been braised with the meat.

CACCIATORA. Italian for "Hunter Style". With pickled peppers, mushrooms, and tomatoes.

CARUSO. With chicken livers.

CHASSEUR. French for "Hunter Style". With chicken livers.

CONSOMMÉ. Double-strength broth, fortified with ground meat which is cooked in the soup to add juice.

DUXELLES. A sauce with fine-chopped ingredients.

FLAMAND. With string beans and onions which have been cooked with the meat.

FLORENTINE. With spinach. (Except Zucchini Florentine, which is breaded and French-fried.)

GRILLE. Broiled, usually over charcoal.

HUSSARD. A sharp, nippy sauce with a tomato base.

JARDINIÈRE. With young vegetables.

JERUSALEM. With artichoke.

MARCHARD. Added while cooking

MARENGO. With olives, tomatoes and mushrooms.

NIÇOISE. With artichoke and Cream Sauce.

PARISIENNE. With Parisienne potatoes and wine sauce.

PIÉMONTAIS. With Parmesan cheese.

POTAGE. A soup, usually thick.

PRINCESS. With asparagus, mushrooms and cream.

ROBERT. With crab legs.

RUSSE. With caviar or sour cream sauce.

SAUTÉ SEC. Fried dry, with very little sauce.

SCALLOPINE. Small veal cutlets, two or three to the order.

SUISSE. With Swiss cheese, mushrooms and chives.

TETRAZZINI. With chicken julienne, mushrooms and Cream Sauce.

ZINGARA. With tongue julienne, hard-cooked white of egg and truffles.

GLOSSARY AND TABLE

Words and terms used by professional chefs and in this book which may be unfamiliar.

AU GRATIN. To brown under broiler.

BARBECUE SPICES. These are now packaged and sold by fine food stores (including The Brown Derbys). If not obtainable, mix your own using chili powder, celery salt, garlic, coriander, paprika, salt and pepper.

BELL PEPPERS. The same as green peppers.

BEURRE MANIÉ. (burr mahn-YAY). Melted butter and flour. Used as a thickening agent.

BEURRE MEUNIÈRE. (burr moon-YAR). Melted butter, light brown in color.

BEURRE NOIR. (burr nwah). Melted butter, burned black.

BEURRE NOISETTE (burr nwah-ZET). Melted butter, deep brown in color.

BLANCH.. To clean, place in water, bring to a boil, remove and wash again.

BRAISE. To half roast, half steam, with the lid on and plenty of moisture in the bottom of the pan.

BREADING. Usually means dipping in flour, then in egg batter, then in bread or cracker crumbs.

CHIVE. A small member of the onion family. If not obtainable, use green onion tops for garnishing or minced on-ions for flavoring.

CHORIZO. Highly seasoned Spanish or Mexican sausages. If not available, use kosher, Italian or plain salami.

CLEAR STOCK. Water in which meat or bones have been cooked. Substitutes: salted water, canned consommé or canned chicken broth.

COCOTTE. A small, flat-bottomed china cup holding 1 egg (3-4 oz.), usually mainly for cooking eggs.

COURT BOUILLON. Fish stock, wine, vinegar, vegetables and seasonings, used for poaching fish.

EGG BATTER. Beaten egg, diluted with half the amount of milk. Used for coating chops, croquettes, et cetera, before dipping them in crumbs.

ENGLISH MUSTARD. Dry, powdered mustard, very sharp in flavor.

FOLDING. Lifting the cake mix or dough with a pastry whip or French whip and allowing it to fall slowly through the wire loops, continuing until the components have become well mixed.

FRENCH TRIMMED. Meat close-trimmed with most of the fat removed.

FRENCH WHIP. A hand whipper or beater, consisting of stiff wire loops and a handle.

GLAZE. To pour gravy over or to brown without cheese.

GRENADINE. A small, thin beef filet steak, ¼-in. thick and 2½ inch in diameter.

GUMBO FILÉ (FEE-lay). Tender young sassafras leaves, dried and powdered fine.

JULIENNE. Shredded or cut in long, thin pieces.

LEEK. A member of the onion family, similar to the scallion and shallot.

MARINADE. Any pickling liquid.

MARINATE. To soak in, coat with seasoned dressing, or pickle in order to acquire a flavor.

MEDALLION. A slice, as of lobster or chicken, about ¼-in. thick and the size of a medal.

MIXING. Blending a cake mix or dough by holding the whip vertically and pulling or stirring it through the mixture with a steady, circular motion.

NEW YORK COUNT. A large-sized Eastern oyster, shucked and canned raw.

"OVER HOT WATER". In a double-boiler or similar arrangement.

PASTRY CREAM. Any cream which can be whipped or which contains over 30% butterfat.

PATAPAR PAPER. A strong vegetable parchment paper. Used for pastry cones and cooking vegetables or fish "in paper".

PEPERONCINI. Small, sour Italian peppers.

PEPPERCORNS. Whole black pepper.

PILAFF. Rice cooked 20 minutes in three parts of stock to one of rice, then drained, buttered and seasoned. The rice should remain in individual kernels.

REDUCE. To boil or simmer until thicker and partially evaporated.

SALAMANDER. A gas or electric broiler used in restaurants.

SAUCE VEGETABLE. A combination of spices, pepper, bay leaf and chopped carrots, celery and onion, used in roasting.

SAUTÉ. To fry quickly with little grease.

SHALLOT. A small, highly seasoned member of the onion family. If not obtainable, very finely chopped green onions may be substituted.

SHOULDER CLOD. Round bone roast cut from shoulder of beef and boned.

SMOKED SALT. Hickory-flavored salt used in barbecuing.

SMOTHER. To brown in oil, butter or other fat, using a heavy pan, preferably a black skillet; then cover with heavy lid and heat in slow oven, or over slow heat, in the meat's own juice.

SPICE BAG. A container made of cheesecloth and similar to a tea bag, in which spices are placed, enabling them to be removed easily after the cooking has been seasoned.

TIMBALE. A mold, smaller than coffee-cup size, used for shaping or cooking rice and for baking eggs, salmon or cheese.

TOURNEDOS. A small beef filet 1½-in. thick and 2½-in. in diameter.

TRUFFLE. An underground member of the mushroom family, cured in wine. Imported from France.

WHOLE BUTTER. Butter in solid form.

MEASUREMENTS AND ABBREVIATIONS

3 (tsp. (teaspoons) = 1 tbs. (tablespoon)
2 tbs. = 1 oz. (ounce), liquid
4 tbs. = ¼ cup
16 tbs. = 1 cup
2 cups = 1 pt. (pint)
1 pt. = 1 lb. (pound), liquid or fat
4 cups = 1 qt. (quart)
1 No. 2 can = 2½ cups

GENERAL RULES

All measurements are level, unless otherwise specified.

All heats are Fahrenheit.

Oven temperatures: Very Slow—250°; Slow—300°; Moderate—350°; Hot—400°; Very Hot—450° and over.

Ingredients are listed in the order of their use (mostly). Flour for dredging and other breading materials are usually not listed as ingredients. This also applies for egg wash, butter for dipping or coating, and salt and pepper for seasoning.

Where English muffins are specified but not available, substitute white toast.

Brown Derby Diable Sauce is a new, secret formula which was developed and is being marketed by The Brown Derby Hollywood Products Corporation. If not obtainable, substitute Escoffier or A-1 Sauce.

When cutting recipes in half, a helpful short cut is to substitute "tablespoon" for "ounce" (liquid or fat) and "cup" for "pound" or "pint".

Every home should have at least one heavy skillet of iron or aluminum. It is the all-purpose restaurant utensil, used for frying, roasting, braising, poaching and preparing sauces.

The Vine Street Derby is
the same great restaurant it was...

THE CHRISTMAS
BOB HOPE & BOB COBB THREW
A PARTY FOR 100 SANTAS

It was 1949. Bob Cobb, owner of the Brown Derby Restaurants overheard a complaint by a 70-year-old actor who had played Santa Claus in the movie "Miracle on 34th Street."

"There is no Christmas for Santa Claus," moaned the erstwhile Kris Kringle.

Cobb took it to heart. He contacted comedian Bob Hope and they decided to have a party for Santas. A few days before Christmas they rounded up every department store Santa they could find. More than a hundred in all!

The Vine Street Derby provided the food and Hope, in a white beard and pillows, provided the jokes.

The Santas swapped stories of little kids who pulled beards and tweaked noses.

Very little has changed at The Brown Derby since that Christmas. The food is still prepared with loving care. The service is still considerate. The prices are still reasonable.

And it's still the best place in town to throw a party...for Santa Claus or anyone else who deserves one.

Even if it's a party for two.

INDEX

The Vine Street Derby is the same
great restaurant it was when...

GEORGE BURNS FOUGHT HIS WAY THROUGH A SNOWSTORM TO FETCH GRACIE A HAMBURGER ON RYE.

It **happened** in 1949. During the great Hollywood snowstorm. Everyone stayed inside. The streets were treacherous, and no one was prepared for the cold.

But Gracie Allen had a yen for a hamburger. On rye. And not just any hamburger on rye. A Brown Derby hamburger on rye.

So George Burns, the long-suffering husband and partner, put on his heaviest coat, stuffed his pocket full of cigars and fought his way through the snow and snarled traffic to fetch Gracie her sandwich.

That's Hollywood. And that's the Brown Derby. It hasn't changed much over the years. The food is still great. The service is considerate. And the prices are reasonable.

And there are a lot of famous and not-so-famous people who would brave rain, sleet, snow or gloom of night to get to the Brown Derby.

www.ingramcontent.com/pod-product-compliance
Lightning Source LLC
Chambersburg PA
CBHW062016090426

42811CB00005B/872